THE PUBLIC ATION

GUEST EDITORS

MARK WALLINGER
MARY WARNOCK

PEER

ART FOR ALL

THEIR POLICIES AND OUR CULTURE

CONTENTS

8 **Andrew Brighton and Ingrid Swenson**
Preface

10 **Mary Warnock and Mark Wallinger**
Introduction

12 **Bob and Roberta Smith**
postcard

14 **Chris Smith**
Government and the Arts

16 **Mark Ryan**
Manipulation Without End

18 **Gerry Robinson**
An Arts Council for the Future (extract)

20 **Department for Culture, Media and Sport and the Arts Council of England**
An Agreement

22 **BANK**
Just imagine…

24 **Brian Sedgemore**
Politics and Culture: the State and the Artist

26 **George Walden**
Contemporary Art, Democracy and the State (extract)

30 **Ian Breakwell**
Half the Work

32 **Stella Santacatterina**
Clarification of a Few Political Points

33 **Art in Ruins**
everyone is an artist

34 **Lord Bragg and Lord Gibson**
House of Lords Debate: The Arts (extract)

36 **Andrew Brighton**
Towards a Command Culture: New Labour's Cultural Policy and Soviet Socialist Realism

42 **Ben Gibson**
The Art of the State, or Laisser-Faire Eats the Soul: British Film Policy

48 **Jeremy Deller**
Unconvention: Artist's Statement

49 **Matthew Higgs**
Unconvention: Introduction to exhibition publication

50 **Arthur Scargill**
Unconvention: an Address (extract)

53 **Centre for Visual Arts, Cardiff**
press statement

54 **Earl of Clancarty, Lord Freyberg and Lord McIntosh of Haringey**
House of Lords Debate: Arts and Sport (extract)

58 **Nicholas Murray**
Culture and Accessibility

64 **Adam Chodzko**
poster

65 **Richard Grayson**
Greek

66 **Ken Worpole**
When Worlds Collide

68 **Helen Gould**
Creative Exchange: The Forum for Cultural Rights and Development

70 **François Matarasso**
Freedom's Shadow

72 **David Batchelor**
A Brief Reply to François Matarasso

74 **Roland Miller**
The Artist's Dance; letter to Peer (extract)

76 **Richard Noble**
Accessibility for All, Freedom for the Few

78 **Ian Breakwell**
The Caller

80 **Antony Gormley**
Total Strangers

82 **David Bartholomew**
The Proposed Sculpture

84 **Funding Application**
Hackney Wick Single Regeneration Budget Community Chest

86 **Martin Creed**
Work no. 203

88 **Joan Key**
statement

89 **Christopher Mansell**
8 + 3 = 11, 6 + 5 = 11

90 **South London Art Gallery**
Attendance chart

92 **Charles Saumarez Smith**
Museum as Memory Bank

94 **Adam Chodzko**
Cleaner (a Story)

96 **Janette Parris**
Plank drawing

98 **Jes Fernie**
I Ate Prunella Clough; Soup

101 **Penelope Curtis**
Letter to Peer

102 **Big Sister**
Beware the Influence of Public Opinion

104 **Roger Cook**
Pierre Bourdieu, William Blake and the Battle for the Autonomy of the Arts

106 **Lord Freyberg and Baroness Blackstone**
House of Lords Debate: Art Colleges (extract)

110 **René Gimpel**
statement

112 **Jean Fisher**
The 'Proletarianisation' of Art

114 **Michael Madden**
A Warning from a Trade Unionist

115 **Graham Higgin**
Lotting the Lottery

116 **Alex Sainsbury**
The Total Quality Culture

118 **Arts Council of England**
Christmas card

120 **John Pick**
The Two Faces of Chris Smith

122 **David Heathcoat-Amory**
The British Art Market

124 **Stewart Home**
Why Public Subsidy and Private Sponsorship Can't Save Art from Complete and Utter Irrelevance

126 **Terry Atkinson**
Eurostar Avant-Gardism Secured in Both Directions by Dumbing Down from London and by Wising Up from Paris

129 **Gerry Robinson**
The Creativity Imperative: Investing in the Arts in the Twenty-first Century (extract)

130 **Sacha Craddock**
Art Between Politics and Glamour

132 **Mark Wallinger**
Fool Britannia: Not New, Not Clever, Not Funny

136 **William Furlong**
Conversation Piece

Selected texts 1945–1997

142 **Lord Keynes**
The Arts Council: Its Policy and Hopes

144 **Wyndham Lewis**
Bread and Ballyhoo (extract)

145 **The Arts Council of Great Britain**
Basic Policy of the Arts Council (extract)

146 **Jennie Lee**
A Policy for the Arts: The First Steps (extract)

147 **Rt. Hon. Viscount Eccles**
Politics and the Quality of Life (extract)

148 **The Arts Council of Great Britain**
Report of the Community Arts Working Party (extract)

149 **The Labour Party**
The Arts and the People: Labour Party Policy Towards the Arts (extract)

150 **Kingsley Amis**
An Arts Policy?

156 **Raymond Williams**
The Arts Council (extract)

158 **Sir William Rees-Mogg**
The Glory of the Garden (extract)

159 **Geoff Mulgan and Ken Worpole**
Saturday Night or Sunday Morning? (extract)

162 **The Arts Council of Great Britain**
Towards a National Arts and Media Strategy (extract)

166 **Terry Dicks and Tony Banks**
House of Commons Debate: The Arts (extract)

172 **Chris Smith**
A Vision for the Arts

174 **Gilbert and George**
Postal Sculpture

175 **Notes on the Authors and Artists**

180 **Index**

Preface

Andrew Brighton, Trustee, Peer

Ingrid Swenson, Curatorial Director, Peer

At the beginning of his *New Statesman* lecture at the Banqueting House, London, in June of 2000, the Chairman of the Arts Council of England, Gerry Robinson, stated: 'This is a great time to be talking about the arts'. We at the independent arts charity, Peer, agree with this, but probably for different reasons. We want to talk about the arts because it seems that much has recently been happening in the relationship between cultural practitioners and policy makers. The dynamics of this relationship beg fundamental questions about the principles of State support for the arts, and the genesis of *Art For All?* was a sense of the inadequacy of much of the discussion of these questions. This book therefore sets out to raise and inform the level of debate.

The majority of the material in *Art For All?* arises from a selection of contributions made after a nationwide call for submissions through advertisements – in *Art Monthly* and the *Times Literary Supplement* – editorials, widely distributed press releases and a poster campaign. Other material has been 'curated'; that is to say, recent and historical documents and texts have been selected in order to broaden or contextualise the debate. Though they are often in extracted form, we have let the contributions stand on their own, without editorial comment, in order to provide a flow of argument and counter-argument. The balance, if ever one can be democratically struck, was ultimately the decision of the distinguished guest editors, Mark Wallinger and Mary Warnock, and we are extremely grateful for their time, clear thinking and support.

Much of what has been written about arts policy is perhaps necessarily boring. Most serious publications on this subject are either institutional reports or descriptions of the structure and history of modern arts administration. As such, they are a minor part of the literature on public administration and management. There is little to distinguish their language and assumptions from any other area of public-sector reporting and history writing. *Art For All?* gives public voice to views from artists, curators, critics, cultural commentators, politicians, teachers and others. The way in which it has been edited and produced reflects its aspirations to the condition of art publication rather than to the language and logic of management and political overviews. It has been modelled more on Wyndham Lewis's *Blast* than on Government white papers or Arts Council reports.

A factor that makes many discussions of 'the arts' seem empty, full of gesturing towards nothing precise, is that they are often predicated on something we perceive to be a mistake – the very idea that there is such as thing as 'The Arts' as a homogenous entity. In Britain, what the establishment usually has in mind when it speaks of 'the arts' is the performing arts. The different histories, ideologies and political economies of specific art forms get lost in what are, at least for the visual arts, inappropriate generalities. While this book represents views from other cultural arenas, there is a predominance of responses from those in the visual art world.

As this collection of texts and images demonstrates, the shifts in thinking about arts funding have a longer history and more diverse origins than simply the current Government's position. Without doubt, *Art For All?* raises political issues, but it is not intended to be party political. This said, the emphasis lies in a concern with the basic principles of public-sector arts funding. We believe that these principles have not been sufficiently discussed, in part because of the character of some criticisms made by the great and the good. Prominent arts professionals have tended to reduce the discussion to demands for increased funding for the arts. The amount of money the State should give to support culture seems to us secondary to the question of why there should be public support at all. Furthermore, debates tend to be dis-tracted from these questions by 'newsworthy' arts grandees accusing particular politicians of having philistine tastes. This should be irrelevant. Policies may be philistine in the sense that they are damaging to the arts, just as policies for health may undermine the health service. But both would suggest political incompetence and misconception rather than personal philistinism or the love of bugs and disease.

Some contributions call for the abolition of State arts funding and pour contempt upon arts administrators. Others advocate more or different funding and administration. There are jokes, polemics, considered arguments, pieces of evidence, documents, anecdotes and images.

Art For All? is a book about a complex culture, and its diverse mode of presentation honours that characteristic. Perhaps a primary source of the unease that gave rise to it is the sense that our political culture can no longer grasp and value this complexity.

Introduction

Mary Warnock, Guest Editor

There has been State subsidy of the arts since pre-classical times, and in what we think of as the greatest periods for art, both in Greece and Rome, public finance was an essential condition, without which architecture and the decorative arts as well as literature and probably music could not have flourished. In *Art For All?*, our attention is confined to the relationship between government and the arts since 1945. We are concerned with an ongoing, contemporary relationship, a source of conflict, irritation and confusion, both in theory and practice.

In this volume, most of the material (apart from the historical documents) happens to be concerned with the visual arts. However, the arguments and opinions expressed are relevant to music, drama and film as well. Literature, on the whole, is less dependent on government support, being reliant instead on the commercial market.

Throughout the diverse texts and views collected here, certain recurrent themes emerge. One is the insistence by successive governments, Conservative and Labour alike, that they must enunciate a Policy for the Arts. This is because they take it for granted that they will have to pay to a certain extent to support artistic activity, and the questions for them, therefore, are: how much? to whom? and with what possible show of justice? However, this assumption is challenged by some contributors, either because of the growth of bureaucracy that follows from it, or because of a perceived threat to freedom (a threat fully understood by Virgil when asked to compose an epic to glorify the Emperor Augustus), or simply because they feel that art should pay for itself.

When the Arts Council was first established, the Treasury allocated to it a sum of money to distribute according to its own judgement. This was an exemplification of the 'Arm's Length' principle, much admired, and on the whole successful in many spheres of activity, until it was gradually eroded in the 1980s. Nowhere was this more obvious than in the distribution of money to universities. Under the Thatcher Government, it was felt that the University

Grants Committee, an Arm's Length body, could no longer be permitted to put in their applications for State funding according to what they regarded as the needs of the universities, so that they could fulfil their own academic plans without regard to what government wanted from them. It was decided that money must come to them from one central body under certain government-laid-down conditions, having regard, among other things, to 'Access', and subject to 'Quality Assessment'. Quality was judged according to fixed 'Performance Indicators'. This is not an exact parallel to what has happened to the Arts Council, but it is enough to show that it is not only the current Government that is obsessed with ways of artificially quantifying the difference between good and bad. Indeed, it was under Richard Luce, a Conservative Minister for the Arts, that a joint body, drawn from the Arts Council, the British Film Institute, the Craft Council and the Regional Arts Boards produced a strategy for the arts and media, part of which is included in this book.

This is a document that repays study, for in some ways it explains the uneasiness, not to say disgust, with current policies expressed by many of the contributors. It also exemplifies the general loss of nerve among those who put together the strategy, sharing with all bureaucrats a terror of being found guilty of a heretical belief in a standard of taste or aesthetic judgement. (One important way of avoiding the necessity of such corporate judgement has been to shift responsibility to the Regions.) It also incorporates some related ideas that are dear to the present Government.

These ideas cluster round what is known as 'Access'. The opposite of 'accessible' is, of course, 'elitist', and it is to the avoidance of this that policy seems above all to be directed. There is an ambiguity inherent in concepts of 'culture' and 'art', and it is here that they are most damaging. If one rules out elitism as a matter of principle, then one has immediately eliminated the notion of 'high' culture, in which, naturally, only some people will be interested. This is not to say, however, that such culture is inaccessible.

For those who want to attend them – and this is not everyone – there could be nothing more accessible than the Proms, for example. Yet, year after year, the series could hardly make a greater contribution to 'high' culture.

The Government's view of culture is reflected in the title of Chris Smith's Ministry – 'The Department of Culture, Media and Sport' – and he has spoken of 'Britain's 450 billion creative industries'. If, in order to satisfy the criterion of accessibility, absolutely anything must count as 'cultural' or as 'art', then the question arises more acutely than ever before as to what should be supported. One answer seems to be that governments should subsidise that which people want. But there is a danger, which frequently emerges in the following pages, that an orthodoxy is becoming established among the bureaucrats, the administrators and the curators as to what it is that people do (or should) want. The Government asserts that to earn State support, art must be 'accessible', but it must also be 'subversive' and 'challenging'. Above all, it must somehow contribute to 'Community'. But some may take John Drummond's view that: 'Failing to differentiate between the good and the indifferent, while sheltering under a cloud of spurious democracy is … not good enough. It is a betrayal of all our civilisation has stood for.'[1]

We hope that the pieces that follow will help to determine whether Government has come up with proper, or indeed intelligible, criteria for excellence in the arts.

1 John Drummond, *Tainted by Experience*, Faber & Faber (London), 2000, p.459.

Mark Wallinger, Guest Editor

What became clear in the course of our discussions whilst editing this publication was not only the range of arguments made, but also the breadth of tone, the sheer variety of language, with which the arguments are expressed. Since it would be difficult to introduce these essays in a tone that could encompass the magisterial, the peevish, the idealistic, the righteous, the absurd and the down-right hacked off, this introduction is not intended as a measured overview, but as a similarly opinionated response from my point of view as an artist …

The need to commodify art, or the willingness of artists to see their practice reified, is essential for securing the money. Subsidised institutions within a mixed economy have inevitably struggled to find ways in which to confer value on art distinct from the market. The visibility and fashionableness of art, and the increasing media profile of certain artists, are an insistent siren call to loosen the public purse strings. So it is perhaps no surprise that initiatives wholly engendered by public institutions require *bona fide* credentials from artists as potential agents of moral improvement before they can get the money.

Funding for artists comes with long ideological and economic strings attached. As an artist, one has to use another language. The ideas, hunches and vacillations that accompany the creation of an artwork have to be banished so that a seamless project can be proposed that can guarantee a calculable return from the potential audience – regardless of race, creed, or colour.

Unable to codify artistic practice according to the artist's experience, the burgeoning ranks of plutocrats, bureaucrats and apparatchiks have evolved a vocabulary and practice of Swiftian inversion, imperturbably Soviet in its incontestable rectitude. The aims of the work have to be pitched like an application for planning permission in a parallel universe, in which the offence to neighbours is measured by the degree of irrelevance one can bring to their lives, or the hope that the response of an indifferent public can feed back as a dividend return on the project.

This is a fundamentalist vision of art in which it is hoped that the viewer will 'interact' with the work to arrive at a prescribed interpretation. Cause and effect must be measurable in order to gauge the success of the work and to justify the jobs of the commissioners – the great-and-the-good and the not-up-to-much.

Prejudices must be challenged, new audiences must be reached, something-or-other must be subverted. One has to deal in absolutes – a world of binary oppositions that are readily identified, diagnosed and neutered. The economics of arts patronage encourage a concomitant economy within the structures they create and deploy, expressing their desire to meet the audience halfway. The language of accessibility has led to an almost unconscious adoption of Reithian values – the mission to educate, entertain and instruct – which have permeated from outreach projects to the galleries and museums.

This itself was a reaction to the sanctification of greed and conspicuous consumption in the late 1980s, when, in the absence of any meaningful debate, a new apolitical orthodoxy gave the opportunity of power and influence to a swill of artists/curators who might previously have found employment in PR.

The subsequent rise of the curator has coincided with the decline of the artist. The continuing fall-out from the collapse of painting as the axiomatic site of the modernist avant garde, and the subsequent hegemony of conceptualism, has required a small army of interpreters, eagerly co-opted by institutions anxious to be identified with the new zeitgeist. This clamour for explanation means that it is becoming increasingly hard to distinguish curators from what used to be called sociologists. Where once an artist's work was analysed in terms of the formal development of themes and subject matter, it is now corralled into the box marked 'Issues', a proper understanding of which is contingent and contextual and for which the individual artist would necessarily have only an imperfect or partial grasp.

The danger comes when the Lottery-funded superstructures – the museums and galleries – expect curators working within a management structure to make far-reaching and disproportionately influential decisions. The fact that they are essentially civil servants means that responsibility for these decisions can be all-too easily diffused through the system. The star curators, impatient for novelty, can dodge in-house and out-house like the hokey-cokey, whereas the artist, once curated, is either collusive with, or powerless to resist, the bowdlerisation of their poetry for inclusion in an anthology of prose.

When decisions and positions hard won and developed over a lifetime are reducible to indicators of cultural diversity, with no regard to individual development, the result is a trite and condescending anthropology of the modern age. Shrinking time into space, the here and now, the better to categorise, catalogue and compare, encourages a kind of historical amnesia where curators can pick and choose from a smorgasbord of narcotic sensation, a baseless landscape of outrage. Art is the new rock 'n' roll. Art is for everyone. Art is the opium of the people.

Bob and Roberta Smith

Postcard

Dear Ingrid 1. Aug 2000
Most Artists are
independently wealthy
"Fat Cats" who do not
deserve or need Public
Money! Arts Council
money should go into
education and Public Arts projects
to encourage those who are not so middle class
as to think of going to "Art school" to make
Arts politi... Art + be creative. Conservative
Does Barone... worse. + What on Earth
all the ... know?
Bob.

To Ingrid Swenson
Shoreditch Town Hall
380 Old Street.
London.
EC1V 9LT .

BOB AND ROBERTA SMITH   Stop It Write Now! 2000
Wall painting
© Courtesy Anthony Wilkinson Gallery, London.
Photographed during Intelligence ...
2000
© Ph... Mark ...hcote
503...495-...2/76... 2.5...0700

Chris Smith, Secretary of State for Culture, Media and Sport

Lecture at the RSA, London – 22 July 1999

Government and the Arts

Just over two years ago, when I spoke at the Royal Academy a few weeks after the general election, I ended with a quotation from Hazlitt. It seems to me now, today, an appropriate place to begin. (I pointed out at the time that I thought Hazlitt had been somewhat unkind to the Scots in what he said, and I still hold to that.) He wrote:

> Scotland is of all other countries in the world perhaps the one in which the question 'what is the use of that?' is asked oftenest. But where this is the case, the Fine Arts cannot flourish, or attain their high and palmy state, or scarcely creep out of the ground to expose themselves to the 'eager and nipping air' of this kind of rigid catechising scrutiny; for they are their own sole end and use, and in themselves 'sum all delight'. It may be said of the Fine Arts that 'they toil not, neither do they spin', but are like the lilies of the valley, lovely in themselves, graceful and beautiful, and precious in the sight of all but the blind. They do not furnish us with food or raiment, it is true; but they please the eye, they haunt the imagination, they solace the heart. If after that you ask the question, Cui bono? there is no answer to be returned.

That sentiment stands as an eternal justifying reason for why the fine arts matter. They matter simply because of what they do for our feelings, our moods, our imaginations, our understanding, our enjoyment, our inner selves. They are an integral part of our self-definition. They provide a window through which we can see others and a mirror in which we can see ourselves.

And because they lead us, sometimes gently, sometimes forcibly, sometimes imperceptibly, to self-knowledge, they also inevitably help both to shape and to characterise a society. The arts are a civilising influence. Indeed, in many ways the arts and civilisation are synonymous. We describe the civilisations of the past more in terms of their arts than of their GDP or even their technology. The success of Medici Florence is measured by the works of art that were commissioned, not by the percentage deals on trade that were done to pay for them. Indeed, the judgment of history on the latter part of the twentieth century will record the achievements of Ted Hughes, of Seamus Heaney, of Lucian Freud, of Barbara Hepworth, of Benjamin Britten and of Iris Murdoch long before it turns its attention to the doings of several hundreds of Cabinet Ministers or captains of industry.

The arts, then, are central to our very beings, and central to our society. But what of the relationship between Government and the arts? This is a potentially explosive combination. Much artistic endeavour is by its very nature antinomian. It disrespects authority or imposed order. It can be highly critical. It can shock. But that does not mean that there should be no supportive relationship between Government and the arts. I reject the arguments of those purists in the world of the arts or those philistines in the world of politics who say that there should be no support. There should be, and for eight reasons.

The first reason is quite simply the centrality of the arts to our understanding of ourselves, something I've already touched on. If art is so important in the texture of our society, then any responsible Government needs to ensure that it is nurtured, encouraged, enabled, and spread.

The second is that you will not achieve real excellence in many art forms without the support of public funds. And the importance of art is diminished if we do not strive for the best. Of course some art will always be able to thrive on ticket sales and private sponsorship alone. And will do it superbly well. But that is not and cannot be true of everything. If we want to ensure that the most challenging theatrical performances, the best of world-class opera or of musical performance are happening here and available to all of us, then we need to provide support from the public purse. Without it, our artistic diet will be poorer, and our lives will be poorer too.

Third, the availability of excellence must not be confined to one part of the country alone. The fact that the Royal Shakespeare Company spends time – a lot of time – performing in Newcastle or Plymouth is of real benefit to communities who would otherwise lose out. The fact that Bournemouth and Birmingham have orchestras of the highest quality, as well as London, is surely important. And the fact that Britain's (and the world's) largest and most varied festival of the arts does not take place in the South-East of England but in Scotland helps to prove Hazlitt's scepticism wrong. Geographical diversity, however, rests on public subsidy as well as on the inspiration of individuals, local authorities and others up and down the country.

Fourth, we must recognize and celebrate the cultural diversity of our country. It is no longer true to conceive British culture as being a monolithic entity; we need rather to speak of British cultures. And a healthy, thriving publicly funded arts system needs to develop organically as society develops, reflecting and sustaining the full diversity and richness of our national identity and our cultural traditions.

Fifth, innovation in particular needs public support. Innovative art sometimes attracts small audiences. Occasionally it may repel as well as challenge. Sometimes it will require courage to say that something difficult should be supported by the public purse. But it should be done, because without innovation, without the pushing of boundaries, without the encouragement of new work, the progress of artistic life is stunted. The support of innovative work of quality will not always receive popular approval. It is why a popularity test should never become the be-all and end-all of contributions from the public purse.

Sixth, public subsidy can allow the widest possible pool of talent within the arts to be trawled and trained – irrespective of personal means or circumstances. Enabling artists to develop as artists is part of what a subsidy system must seek to facilitate.

Seventh, the role that the arts can play in assisting the process of education, both within the formal school and college system and for learning throughout life, is of obvious importance. When David Blunkett and I visited Haggerston School in Hackney last week, we saw the opening of a performance of Macbeth put on by the girls of the school. Not only was it a rumbustious and impressive performance. It had helped to bring out a real sense of self-confidence in all the performers. Time and again the evidence has shown that pupils who engage in music or drama perform better across the whole range of academic subjects. This synergy of arts and education will not be realised unless we seek to assist it to happen.

And eighth, perhaps most importantly of all, public subsidy has to be about enabling the greatest possible number of people to experience and enjoy the arts. This fundamental purpose – that goes most frequently under the rather dry title of "access" – is central to any sensible public policy for the arts. Broadening out the accessibility of the arts – without of course losing any of the excellence in the process – has to be the aim, and it cannot be achieved without subsidy. I lose patience with those who claim that greater access means compromising on quality. That is nonsense, as anyone who went to the Hamlyn week at the National Theatre recently would know. The Hamlyn weeks have brought in to the theatre thousands of people who have never been to the theatre in their lives before. You can tell, from the absence of the usual reverential hush before the dimming of the lights – followed by intense concentration on the stage, the moment the play begins. And if only a small percentage of those people, experiencing drama, live, for the first time, decide to come back again because they loved it so much the first time, then surely that is something to be rejoiced at. Through the establishment of the New Audiences fund that we have made available to the Arts Council, we are seeking to spread these opportunities to more people and more places – and to make some of the follow-up visits more affordable, too.

These, then, are the eight principal reasons, the justifications, for applying public subsidy, from the tax payer, to the arts. Yes we should do it because it's simply a good thing to do, part of being a civilised society. But we do it also for those great purposes of excellence, access, and education, that we have consistently set out. If I had to sum up the central thrust of arts policy it would be simply this: we want to make the best things in life available to the greatest number of people.

I do want to sound one note of warning, however. I believe passionately in the value of art for art's sake. But I do not believe in grants for grants' sake. There are perhaps a few people in the world of the arts who seem to believe that the world owes them a living. I make no apology for disagreeing; for saying that if the taxpayers are putting in, as they should, substantial amounts of public subsidy, then they are entitled to see something in return for that investment. Some sign that those eight principles of public funding are being realised. This is why we have put in place robust funding agreements with each of our sponsored bodies, setting out responsibilities and objectives on each side, and establishing a clear aim for increased artistic activity in return for increased support. And it is also why we have established the new Quality, Efficiency and Standards Team, which will help to look at value for money, at the artistic or sporting or tourism or heritage return for particular programmes, and also link lessons of best practice across different disciplines and organisations. QUEST will help to refine the indicators that we build in to the funding agreements; it will seek to make the important measurable rather than the measurable important; and it will help good art and good management to come together in an entirely practical way.

I am enthusiastic about the work that can be done on this. Instead of creating another bureaucratic body, we are actively seeking to drive up standards, pin down value for money, and achieve more artistic activity. We wish to make the best available to everyone and to do it not by making rhetorical speeches but by enforcing funding agreements that require arts institutions to reach out to the communities around them. Isn't that what any civilised society should aspire to do? And if the arts are a civilising influence shouldn't we seek to extend this to every housing estate, every primary school, every old people's home? That seems to me to be an entirely appropriate function of government in a modern democracy.

So let me make this clear. We believe fundamentally in the fine arts and in the need for Government to support them. We do not disparage the popular arts, but believe in the need for all kinds of powerful and affecting artistic activity to be available to as many people as possible. But we also believe clearly that where public investment is made there must be some sort of return, in artistic value and reach, for the contributing public.

Some people, I have to say, appear to have wilfully misinterpreted what we are seeking to do. So let me set three myths to rest. The first myth is the most obviously wrong: that somehow this Government is uninterested in the fine arts. To those who claim this I would simply say, look at what we have actually done over the last two years:

- We have put in place a three-year funding settlement involving an increase of £125 million for the arts and £99 million for museums and galleries, the biggest ever increase in funding for cultural activity from central government.
- We are giving the institutions we directly support the certainty that comes from three-year funding agreements.
- We have given a firm commitment of a continuing one-sixth share of lottery funds for the arts for the next ten years at least.
- We have put in place a special New Audiences fund to help bring new people to experience the arts, through cheap ticket schemes, vouchers for students, transport in rural areas, touring grants, and schemes to enable schoolchildren to take up empty seats at performances.
- We have encouraged the Arts Council to streamline itself, to make itself less unwieldy, to reduce bureaucracy, and as a result to save some £10 million over the next five years that can be directly used to support the arts.
- We have overseen an increasing devolution of decision-making, both for grant-in-aid and for lottery funds, to the Regional Arts Boards, to bring the decisions closer to the activity on the ground. I want to pay considerable tribute to the work of Gerry Robinson and Peter Hewitt, often in difficult circumstances, in achieving this.
- Together with DfEE, we have established a special fund to enable dance and drama students to get proper grants and assistance to undertake courses at accredited institutions.
- We helped to protect the position of artists and performers in relation to the payment of National Insurance Contributions.
- We have established the National Foundation for Youth Music, with £30 million of lottery funds, to help ensure – together with an additional £150 million from DfEE – that every child who wants to, has the chance to learn to sing or play a musical instrument.
- We have provided funds so that from April of this year every child will be able to go to all our national museums and galleries for free, and from next April every pensioner, and from the year after that wider access provisions for everyone.
- We have introduced a £15 million fund for the 43 designated museums across the whole of England, spreading central funding for the first time widely to the regions.
- We have ensured that the provisions of the New Deal are appropriate to the needs of young musicians wishing to seek a career in music.
- Together with DfEE, we have insisted that art, music, drama, and sport must remain a statutory partof the curriculum in our schools.
- We have established NESTA – the National Endowment for Science, Technology and the Arts – to provide a national fund for talent, enabling people with a skill to develop their abilities and ideas, as well as helping to break down the artificial barriers between arts and sciences.
- We have helped to develop Elliot Bernerd's visionary proposals for the future of the South Bank Centre.
- We have put in place substantial incentives for film-making in Britain, with new tax reliefs, an ending of the Channel Four Funding Formula, a new agreed skills investment fund for training in the industry, the establishment of a British film office in Los Angeles, a new definition for British films, and the establishment of the new Films Council.
- We have emphasised the crucial cultural importance of the BBC, and the need for it to operate especially in a new era of multi-channel television – as a true benchmark of quality in our broadcasting environment.

That's not a bad record for a couple of years. Of course there is more to do, much more; but I would challenge anyone to try and argue, in the face of that, that we are somehow "not interested" in the arts. We are, and I believe we have been proven so by our actions.

There are two areas of work in particular which remain of deep concern to me, and on which I hope that we can make further progress before long. The first of these is the condition of regional producing theatre in this country, from which so much of our acting and producing talent has always emerged, and which provides a lifeblood to cultural activity in many different towns and regions. Some theatres are truly struggling at present, some of them burdened with major financial debts from previous years, and we need to identify rapidly how they can be helped. The second area is similar, and relates to the orchestras, particularly outside London. Again, some are struggling. This is why I have specifically asked the

Note to readers: Pages 14 and 15 were to contain an extract from Chris Smith's Introduction to *Creative Britain* (Faber & Faber, London 1998). The text we wished to use was from the last paragraph on page 22 to the end of the chapter on page 27. Unfortunately, during the late stages of design, the DCMS instructed us not to print this text. In its place we were offered the rather longer lecture reproduced here, but only on the condition that we printed it in full and unedited. We apologise if the resultant type size is difficult to read.

Arts Council to conduct two reviews, one of regional theatre and one of orchestras. Both of these processes are now well under way.

This approach must of course be thorough, and unsentimental. It must be based on rigorous analysis of regional patterns, genuine financial positions, quality of management, and above all quality of artistic work. But it must not assume that simply because a particular configuration of funding support has always been in place that must continue to be the case for evermore. Hard decisions may emerge from these reviews, but let us make sure that the range, viability, accessibility, and excellence of theatrical and orchestral work across the regions of England end up stronger as a result of this process. That must be the aim.

The second charge that is sometimes levelled is that we are engaged – in an overused and facile phrase – in a "dumbing down" exercise; that we are seeking only to support the popular and not the highbrow, and that somehow by arguing for greater access we are endangering the very excellence that the access is designed to enable people to share. What nonsense. Too many use this accusation in lieu of a proper debate about the nature and impact of the arts, and the audience for them. The commercial music and film industries are important and produce outstanding work of real quality, and deserve Government attention – not through Exchequer grants but through a sensible tax regime and good international copyright protection for the value of intellectual property. But to pay attention to their needs does not mean in any way that you are ignoring the needs of the non-commercial sector.

Nor does a commitment to wider access mean a diminution of artistic quality. That's why I want the new Royal Opera House when it opens to have some cheaper ticket prices and to have a less exclusive atmosphere and to do even more education work with schools. But I want to see it doing work of incomparable artistic beauty, just as it has at its best in the past. Elite performance on the stage does not need to be matched by exclusive social performance in the stalls. We need a world-class opera house in our capital city, and I'm pleased that we seem to be on course for securing precisely that ambition. I'm proud we've played our part in helping to secure it. And I'm enormously grateful to Colin Southgate, Michael Kaiser, the private donors and others, for enabling it to happen. Let's share it as widely as we possibly can with our fellow citizens.

There is no contradiction between the aims of excellence and access. Indeed, quite the opposite. They go hand in hand together.

There is a third myth, and it is equally wrong. This is the charge that we have somehow re-labelled the arts as the "creative industries", and that we are only interested in the economic return that the arts bring, not the intellectual or spiritual gain for those who experience them. I hope what I have already said today can shoot down this particular canard. But for the avoidance of doubt, let me just spell out precisely what we believe. We believe with Hazlitt that the arts provide their own justification by what they do for all of us. But we also believe that they happen to have an increasing economic importance in our national life. And that the performing and visual and plastic arts sit alongside a whole range of other activities – commercial music, film, architecture, design, publishing, broadcasting, multimedia, fashion – which are of increasing value to our economy. We have indeed called this whole cohort of industries and activities the "creative industries", because they rest ultimately for their economic value on the creative imagination of individuals, and the intellectual property created by them.

These industries are worth over £60 billion every year to our nation's economy. They are growing at twice the rate of growth of the economy as a whole. We would be foolish to ignore their needs. We do think that it is important to look at the copyright protection measures they require, at the export assistance, at the ways in which the formal education system, at both school and college, can assist, at the access to venture capital that small creative businesses need at the outset. That is why we set out to map the extent and nature of these creative industries, producing our mapping document last December. And it's why we are now turning our attention to the legal, financial and educational requirements they have. There's nothing here to threaten the pure value of artistic activity. Far from it.

Other European Union member states have taken a keen interest in the Creative Industries Mapping Document and have started to undertake similar studies. We are now taking a new position at the forefront of European cultural policy. Perhaps we are witnessing something of a sea-change in our economy in this country, something in which we may be way ahead of most of the rest of the world. It is commonly accepted that we have, over the last three centuries, moved as a nation from an economy largely based on agriculture to an economy largely based on manufacture and trade, to a country where service industries are developing as manufacturing partly diminishes. But perhaps we are now seeing a further change, with the growing importance of knowledge – and creativity-based enterprise taking over from some of the more traditional service sectors as the real generators of growth. Our creative traditions, our command of the English language, and our world lead in many of these fields, are among the reasons for our success. But surely we should be making a real effort to play to our strengths here, and seek to understand how Government can help to secure progress.

So far I have sought to outline how the Government must and can and does support the arts. But what of the future? What are the issues that lie ahead of us, and that must shape the relationship between Government and the arts over the next two years? Partly, of course, we must hold fast to the fundamental approach that we have already set in place: seeking to make the best available to the most. There is continuing work to do here.

But I want also today to set out three challenges for the next few years. They are challenges for us in Government as much as they are for those in the world of the arts. They are things we much tackle together, working in partnership.

The first challenge is to demonstrate very clearly how art and artistic activity can transform the lives and hopes of those who are socially excluded or marginalised. And then to make it happen, on the widest possible scale. Last week we published our Report from the Policy Action Team, set up under the umbrella of the Social Exclusion Unit, to look at the role of arts and sport in promoting social regeneration. It is a very impressive report, and contains a litany of examples of how inspirational people are doing precisely this, here and now, the length and breadth of Britain.

Take, for example, the Look Ahead hostel in Aldgate in the East End of London, which I visited a couple of weeks ago. Home to 160 homeless men and women, it was for years a byword for hopelessness. Staff had to go round in twos and threes for fear of assault. Furniture had to nailed to the floor to prevent its removal or destruction. The next door school playground was littered in broken glass from bottles thrown from the hostel windows. But instead of despairing, the Look Ahead organisation lived up to its name and had the imagination to bring in two people to start using art and a drama and artistic activity to transform the hostel. It is now an almost unrecognizable place. It is covered in art works and mosaics made by the residents. The furniture is beautifully designed, movable and completely intact. The atmosphere sparkles. The residents now work with the teachers and pupils at the next door school to produce art and drama. Some of them put on powerful theatrical performances about homelessness. They publish books of poetry. This is not about gimmicks; it is about real human progress and hope. And it rests on a very simple principle. Involvement in art can give someone, however marginalised they may be from society, a sense of self-worth, a self-confidence, something to live for and to feel proud about. Of course in the battle for social regeneration bricks and mortar and safe roofs and good schools and the chance of a job are vital. But the starting point for all of this has to be a sense that you can achieve something as an individual, that there is something to aspire to in life, that you are worth something as a human being. Involvement in the arts can give you just that.

The challenge for all of us is how to ensure that examples like this can be copied and learned from nationwide. How can we help the same process to begin in other hostels for the homeless, other estates, other difficult or dispossessed neighbourhoods? We can do some things in ways we have already set out: targeting lottery funds particularly on helping areas of deprivation; putting in place the idea of "community halls" that cover a whole range of different artistic and sporting and community activities; developing the concept of bursaries for individuals with talent stuck in a cycle of deprivation; implementing many of the proposals of the Report from the National Advisory Council on Creative and Cultural Education, seeing the education system as a platform upon which to build a wider engagement with the arts. But let's also look together, over the next few months, at other ways of taking this agenda further forward.

The second challenge I would set out is the need for us to apply our artistic values to the quality of our built environment. In some ways the environment around us, especially in urban areas, is the most important field of artistic activity that makes an impact on any of us. It affects us all, very directly. Every day, any day, we walk or pass through areas of real beauty and real ugliness. We see buildings that inspire us and depress us. We enjoy open spaces and squares that invite or repel. We see works of public art that have become local symbols – such as the rightly-admired Angel of the North – and others that have been completely destroyed by graffiti and neglect. And we see what can be achieved, in cities like Bilbao or Barcelona or Glasgow or Birmingham, where art and architecture and public sculpture and urban open space have been looked at as a whole, and where economic and social regeneration has followed in the wake of aesthetic improvement in the public realm.

Richard Rogers' recent report on the urban environment gives us some pointers to the future. In my own Department we have recently established the Commission on Architecture and the Built Environment, which will shortly take over responsibility from the Royal Fine Art Commission. I am delighted that Stuart Lipton has made such an active start in preparing for the formal establishment of the new Commission. And I see its principal task as being to look at how quality can be restored to our buildings and our urban spaces. It's a task for all of us, not just one Government Commission or even one Government Department.

The third challenge is for us to reach out to those who are as yet untouched by artistic experience and activity. 50% of our fellow countrymen and women never ever, in the course of a year, set foot inside a concert hall, a theatre, an opera house, or an art gallery. They never go to any kind of arts event. They do not see the arts as something for them. They associate the arts with other people; the arts, they say, "are not for the likes of us". Yet we know from those who do venture across the daunting threshold just once, that the experience can be every bit as moving and compelling as it is for everyone else. How then do we entice, enable, encourage this unreached half of the population? How do we enable them to come to an experience and understanding of the arts? How do we change the culture of culture, to make the arts more of a natural part of life?

We do it by enabling institutions to invite more people in; by taking art out into places where people lead their everyday lives; by ensuring that subsidised artistic activity reflects the full range and diversity of cultural experience in Britain. We do it by ensuring that our public service broadcasters hold fast to their responsibilities in the arts. We do it by encouraging arts organisations to join the New Generation Audiences Scheme – making unused seats available free to schoolchildren through the internet – or to offer tickets at concessionary rates to children, or pensioners, or students, or those who are unwaged, or to make professional facilities available for use by the local community. And we do it by consciously seeking to avoid the inherent snobbishness of the language some people have used about the arts in the past, encouraging not breaking down an artistic divide in society.

But we in Government, or the Arts Council, or local authorities, cannot do it alone. We need your help in this endeavour. Let's not forget that this week is the first week of the Proms season at the Royal Albert Hall. The starting point of the early Proms, let's remember, was not about patronising a broad audience, but about building from an established basis of popular entertainment to stretch an audience's enjoyment and understanding to a new and higher plane. We need to find new ways of doing the same: connecting with the public taste, but then shaping and extending it.

As part of this, we need to put the end user at the heart of our approach. We have tended in any discussion of arts policy (and I am no exception to this rule) to talk about organisations and companies and institutions and funding mechanisms. We haven't talked enough about audiences, about attenders and participants and publics. We need to. We need to develop not just a language, but an attitude of mind that thinks about both consumers and producers. This isn't about letting consumption levels dictate what is produced. That would be, dangerously, letting the tail wag the artistic dog. It is however about thinking always, in everything we do, about how the work that is being done can most readily be shared with all those who might appreciate it.

Half a century ago J M Keynes, the newly appointed Chairman of the newly created Arts Council of a newly elected Government said 'We look forward to a time when the theatre, the concert hall and the art gallery will be a living element in everybody's upbringing.' That is an aspiration which we share but we do not want to wait another half a century for its realisation. That is why we have put in place a new approach, new structures, new funding agreements and new funds which will enable us to move closer to that goal. My challenge to all those in Britain who value the arts and work in the arts is this:– let us work together so that in ten years time that half of our people who are presently engaged in the cultural life of the country has grown to two-thirds. That truly would be something worth doing. It would bring us closer to that fundamental aim – to make the best things in life available to the greatest number.

Nearly ninety years ago James Oppenheim wrote a poem, having seen the banners carried by the women millworkers in the 1912 Lawrence textile strike in Massachusetts. It stands still as a cry from the heart for the fine things of life to be part of the struggle for better conditions for all.

> Smart art and love and beauty their drudging spirits knew.
> Yes, it is bread we fight for but we fight for roses too!

A useful reminder, perhaps, to any Government. We won't ignore it.

Mark Ryan

Manipulation Without End

Browse through any brochure, policy document or mission statement from the culture industry and you will find the same words and phrases popping up over and over again: 'accessibility' and 'relevance', 'promoting social inclusion and cultural diversity', 'empowering the learning and creative society', 'putting people first'. This sort of language, repeated ad nauseam, could be brushed off as little more than padding for dull speeches, but that would be to miss its significance. Choice of words is always revealing, and when a certain group of people come to share a fixed language, that language can reveal much about the thinking of the group as a whole.

Cultural language today is, with few exceptions, very bad language. Precision of meaning and the clear statement of aims is largely subordinated to another set of concerns: to insinuate a set of messages, the meaning of which often lies beyond the words themselves. Because the words have no clear meaning, the writer or speaker comes to rely on a set of assumptions as to how different elements of his or her audience will interpret these words. The meaning may be vague, but everyone will nevertheless know what the message is.

To get a sense of the vacuity of the language, let me make a comparison. 'An island of coal surrounded by a sea of fish' – this was how Aneurin Bevan, Minister for Health in the post-war Labour Government described his vision of Britain. Fifty years later, David Puttnam, director of *Chariots of Fire* and soon to be appointed a key advisor on science and culture by Tony Blair, self-consciously chose to update Bevan's vision in these terms: 'an island of creativity surrounded by a sea of understanding'.

The first thing we notice is that whereas Bevan uses two simple nouns of one syllable each, 'coal' and 'fish', Puttnam uses two of the most complex words in the English language, one of five syllables, the other of four. 'Coal' and 'fish' conjure up a clear and immediate image, while to the ear they balance each other perfectly. 'Creativity' and 'understanding', as Puttnam uses them, are by contrast vacuous and pretentious words that make a nonsense of the island/sea duality that served Bevan so well. Bevan's vision gives us a simple and immediate image of Britain, and at the same time one rich in historical and literary allusions. Puttnam's, on the other hand, is as empty as an inflated bladder. The update of Bevan's vision is all the worse when you consider that Puttnam is supposed to be a man of culture, unlike Bevan who left school when he was thirteen to work down the mines.

Puttnam's vision illustrates one of the chief characteristics of the new language. Rather than giving expression to a world that already exists, the language creates a world of its own, a virtual world, related more to how people might want to view things than to how they really are. Consider those terms 'creativity' and 'understanding'. Not only are they very complex words, they have also become extremely vague in their meaning in recent years, largely as a result of their use by the culture industry. 'Creativity' could refer to an artistic or intellectual process, but the very definition of such a process has now become so loose and subjective as to be itself meaningless. According to Arts Council boss, Gerry Robinson, 80% of a child's mental activity is creative, whereas with an adult it's around 1 or 2%. Used in this way, 'creativity' appears to mean lack of inhibition, a definition that might suggest that the most intelligent people are in fact the least creative, and that a vast reservoir of creativity already exists, which we have ignored. Or take the proclamation that we now work in a 'creative economy'. Here, the term 'creative' has simply replaced the word 'service', i.e., not manufacturing, which means that domestic servants and shop assistants, for example, are now classed as 'creatives'. As for 'understanding', this word is gradually shedding its proper meaning of intellectual effort directed at a particular problem, and acquiring a more emotional definition – having a generally tolerant and easy-going attitude. In other words, anybody can have the power of understanding so long as they chill out and try not to understand too much. Language such as Puttnam's can endow the everyday and banal with deep philosophical significance and make us feel as if we live in a world bursting at the seams with creative energy.

The fantasy language of the new elite works by massaging our conceit. 'Coal' and 'fish' are tough, blunt words that tell it like it is. 'Creativity' and 'understanding' on the other hand are soothing and emotionally uplifting words that switch off the critical faculties and turn on a variety of subliminal feelings. Their length and vagueness act almost as a deterrent against too close a scrutiny and instead invite the listener to surf along and enjoy. To those in the creative industries whom Puttnam was addressing, the message that they were to define the essential character of the new Britain must have been nice to hear. But taking the message to a broader public is more intoxicating still. 'An island of creativity' sounds great. We don't have to worry about the hard graft of work anymore. Now we might all be able to pursue our favourite hobbies all day long and make a fortune at it while all those foreigners bob around in their sea of understanding awaiting our scraps of brilliance. The harsh reality that Britain's creative industries are losing out to America and Europe on nearly every front gets swept away in the waves of Puttnam's exalted vision.

Pronouncements from the culture industry regularly come in torrents of flattery that tell us what a fascinating and culturally diverse society we live in. The past was another country, grey, uniform and hierarchical, where everybody was miserable and unhappy, performing mind-numbing work and with little opportunity to express their creative selves. In future, however, we will all define for ourselves the rules by which we wish to live, free of any external constraints. Only one thing holds us back: the forces of conservatism and elitism trying to impose their out-dated values on us. Once we chuck them overboard and give free rein to self-expression, our true brilliance will surely blossom.

Here, we come to the great paradox of the new language. Fantastic and indeterminate as it is, the language nevertheless manages to create a Manichaean world of good and bad, railroading us into a fixed pattern of thought. There are good words and there are bad words. 'Diversity' is good *per se*, 'exclusion' is bad. Who could be for exclusion, or against diversity? When the new elite says we must tackle 'social exclusion', such a statement could mean a lot of different things. 'Social exclusion' sounds like a nasty thing because of its vague association with poverty and deprivation. However, like most key terms in the language of the new elite, 'social exclusion' is a radically subjective concept. Anybody can be socially excluded if they feel that way, or what is more often the case, if the new elite thinks they should feel that way. In practice, this sort of language works as a system of veiled threats. The museum or gallery that is not prepared to turn its collection into a children's playground is being exclusive. The university with strict entrance tests is being exclusive because it values the education it gives over the

feelings of its applicants. Just imagine one of the new notables giving a speech on museums. If he came out straight and said in plain and simple English 'we believe museums should make people feel good', he may not get a great response. Rephrase that in the following terms: 'we believe museums must tackle social exclusion', and it works. An attack on culture is rebranded as a social and moral crusade. Anybody who dares take issue with him will be immediately branded a snob and an elitist.

Although the precise meaning is unclear, there is never a doubt as to what the new language intends. The artistic director who is concerned only with the merit of his work, when he hears that he must tackle social exclusion, knows that he is being warned. Perhaps he is thinking too much about art and not enough about The People. On the other side of the fence, speaking the language is like joining a Masonic lodge. You become 'one of us'.

The emphasis on The People, or on putting people first, sounds at first like a rehash of Stalinism. However, there is one crucial difference: Stalinist populism had a definite aim, a clear vision of the future, twisted as it was. The language of Stalinism was an attempt to cover up the brutal means by which it hoped to achieve its ends. The new elite, however, has no such vision; it is devoted only to keeping in with the public. That is why the language is about fantasy, flattery and manipulation rather than about

concealment. Lacking the discipline of any clear aims, art, culture and language become for the elite no more than instruments to keep people happy and itself in power. The language of the elite is above all the language of the demagogue.

Gerry Robinson

An Arts Council for the Future

Extract from *An Arts Council for the Future*, The Arts Council of Great Britain (London), 1998

[...] Too often in the past, the arts have taken a patronising attitude to audiences. Too often, artists and performers have continued to ply their trade to the same white, middle-class audiences. In the back of their minds lurks the vague hope that one day enlightenment might descend semi-miraculously upon the rest, that the masses might get wise to their brilliance. Ian McKellan's example in quitting London for Leeds may be a strong sign that this is an attitude that just won't do any more.

If we believe that experience of the arts can inspire, can lift the spirit, can add a third dimension to our lives, surely it is nothing less than our duty to go out and seek to spread what can be a life-transforming experience. [...]

At the same time as we redefine our preconceptions of the audience, perhaps it is also time for us to review our tendency to see the arts as somehow segregated from the real world. Even those who love and share the arts can at times compartmentalise them, regard them as a kind of bolt-on extra to reality. The truth is, the arts are the real world, in exactly the same way that commerce and the City are parts of the real world.

The last census suggested that around 650,000 were employed directly in Britain in what we might call the 'cultural industries'. Between 1981 and 1991, those in artistic, creative and related occupations increased by 34% at a time when general employment rose by just 4.6%. Without waiting for the next census, experience tells us that there has been a further significant expansion in the arts' role as an employer and as a generator of revenue.

Looking at the broader picture across the country, turnover for artists, sculptors, authors, composers and designers now stands at around £2.5 billion compared to £1.1 billion five years ago. The music sector is said to bring £2.5 billion to the UK economy and to account for 115,200 full-time and 160,000 part-time jobs. The arts and cultural tourism are among the fastest growing areas of tourism demand, netting nearly £5 billion in revenues each year. [...]

Now, perhaps some people might suggest that the Arts Council – or the arts – has no part in helping this Government, or any government, with its New Deal. I would turn the question round: why should the young and long-term unemployed only look to, say, clerical or construction work as their routes out of benefit? Why not look to work in the creative industries? Why shouldn't the arts play as social a role as, say, manufacturing? And why shouldn't the arts help lift depressed areas out of despair? Why aren't they central to it?

In the field of health care, there is also increasing evidence of the ability of the arts to help with patient recovery rates. Two years ago, the *British Medical Journal* published the results of a nine-year study that, after taking into account other factors such as lifestyle, income and housing, demonstrated a significant relationship between the degree of attendance at live cultural events and recovery of health. [...]

Naturally, there may be some fears among artists and arts companies that to take a broader view of the arts within society and the economy is to threaten the spirit of innovation and experiment, perhaps even the genius that is the true creative force behind challenging work. Some have seen the appointment of a businessman to the Chairmanship of the Arts Council as a threat to the very life-blood of the arts.

But, if we take that view, we underestimate both the robustness of the arts and the absolute refusal of the artist either to accept limits to the parameters of his or her work, or to yield to restraints on his or her imagination. Really, we should have more confidence in our arts and artists than that. [...]

Yes, traditional art forms are hardy and capable of innovation and reinvention, but flexibility has always characterised the arts and artists. In the past, the Arts Council has tended to distribute its budget largely according to art form. Perhaps it is time now for a funding system better adapted to that flexibility.

But before we consider some of the implications of that, could I first make a plea that we do not let ourselves be sidetracked by what I believe to be a bogus debate. The Government and the Arts Council's shared belief that the arts must not be a secret garden seems to have set some alarm bells ringing and raised concerns that the new millennium will be a new era of philistinism, that 'high art' – for want of a better phrase – will somehow be crushed by popular art.

It was a fear articulated by Professor George Steiner in this year's Proms lecture. He claimed then: 'A philistine, almost vengeful mood is being orchestrated to put in question the role of serious music. Our political masters and their minions would have it that grand opera, that symphonic orchestras and the halls they require are somehow luxuries. These, we are told, are the toys of the elite, inimitable to the robust joys of populism.'

Not only do I believe Steiner is wrong in his identification of 'a vengeful mood' against 'serious music', the more critical flaw is his suggestion that high art and popular art are somehow foes that cannot co-exist.

In fact, they are both essential links in the same complex, artistic chain. They feed off one another; they grow alongside each other. Everyone appreciates that the gateway to Birtwhistle and Cage can be Strauss or Mozart. A love of Betjeman can lead to appreciation of TS Eliot or Simon Armitage. And yet it isn't always the case that the route to so-called high art begins at the popular end of the scale. This is a two-way highway. [...]

So, it simply is not the case that popular and 'high' art are mutually exclusive; and we should not be distracted by nightmares of a new era for the arts in which innovation and experiment are crushed and the philistine triumphs. We should not fear taking the arts to a wider audience or crossing art-form boundaries to challenge those audiences. Exposure enriches our art. It doesn't cheapen it.

And the doom-mongers either show insufficient confidence in the robustness of art, or they wish to preserve it for an elite. Whatever their reason for despair, they are misguided.

For ourselves at the Arts Council of England, as we take on a new enhanced, national strategic role, the challenge is to create the circumstances that will allow creativity to flourish and in which artistic risk-taking is encouraged at the same time as breaking down barriers that limit the arts' exposure across society. [...]

With that platform of extra resources, the Arts Council is poised to bring about a revolution in the way in which artistic priorities are set and decisions taken about funding since the organisation was founded in 1946. But what will it mean? It will mean:

- a clearer national, strategic role for the Arts Council;
- a major devolving of decision-making to the regions;
- a leaner but more effective Arts Council;
- a better mechanism for setting artistic standards across the country;
- a more confident advocacy on behalf of the arts by the Arts Council.

Those imposing institutions, the Arts Council and the British Council, by their mere existence serve to conceal from the public the neglect of contemporary art. It would be far better, from the artist's standpoint, if they were not there. Things could scarcely be worse: and without these make-believes it might become plain to the public how desperate things are.

Agreement between the Department for Culture, Media and Sport and the Arts Council of England

Extract, 1999

[...] **VI. Performance Indicators**

[...] 21. The purpose of performance indicators is to inform DCMS's overall assessment of ACE's achievement of the Department's goals for the arts, detailed in Section II. But indicators are not a crude on/off switch for DCMS funding of ACE: they will provide the basis for a continuing dialogue on how to maximise the return on the taxpayer's investment in the arts. In addition, to avoid skewing funding and the related outputs, no individual indicator should be taken in isolation: the ten goals and their associated indicators should be in balance with, and complementary to, one another.

22. The performance indicators assigned to ACE in this agreement relate directly to DCMS's goals for the arts, as well as to ACE's own Charter (which also underlie ACE's most recent Corporate and Business plans), and fall into three categories: those that give a robust indication of ACE's performance now; those that require some development over the three-year period of this agreement; and those for which there is not yet a satisfactory indicator, but for which there is a clear requirement for measurement and a concomitant need to develop new indicators over the coming period. Additionally, indicators are included here that reflect the overall health of the arts, but which go beyond those outputs for which ACE is directly responsible (these are clearly marked with an * in the following).

23. In the course of this agreement, as the new planning processes become more firmly established, we would expect performance against targets to become easier to measure. All indicators outlined here will be re-evaluated and amended as necessary in the annual review of this agreement, though we recognise the need to keep such adjustments to a minimum in the interests of establishing stable indicators.

Goal 1: Encourage Excellence at Every Level

24. The performance indicators agreed for this goal are as follows:

(1i) A statement on the introduction during the first year of this agreement of mechanisms for the assessment of artistic quality of subsidised arts organisations, including assurance that regular and development funding are all informed by such quality assessment.

(1ii) A statement of ACE's assessment of how nationals and other leading English companies compared during the first year of this agreement to similar organisations in the same field in other parts of the world, by peer review body.

Goal 2: Encourage Innovation at Every Level

25. The performance indicators agreed for this goal are as follows:

(2i) The number of commissions of new work by funded organisations.

Table 2

Number of new commissions by regularly funded organisations[1]	
1995–96 (actual)	2,060
1996–97 (actual)	2,278
1997–98 (actual)	2,071
1998–99 (forecast)	2,200
1999–00 (target)	2,300
2000–01 (target)	2,375
2000–02 (target)	2,425

1 In 1997–98 the sample size was 397 of an entire population of 546 regularly funded organisations; the survey sample is grossed up to reflect the larger figure.

(2ii) A statement providing evidence that regular and development funding is informed by assessment of innovation.

Goal 3: A Thriving Arts Sector and Creative Economy

26. This goal reflects the responsibilities of DCMS and ACE to promote the economic health of the arts seen as an industry and an employer. While the outputs from ACE funding can be regarded as a catalyst for, and a mirror of, the general wellbeing of the arts, a variety of factors beyond ACE's control – not least the economic cycle – affect the overall health of the arts sector. 3i and 3ii therefore provide background information rather than benchmarks against which ACE's performance alone can be directly assessed; 3iii and 3iv, in contrast, will specifically reflect progress on issues for which ACE has direct responsibility.

27. The indicators agreed for performance against Goal 3 are as follows:

(3i) A statement of progress made in promoting the health of the arts economy (including small businesses and craftspeople) over the first year of this agreement, drawing as far as is possible on quantitative indicators, with proposals for indicators against which progress could be assessed in subsequent years.*

(3ii) The amount of commercial sponsorship secured by the arts and crafts sectors, as measured by Arts and Business (formerly the Association for Business Sponsorship of the Arts); see Table 3.*

Table 3

Total sponsorship (£M)[1]	
1995-96	80
1996-97	96
1997-98	115
1998-99	111[2]
1999-00 (target)	119[2]
2000-01 (target)	127[2]
2000-02 (target)	134[2]

1 The survey sample is grossed up to reflect the entire population. It includes general business sponsorship, corporate membership, corporate donations, capital projects, support in kind, and prizes.

2 Targets will be reviewed when the actual figure for 1998/99 becomes available.

(3iii) A statement on steps taken to improve partnership arrangements with other funding bodies, including local authorities and European Union.

(3iv) A statement of achievements in the first year of ACE's assumption of policy-making responsibility for the crafts, drawing wherever possible on quantitative assessments of the health and crafts sector.

Goal 4: More Consumption of the Arts by More of the People

28. The outputs from ACE funding can be regarded as a catalyst for increased consumption of the arts, while not determining overall levels of consumption in themselves. Indicators 4i and 4ii therefore provide useful background information, rather than targets against which ACE performance can be directly assessed; five-year rolling averages are used as these are statistically extremely robust, though the underlying year-on-year trends are also of interest (in 4i in particular, the aspiration is that 50% of the population will have attended an arts event in 2001–02, though the five-year average is likely to be marginally lower). 4i and 4ii can also indicate trends in arts consumption, particularly by socio-economic groups, which DCMS may wish to discuss with ACE. In particular, we expect ACE to encourage funded arts organisations to promote consumption by as wide a section of the population as possible, including people with disabilities. ACE will encourage funded arts organisations to follow best practice in making such arrangements.

29. We will also seek to develop other indicators for consumption which, in addition to the following, specifically reflect ACE's own achievements towards this goal. The performance indicators agreed for this goal are as follows:

(4i) The proportion of the population attending arts events; see Table 4.*

Table 4

Five year rolling average	% of adults who attend any of the eight arts[1]
89/90–93/94 (actual)	46.53
90/91–94/95 (actual)	46.87
91/92–95/96 (actual)	47.25
92/93–96/97 (actual)	47.70
93/94–97/98 (actual)	47.76
94/95–98/99 (forecast)	47.98[2]
95/96–99/00 (target)	48.22[2]
96/97–00/01 (target)	48.46[2]
97/98–01/02 (target)	8.612

1 The eight arts comprise: plays, opera, contemporary dance, ballet, classical music, jazz, art galleries/ exhibitions, and 'any performance in a theatre'.

2 Targets will be reviewed when the actual figure for 1994/95–1998/99 becomes available.

(4ii) The proportion of the population attending arts events regularly (at least twice a year); see Table 5.*

Table 5

Five year rolling average	% of adults who attend one of the eight arts at least twice a year[1]
89/90– 93/94 (actual)	24.65
90/91– 94/95 (actual)	24.85
91/92– 95/96 (actual)	24.98
92/93– 96/97 (actual)	25.19
93/94– 97/98 (actual)	25.19
94/95–98/99 (forecast)	25.18[2]
95/96– 99/00 (target)	25.24[2]
96/97– 00/01 (target)	25.31[2]
97/98–01/02 (target)	25.38[2]

1 The eight arts comprise: plays, opera, contemporary dance, ballet, classical music, jazz, art galleries/exhibitions, and 'any performance in a theatre'.

2 Targets will be reviewed when the actual figure for 1994/95–1998/99 becomes available.

(4iii) Attendance at funded organisations by art form; see Table 6.*

Table 6

Attendance at regularly funded organisations (millions)[1]	
1995–6 (actual)	21.575
1996–7 (actual)	23.531
1997–8 (actual)	22.022
1998–9 (forecast)	22.500[2]
1999–00 (target)	22.750[2]
2000–01 (target)	23.000[2]
2000–02(target)	23.250[2]

1 In 1997–98 the sample size was 397 of an entire population of 546 regularly funded organisations; the survey sample is grossed up to reflect the larger figure.

2 Targets will be reviewed when the actual figure for 1998–99 becomes available . These targets encompass the 300,000 new opportunities to experience the arts announced in the 'Comprehensive Spending Review'.

(4iv) A statement of progress in developing new indices to improve and/or replace 4i to 4iii above.

(4v) A statement of achievements in creating new audiences under the auspices of the New Audience Fund over the first year of the agreement, drawing wherever possible on quantitative indicators.

(4vi) A statement of progress in promoting attendance at funded organisations' events by ethnic minorities, drawing wherever possible on quantitative indicators.

(4vii) A statement of progress in promoting attendance at funded organisations' events by people with disabilities, drawing wherever possible on quantitative indicators.

(4viii) A statement of progress made in the first year of this agreement on promotion of the use of the Internet and other modern communications technologies by funded organisations in support of broadening access to the arts. [...]

JUST IMAGINE CLOSING DOWN
THE CHISENHALE, THE TATES,
THE SHOWROOM, CAMDEN
ART CENTRE, SOUTH LONDON
GALLERY, THE SERPENTINE,
THE PHOTOGRAPHERS
GALLERY, SOUTH LONDON
GALLERY & THE HAYWARD,
AND TAKING ALL THAT
MONEY AWAY FROM ALL
THOSE CURATORS & STATUS-
MONGERS & BUREAUCRATS &
MONEYMEN & MANAGERS,
THEN GIVING IT TO ARTISTS,
WHO WOULD SET UP LOADS OF
TEMPORARY, MORE EXCITING
SPACES FOR LOTS OF ARTISTS
TO SHOW IN, AND THERE'D BE
MUCH MORE ART AROUND
BECAUSE THE MONEY WOULD
GO SO MUCH FURTHER THAN
IT DOES NOW AS IT WOULDN'T
BE SPENT FUELLING THE

CAREERS OF ALL THOSE WHO <u>PRETEND</u> TO BE THE FRIENDS OF ARTISTS BUT ARE REALLY THEIR LAZY, POWERFUL, ENEMIES...

<u>JUST IMAGINE ALL THAT ART!</u>

IT WOULD MAKE LONDON A <u>PHOENIX</u> REBORN FROM THE ASHES OF BUREAUCRACY!!

<u>LET'S DO IT!!!</u>

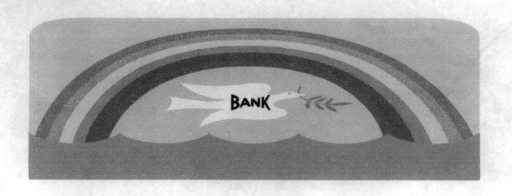

Brian Sedgemore, MP

Politics and Culture: The State and the Artist

If, as I believe, politics is culture and culture is politics, then it was inevitable that the arms-length principle would die with the creation of an independent arts Ministry in 1979, then called The Office of Arts and Libraries, run by a Minister for the Arts. The Ministry was absorbed into the Department of Education and Science in 1981 but became independent again in 1983. The Department of National Heritage was created in 1992 as a Ministry of Culture. The Department for Culture Media and Sport was created in 1997.

But, of course, the row about creating a Department of Culture was not just a row about creating a title, or about the association of the word 'culture' with what went on in Nazi Germany and Soviet Russia, but about the nature of culture itself and the aims of politics.

My new *Collins Concise English Dictionary* gives three definitions of culture:

- *The total of the inherited ideas, beliefs, values and knowledge that constitutes the basis of social action.*
- *A particular civilisation at a particular period.*
- *The artistic and social pursuits, expressions and tastes valued by a society or class.*

There's enough to work on there. But at the outset, and I'll came back to this, please note that there is no mention of art or culture being an instrumental branch of macro-economic policy, the Thatcherite theory that is now part of New Labour practice and thinking.

From Victorian times through to the 1960s, culture was often described in terms of the best that there is in civilisation. The views of Keynes, who subscribed to this idea, were little different from those of Matthew Arnold. The term 'best of civilisation' connoted a moral and aesthetic value that challenged barbarism and materialism. Inevitably, this elitist view retreated in the face of commercialism and the growth of mass culture.

More recently, Raymond Williams redefined culture as 'a whole way of life'. This definition changed somewhat when we became a nation of consumers and shopping addicts, not merely in supermarkets, but in fashion stores and auction rooms. Consumerism is now the new religion. Businessmen and politicians welcomed the change, in part because consumption means production, higher profits and fewer balance of payments problems. Sensing, perhaps anticipating, the change, Gramsci saw this culture as a way in which the ruling elite created a new ideology that kept various groups in power by consent rather than through a command culture.

However, trouble came for politicians with the rise of postmodernism, structuralism and its antithesis. At this point, the notion of cultural value spun out of control and left us all with the headache of relativism.

Politicians, whilst trying not to debate the issue, have a natural and maybe unconscious desire to keep the notion of cultural value intact because culture is now a matter of public policy in all Western democracies. Culture, as seen by most politicians is instrumental in:

- upholding countries' traditions;
- creating national identity;
- creating jobs and wealth, through the growth of cultural industries;
- solving balance of payment difficulties.

What need, then, have politicians and their bureaucratic elites for truly creative art, when what we are now talking about is buying and selling commodities? Is it any wonder that we have too many artists interpreting the world rather than creating it or mediating between the world as it is and the world as it ought to be?

In his book, *Creative Britain*, our Secretary of State for Culture repeatedly tells us that he values the arts for themselves (and I believe him

because I know him), but in page after page, chapter after chapter, we are overwhelmed by the instrumental view of art. If, as I believe, culture is politics or a way of life, then the notion of instrumental art is both offensive and misconceived.

Throughout *Creative Britain* it seems to be assumed that if the arts are good for the balance of payments then, by definition, they are good for people. The possibility of a dichotomy is nowhere to be seen. If you want to see such a dichotomy, just walk down the Golden Mile in Blackpool and purchase some of the tinsel; or watch some dumbed-down, cheaply produced TV programmes on all the channels, including the BBC – look out for further dumbing down as global companies go digital; or pay £70 for the second or third Manchester United football shirt for your son so that he can hang cool in front of his mates. Cool Britannia is really commercial, greedy, consuming Britannia. The genie of the cultural bottle is out and there is no way to put it back within a prevailing ideology that sees markets as the correct solution for most political problems.

In opposition to this view, we have Roger Scruton, a right-wing commentator, telling us that if a market solution leads to the lowest common denominator, then 'the result is not very edifying – but the results of democracy seldom are'.

In more populist terms, the philistine asks, 'If the arts do provide so much to their audience, why are the audiences not willing to bear the cost?' The philistine goes on to remark that insolvency *per se* does not normally constitute grounds for public subsidy. How should we reply, as reply we must? I'd welcome your suggestions.

I myself come from the school of thought that says, if you walk into a gallery where Picasso's *Weeping Woman* is hung and wince because you can experience her pain, then you'll never be able to put a price on my 'wince' and I certainly don't want some dismal economic Johnny exploiting me with a monopolistic charge.

There's another problem for artists and the Government. In his book *Labour Camp*, Stephen Bayley, the renowned designer, excoriates New Labour politicians for confusing style with substance in the field of culture. He writes:

The Nazis and the Soviets used rigid censorship and highly persuasive propaganda. They exploited sentiment. The dictators of each country, at least presentationally speaking, attached a central role to the arts (although experimentation and dissent were not so much discouraged as ruthlessly crushed). It is, I think, not such a huge distance between party line and the vile Mandelsonian neologism 'off message'. And they invoke the 'People'.

Exaggerated it may be, but it is disturbing that such a distinguished non-political designer should feel compelled to write this.

Artists desecrate, illuminate, inspire, initiate aesthetic research and visual literacy, subvert established ideas and institutions, and make us think. It's the potential for subversion that makes New Labour leaders feel uneasy.

The Prime Minister, Tony Blair, really does believe that you can have politics without conflict. As such, the notion of subversive art becomes not merely offensive, but meaningless. What is there to subvert? Dare I answer my own question by saying that New Labour cries out to have its piety and authoritarianism subverted?

As I myself said in a contribution that I made at the Tate Gallery on the future of fine art in a symposium convened by the Wimbledon College of Art:

New Labour wants art that is as pungent as processed cheese, as soul-searching as a conversation between Po, Lala, Dipsey and the

other Teletubby, as original as Dolly the Sheep. As part of the politics of contentment, New Labour wants colours that don't clash, textures that don't distort and shapes that Cubists wouldn't understand. 'Turner in; Conceptual Art out' should be the slogan that hangs outside the Tate. And please keep that painting that depicts Stanley Spencer's aching balls away from Tony's children. Surely there are less traumatic ways to express impotent love.

Of course, the Prime Minister's belief that you can have politics without conflict and art to match is a fantasy, born perhaps out of Rousseau's concept of the existence of the General Will, or possibly from the later idea of 'wish-fulfilment dreams'. Basically, politics is about mediating between competing claims in a world of scarce resources. In that sense, conflict is its bedrock.

The threat to artists and free cultural expression is that deep down, New Labour is every bit as philistine as Old Toryism. New Labour wants the People's Art – art, that is, that keeps the people amused, contented and quiet – but just doesn't want to pay for it. It doesn't want palm prints of Myra Hindley, or visual satire that mocks the most powerful image in Western Christendom.

This cultural debate will go on precisely because it is at the core of politics. In the meantime, my demands are modest. I would like to see the Arts Council abolished – really abolished and not replaced by a pale imitation of the existing body. For the sake of transparency and accountability, I would like to see all the major national orchestras, and not just those in London, all the major galleries in the country, all the major museums as well as the Royal Opera House, ENO, the National Theatre and the National Film Theatre, funded directly by the Department of Culture. These are neither regional nor London bodies and we should not pretend that they are. Parliament should then scrutinise the funding through a Cultural Select Committee.

Other arts expenditure should be made by Regional Arts Boards (RABs). Each should be given its share of the Lottery money for the arts. Should elected regional government ever arrive in Britain, then these RABs would be accountable to the elected regional authorities. If that does not happen, then the RABs should account for their spending to the relevant Cultural Select Committee. Appointments to RABs should be scrutinised by elected bodies, and maybe Parliament, after having been advertised. People should be allowed to nominate themselves. Maybe RABs should be directly elected.

The principle of additionality – i.e. that Lottery money for the arts would be additional to current government spending – should be strictly adhered to. In breaching this principle, the Government is perpetrating a fraud on those who play the Lottery. The Lottery should treat the Hackney Empire in my constituency with the same respect and generosity as it treats the Royal Opera House. The Secretary of State for Culture should publicly state his support for freedom of artistic expression by upholding the right of authors to blaspheme and to mock Jesus, God, Allah, Mohammed or whomsoever, without fear of death by *fatwa*.

Every local authority should by statute be obliged to draw up policy on the arts for its area. Luvvies and Noel Gallagher should stop visiting Downing Street. Britpop and Cool Britannia should be finished off. More artists should mediate between the world as it is and as it ought to be. And we politicians should accept that cultural fragmentation no longer makes it possible to express national identity though cultural forces, precisely because the notion of national identity is dead.

Our culture would not change much, but every progressive move helps.

George Walden

Contemporary Art, Democracy and the State

Extract from *Contemporary Art, Democracy and the State*, a paper delivered to the Philosophy Department, St. Andrew's University, 2000

[...] Personally, I do not believe that British contemporary art is either exciting or innovatory; indeed, I do not find it of much value or interest at all. Some of it is capable of affording entertainment or distraction, but if those are the criteria, in terms of wit, intelligence, originality, social commentary or philosophical undertones it rarely rises to the level of the most accomplished American TV shows such as *The Simpsons*. Popular art forms at their best are genuine and alive. Works invested with the title of 'fine art' can frequently leave us unmoved and indifferent because they are in every sense inauthentic.

In so far as our contemporary art enjoys the support of an all-party parliamentary consensus, and is vociferously championed by public bodies such as the Arts Council and the BBC, I am conscious that my views may appear arrogant, undemocratic – even subversive. I can only hope that, in the arts as in other fields, our democracy feels confident enough of its stability to tolerate dissenting voices. This is not the place to elaborate on my reasons for declining to accept the guidance and authority of the State and of government-appointed organs on aesthetic matters. I do not intend to go through the various schools of Pop Art, Minimalism, installations and suchlike. Though capable of infinite scholastic refinement in the hands of their votaries, they can be seen as adding up to a single, continuous movement. My criticisms may appear broad-brush, but one of the

problems of Conceptual art is that it leaves itself open to conceptual criticism. Of the characteristics of contemporary British art I shall say three things, which I believe are pertinent to the argument.

First, much of it appears to me to be both derivative and residual: pallid or gaudy offshoots of genuinely exciting and innovative artistic movements that flowered in Russia, France and later, America, in the first half of the twentieth century. Second, I believe that the tardy adoption of these styles in Britain, far from being proof of our openness to the 'new', is an aspect of our national conservatism in the arts: only when a style has lost its power to sting do we feel ready to espouse it in safely diluted, popularised versions. In that sense, British contemporary art is akin in spirit to the genteel imitations of Cézanne by painters in the Bloomsbury circle: his noisiness notwithstanding, conceptually speaking Damien Hirst is Duncan Grant. (It may be more than coincidental that Mrs Bottomley is, I understand, a distant relation of Bloomsbury.) It must also be confessed that in our less fruitful periods of art, as a country we have frequently shown a weakness for the mimetic and backward-looking in our artistic styles. In the nineteenth century, we had the mock Gothic of the Pre-Raphaelites, the mock Japanese of Whistler, and the mock classical of Lord Leighton. Today, we have mock revolutionary art. Third, I believe that it is this same conservatism that has led us into a situation

whereby State-modernism – for want of a better term – has become the official academy: which is to say, the primary medium for conformism in the arts.

Official patronage of the arts has always existed in one form or another, though in the past, the donor tended to call the tune. The popes did not commission or subsidise portraits or tombs in which they risked being depicted like creatures from Gilbert and George. The Victorians did not build museums and galleries to be filled with socialist propaganda. And the Soviet Union confined its considerable largesse to artists who produced nothing else but socialist propaganda. In modern democracies, all that has been stood on its head: the elected authorities frequently find themselves financing works of art in which their beliefs are vilified or caricatured – which does not prevent them from applauding the artists in question. The modern patron, it seems, has turned masochist – though, again, it would be a mistake to take things at face value.

Comparisons have been made between British State-modernism and Socialist Realism. There is truth in the analogy to the extent that, in both cases, a closed market is established, complete with an enforcing bureaucracy, from which dissidents are excluded. Yet the comparison is essentially a rhetorical distraction, leading us to lose sight of what is most important in the argument. The point is that

Britain is not a totalitarian country. How is it that a democracy can voluntarily acquire a quasi-official artistic style at all, let alone one that portrays itself, and is accepted by a majority of critics, as 'revolutionary', 'anarchic', or 'subversive'? How, in other words, has the State come to embrace its own opposite in the arts? And how is it that artists fail to see that they are being asphyxiated in the embrace?

The answer, I believe, lies not in a conspiracy, as some of the beleaguered opponents of modernism suggest – the art world can be a paranoid place – but in the far more familiar human failings of make-believe and self-deception. The key word is 'mime'. Artists go through the motions of biting the hand that feeds them, while the State, rich collectors, critics and the media go through the motions of wincing at the pain. The art in question – a mimicry of older styles – induces mimetic responses amongst its apologists and promoters. Defenders of State-modernism insist that it tells us much about the contemporary art world, not least through its powers of irony. It certainly does, though – ironically – not in the sense its defenders like to think. One irony, like one train, can hide another – and it is the hidden irony that does the damage. What inauthentic modernist art tells us about contemporary life is the inauthenticity of society's artistic critique of itself, even at the level of irony, and about the collusive myths of advanced democracies.

PERSONALLY, I DO NOT BELIEVE THAT BRITISH CONTEMPORARY ART IS EITHER EXCITING OR INNOVATORY; INDEED, I DO NOT FIND IT OF MUCH VALUE OR INTEREST AT ALL

This is not to say that the artists or their work are frauds in the usual sense. Like method actors, they have entered into the spirit of the style they are impersonating. Even as they lay claim to originality, they are miming, in all earnestness, a defunct tradition: striking the bold or anarchic stances of early modernism for all the world as if their work were not taught as orthodoxy in art schools financed by the State, and with approved curricula. And just as actors sometimes continue to mime their favourite character off-stage, and to that extent become the character, think of themselves as the character, so artists play out their mimetic role in all sincerity. They genuinely see their work as being a challenge to society and its values, as if they themselves were not part of a sophisticated and well-established enterprise from which they show no disinclination to profit. Supposedly free, antinomian spirits accept prizes at dinners graced by Ministers whose subsidies keep the awarding institution afloat, and where speeches are made solemnly pronouncing their offerings to be ground-breaking, whereas they are mostly in a style that will soon be a century old. It is not so much the art that is surreal and disturbing, as the dinners.

Ministers and the arts officials they appoint have their assigned parts in the mime, behaving as if contemporary art were indeed excitingly 'subversive'. It is a role they are fated to play. If they did not, there would be no virtue in their ostentatious tolerance. Again, the mimicry

is, as it were, unaffected. Politicians are entirely genuine in the warm sincerity of their condescension to the arts. It comes, as we must now all learn to say, from the heart. It is a game that Ministers are well-suited to play. In treating the 'challenge' of contemporary art as if it were real, they are mimicking the democratic process in Parliament itself, with its set-piece jousts and stagy confrontations, while the business of the House is fixed through the usual channels by amicable agreement.

It could be argued that this element of sham and simulation, far from being lamentable, is progressive. To have reached a stage of democratic tolerance where governments subsidise 'oppositionary' art much in the way that the salaries of the opposition who abuse them in the House of Commons are paid from official funds, is evidence of an advanced civilisation. In this state of affairs, it is tacitly understood by everyone that, with the artists as with the opposition spokesmen, the denunciation of the authorities and all their works is largely for the form, that their bark is worse than their bite, and that their underlying respect for the institutions of the State, democracy, the workings of the market, and conventional social mores is not in doubt. Yet that would reduce the creative artist to the position of mere participant in a system of checks and balances: at best to the role of a kind of loyal opposition, at worst to that of court jesters trained by the State for the delectation of the authorities and

the public. Hardly a role that an authentically disturbing artist would wish to play.

So it is that the State has enfolded its artistic opposition. By unwritten agreement, old notions of approved and non-approved, conformist and non-conformist, academic and innovatory art have been stood on their heads. There is no doubt as to who has got the best of the bargain. Artists cannot expect to enter such agreements and to preserve their fire-power intact. As the erstwhile *refusés* have been ushered into the official salon by nervously deferential authorities, in accordance with convention, they leave their weapons at the door.

A striking aspect of British contemporary art is the low level of critical exegesis that surrounds it. One might have thought that, if the art were as outstanding as is claimed, its critical language would be on a similarly elevated level. Yet with the possible exception of Tim Hilton, people of the calibre of Clement Greenberg, Robert Hughes or the former *New York Times* critic, the British-born John Russell – whatever one thinks of their view – are conspicuously lacking. It is characteristic of semi-official orthodoxies that the writings of their supporters should be obscure, jargonised and defensive, and in relation to contemporary British art, that, largely, is what we get. (The discourse of progressive educationalists, another elderly orthodoxy, is remarkably similar.) The response of artistic power-holders to adverse

comment is reminiscent of the nervy reactions of a fragile regime. The mildest doubters are treated as out-and-out reactionaries, on the principle that if you are not with us, you are against us.

This polarisation has its own, internal logic. Depending as it does on a synthetic conflict between art and authority, State-modernism encourages a Manichean approach to criticism, in which disputes are dramatised as those between elitism and egalitarianism, between constraint and liberation, between the old and the new. The smaller the opposition, the more stagy the polarisation. Despite occasional flurries of publicity, contemporary art is suffering from a lack of hostility. Critical indifference, or the tepid enthusiasms of conditional supporters, is insupportable. Hence, the stubborn attempt to provoke an argument, whether it be by a display of human excrement, or a portrait of Myra Hindley. As energy drains away in a closed, entropic system, increasingly laborious means are necessary to bludgeon the adversary into reacting, to give at least a semblance of reality to the mime.

Smothered in official approbation, praised by compliant critics, established as orthodoxy in art schools, cosseted by indirect subsidies of every description, and with the lure of financial success for its most successful practitioners, late modernism finds itself in the position of the classic academic schools of art – but with a major difference.

In the past, reigning styles were challenged, or obliged to re-invent themselves, by new, more dynamic movements. State-modernism faces no such challenge. Exhausted as it is, there seems nothing to replace it. No-one seriously suggests that a new and vibrant style of art is waiting in the wings. If the Tate, the Royal Academy and the Serpentine Gallery (of which the late Princess Diana was a patron – note the collusion of royalty in the game) were to be taken over by insurgents, and a show of exclusively figurative art staged, with the exception perhaps of Lucian Freud, it would be a wan, pallid thing. A full-scale counter-revolution involving a return to pre-modernism is both technically impractical and aesthetically undesirable. Short of a general collapse of the market – predicted some years ago by one of modernism's most discriminating critics, Robert Hughes, but yet to come about – I see no chance of an aesthetic re-evaluation. I believe Mr Hughes underestimated the institutional underpinning for what I have called a 'closed system'. In that sense, the comparison with Socialist Realism is valid: it took the collapse of Communism to get rid of that.

As for us, in our democracy as in our art, we appear to have reached a sort of stasis. The mime of democracy must go on, if only because no-one can think of a better piece of theatre. Art has become caught up in the game of fictitious oppositions. In the short and medium term, I do not see how this situation can change. What we are seeing is an arts cartel in the process of formation – the first of its kind in history. It is as if society had taken a major holding in a hostile enterprise, on the understanding that old products and brand names will be retained. The strategy – albeit unconscious – is working brilliantly.

Public protest – such as it is – is increasingly handled by the arts establishment in the same way as government departments. When inflation leaps, or the trade gap widens, the Treasury says 'Not too much weight should be placed on a single month's figures'. Should the figures be good, it insists that they indicate the underlying strength of the economy. Illogicality has never troubled Ministers' press departments, and shows no signs of troubling our public galleries.

If a new exhibition is ignored or heavily criticised, then that is proof of its worth. The avant garde is, by its nature, in advance of its time. And should a controversial show draw the crowds, the attendance figures are quoted as proof of its worth as well. In other words, the art is good when it is popular, but being unpopular doesn't make it any less so. Hostility validates art, as does popularity. Like all Groucho Marx logic, the position is impregnable. In its public relations as in its mimetic conflict with authority, like some quasi-privatised public utility from whom you are forced to buy whether you like it or not, State-modernism has cornered the market.

'Accessibility' is important in the theatre of British contemporary art – a theatre based, like much of democracy itself, on a solemn fiction. The reaction of the contemporary art theorist to the protest that 'anyone could do it' is a beaming affirmation. The new canon is easily learnt. Nothing could be further removed – to take an extreme example – from the complex skein of mythology, religion, classical references of Poussin, or the intricate, hard-to-read surfaces of a Titian or a Degas.

Duchamp's readymades have been invested with a democratic, egalitarian ethos as the art of the everyday – the very opposite of what was essentially an intellectual *jeu d'esprit*. His black, destructive humour has been lightly ironised, playfulness being a democratic virtue. As we enter some contemporary exhibitions, the words 'jolly' and 'larky' frequently come to mind [...] Here is a palace of harmless 'fun' – a word increasingly found in the prospectuses of galleries. Alternatively, the exhibits are of the plaintive or anarchistic variety, appealing to the kind of inchoate resentment that Rousseau and others warned would be a concomitant of democracy. That is the 'subversive' element. There can also be the quirkiness and cult of originality dear to the British sensibility. In other words, like a fairground with its sexual raucousness, its distorting mirrors and House of Horrors, something for everyone.

Yet however 'disturbing' the object, the key word is play: just kidding. Contemporary art falls four-square into the bread-and-circuses aspect of modern democracy, best summed up in the advertising business. It is fitting that the biggest private collection of contemporary art in Britain belongs to one of the Saatchi brothers – a name that conjures every aspect of late modernity: the ephemeral, quick-money world of virtuality and make-believe, in which everything from art to Conservative politics can be turned into hot properties – though some sell better than others.

Like commerce itself, we are unlikely to see an end to the process. Democracy is a settled state. Apart from a few adjustments here and there, it is not something we strive to move on from. We have got what we wanted and are stuck with it. In this sense, contemporary art is a true mirror of the times. All we can do is make faces in the glass: amuse ourselves, frighten ourselves, distract ourselves. The alternative is to turn aside, close our eyes, and analyse the situation. The trouble with doing this is that, in thinking about art and society in a late twentieth-century democracy, we shall begin thinking thoughts we would prefer not to hear. Perhaps because they are genuinely rather than factitiously disturbing.

Ian Breakwell

Half the Work

'The context is half the work' was a maxim of the Artist Placement Group (APG) who, during the 1970s instigated a series of creative collaborations between government departments and artists, including myself with the Department of Health and Social Security. The intention was not to recreate the traditional relationship of patronage, but rather to involve artists uncompromisingly in the day-to-day work of government organisations at all levels including policy and decision making.

There has since been no equivalent to APG's pioneering initiative, and the alienation of artists from social policy is now entrenched. Despite a majority of the most visible contemporary artists in the UK using explicitly figurative content encompassing a kaleidoscopic range of aspects of the business of living, their opinions are never sought about anything other than the business of art. No artist ever features in any newspaper, television or radio debate on current affairs, social or moral issues. Official perception is still that art should keep its proper place.

Yet, and on a lighter note, even when art is confined to its separate and 'proper' place, its context is habitually affected by that everyday life from which it is, in fact, inseparable.

left Department of Health and Social Security, Euston Tower, London, 1970s, photographer unknown
above Ian Breakwell working on APG Placement in the offices of the Mental Health Group (Architects Division) at DHSS Headquarters, London, 1976

Ian Breakwell   31

Stella Santacatterina

Clarification of a Few Political Points

Social and political issues cannot be the direct subject of art. This fact is made evident by the earlier failures of the historical avant garde and the philosophical background of the twentieth century. Heideggerian propositions suggest that the catastrophe of modernity has already happened and that art moves in its own zone, which is not that of daily reality. In relation to its cultural context, art operates vertically, escaping any direct correspondence with the social or political, since otherwise it would lose all capacity to reflect critically upon them. An art that is 'accessible', or reflects only daily reality, derives from an impoverishment of thought dispossessed of any imaginative faculty – it is less than reality itself and neutralises any possibility of nourishing the viewer's experience.

In the contemporary scenario, the declaration of the Minister for Culture, Chris Smith, that arts should 'deliver access, excellence, innovation and educational opportunity in accordance with the Government's wider social, educational and economic objectives', reminds us of Walter Benjamin's famous comment that whilst Fascism tends to aestheticise politics, Communism tends to culturalise them. Smith's statement alarmingly combines both tendencies, producing a self-defeating agenda since, where art becomes circumscribed through prescriptions generated by authoritarian control, it necessarily ceases to be art at all, becoming merely a decorative screen to mask the lack of courage in support of open and genuine experimentation. Unfortunately, education nowadays means little more than the accumulation of information, not self discovery or understanding and experience in the world. But it should not be the responsibility of art to cover the lack in the education system; art should in fact resist all forms of institutionalisation in order to remain art. Moreover, to speak about the 'social responsibility of the artist' is to impose a moral obligation that is more properly the province of all human individuals, whatever their profession.

Significantly, Smith's pronouncements and those of New York Mayor Guiliani regarding the 'Sensation' show in the Brooklyn museum may be seen as two sides of the same coin. In Smith's case, the language is couched in terms of 1950s postwar, left-wing party rhetoric; in Guiliani's case, his accusation of 'degenerate' art takes the form of a censorial appeal to 'good taste'. The adjective 'degenerate' implies that there is some ideology behind the work. However, already the detritus of both past high and popular culture, most of the 'Sensation' work is hardly provocative, needing no adjective whatsoever; a thoughtless object produced by a thoughtless subject, it asks nothing more than to be legitimised as such and absorbed by the economic system of commodities. Above all, this invasion of the political into the cultural debate highlights the impotence of the political itself, which, having lost its ability to change the forces of global economy, can now attempt to exercise control only over culture.

Lord Bragg and Lord Gibson

The Arts

Extract from House of Lords Debate, Hansard (London), 10 February 1999

The Arts

Lord Bragg: [...] I believe the evidence shows that in the past twenty-one months the arts are well set to be better governed and better managed than ever before. With the increase in the length of life that we are promised, and the increase in leisure, they need to be. They are vital capital for our future. At last the arts in Great Britain are poised to build on the superb platform of opportunity constructed by Jennie Lee in the 1960s, when boldness was our friend and we saw the arts as a Promised Land. In that seminal decade, the arts bloodlessly and seamlessly embraced liberty and equality, quality and fraternity – very heaven. Now it has come again. Without question, there is much to do, but much has already begun.

There is much that is not yet right. Companies that hoped that Chris Smith would slip into a telephone box and emerge as a Superman instant fixer have often been disappointed. Telephone boxes, perhaps, are too transparent for that these days. It takes time to clear up some of the silt of eighteen years; it takes time to dig new, navigable channels; and it takes time, once a course is agreed, to make it clear to all. But from what I see, the will, the vision and increasingly the means are there. The question, as always, is how to fit the amplitude of a visionary landscape into the frame of political possibility.

I believe that the Government has made an impressive beginning, the more impressive because it has worked within budgetary constraints and against a *Bleak House* inheritance, which of course notched up achievements, but also left neglect, bungle and cynicism – a tradition that Conservative councils like Westminster carry on regardless, trampling over the arts with loutish indifference.

If I seem to contextualise too dramatically, it is because I believe that it is essential that what the government is doing now is seen in context; otherwise it will be most unjustly accused of debts and failings not its own. We cannot be dragged down by a past created by others. Today, vitally, the arts need the commitment of confidence; a new start is, in itself, an agent for confidence. It has been badly lacking.

One growth industry in the Conservative years was the culture of complaint. I know; I was part of it. We all knew that the high road to applause at any arts gathering was to attack the Government. The attacks had reason. But then it became an addiction, and the complaints clique has observed no alteration. But now, I submit, the tune has changed; the show has moved on. Complaint must take a look at evidence.

In a fraction of the total time that will, I trust, fall to its lot, the Government has already stabilised, organised and revitalised the arts, both now and its future prospects. Of course there have been omissions, errors and failings, but they are as nothing compared with what went before, and they are as nothing compared with the successes of the last mere twenty-one months.

Let us look around the estate at the first crop. It is a fair time to take stock: in education, £180 million over three years for music funding and £30 million for the Youth Music Trust. Out of that will come a country in which all children will have access to musical instruments at school, to music teaching and to the riches of music. We will play and sing as never before. We now know it has been proven – in America, but it was a good study – that listening to Mozart when you are young makes you smarter, not only at music but at all learning.

Dance and drama students will now enjoy new schemes of support that will radically reinvigorate those two great arts, lately dying at the roots from a thousand cuts. The academies were threatening to become finishing schools for the wealthy only. These and other measures will unlock dreams and talents that can change society.

Access is another pillar of Labour policy. The sum of £5 million a year is to go into the new audiences fund; there is to be free access for children and old-age pensioners to museums, and more to be hoped for; and all the Arts Council grants are linked to wide access.

As to excellence – which is the third part of the core, with access and education – there will be large increases, to use a shorthand, for the National Theatre, the London Symphony Orchestra, The Art Angel, which gets a 100% increase, the orchestras in Bournemouth and Birmingham, and so it goes on. In broadcasting – the most interesting for me – the Government are setting the legal framework for digital. Digital could, among other things, bring the full harvest of the arts to the British public. Niche channels will, I believe, proliferate for poetry, painting, opera, dance, classical music and golden oldies – a thousand channels could bloom – and at last the best would be available to the most, when we want it and in depth. It will be a new-found land.

As to the Arts Council, it has brought the Opera House (that rather sad symbol of arts governance over the past decade), under control – a remarkable feat. It had been 'a shambles' according to the former Chairman of the Arts Council, my noble friend Lord Gowrie. The Arts Council has now pointed it in a good direction.

The Arts Council gained a huge overall increase in funding – £125 million over the next few years – and there is more regional funding and increased power for the regions. For me, that is most important. I disagree with the noble Lord, Lord Freyberg, on this issue. Of course the regions have to be run with enlightened efficiency, but so does everything. My friends in Northern Arts and the other nine regions have warmly welcomed the radical changes of Gerry Robinson and Peter Hewitt of the Arts Council. I believe that this will encourage local authorities to release money and release enthusiasm, which, so far, has very largely not been present. So welcome to Gateshead Music Centre; welcome to Keswick's Theatre by the Lake; and welcome to the same story that is being unfolded elsewhere and which will gather in force over the years.

I have argued this case because I believe that it is right that what is now so positive should be stressed, and these are just a few headlines. We must throw off what Richard Hoggart called 'the poverty of ambition'. He meant the working classes in the 1930s. Over the past two decades, I fear, it has infected the whole. Internally, individually, where it matters so much to each of us, the arts can be revolutionary. We as a nation can grow into Shakespearean ambitions. Why not? The foundations are laid; the game is afoot. I hope that Jennie Lee is looking down at her old party and perhaps even raising a glass as she sees her soul go marching on.

Lord Gibson: My Lords, I speak as a one-time Chairman of the Arts Council – some may say it was a very long time ago, but to me it seems like just the other day. I hope that the noble Lord, Lord Jenkins, who was Minister for part of the time that I chaired the Council, has the same recollections. We had happy times together, despite an occasional disagreement.

As I look at the council today, I am concerned that it seems to me, in spite of the optimism – not to say euphoria – of the noble Lord, Lord Bragg, to be squeezing itself out of existence. On the one hand, it is devolving to the regions almost all decisions about grants to the arts. I am not against that process; my own instincts are very much the same. We started the Regional Arts associations in my time. But it is a matter of extent. I just hope it turns out to be practical and for the best. On the other hand, the Arts Council is left with the national companies as regards which Government Ministers increasingly seem to feel the need to intervene.

I am not sure whether that is a very happy process. I sometimes wonder whether the Government intends the Arts Council ultimately to become a purely advisory body. I hope not, because I strongly believe, as most noble Lords have underlined this afternoon, in the arm's-length principle and I deplore any trend away from it. We used to set great store by it. It was the reason for our creation and the basis of our operation. It was the whole reason for our existence. It was considered a great achievement. I think it is still considered a particularly British way of doing things.

When I chaired the Arts Council I was invited by the French Government to go to France to have a look at the way they subsidised the arts, and by German city governments – Munich, Hamburg and Berlin – to do the same there. I enormously enjoyed it. It was very instructive and I learnt a great deal. But I came away envying the size of subsidy more than the system and I came to recognise that the larger the subsidy, inevitably the greater the political involvement in the arts. I did not want us to adopt that system here. I thought we had the best. I think that what I saw in France and Germany is beginning to happen here. […]

Andrew Brighton

Towards a Command Culture: New Labour's Cultural Policy and Soviet Socialist Realism

Reprinted from *Critical Quarterly*, vol. 41, no. 3, Autumn 1999. This essay was first given as a paper at the Annual Conference of the Association of Art Historians, 1999, and a shorter version appeared in *The Guardian*, Monday 12 April 1999

This essay argues that a change has taken place in the rationale of State support for the arts in the United Kingdom. The arts are now thought of as an instrument of social policy. With the election of the Labour Government, tendencies within the arts and the arts bureaucracy have conjoined with the political vision of the Government to initiate a reshaping of State support. By a comparison with Soviet Socialist Realism (SSR), I will sketch the character of this new rationale and its administrative implementation.

The Decline of Autonomy

The development of public support for the arts in the post-war period was part of the development of the welfare state. It was one of the means whereby capitalism, in Maynard Keynes' words, could be made good enough. The political will to create and sustain the growth of arts support is attributable to the cultural interests and influence of the increasingly powerful and numerous educated, the professional classes – in other words, intellectuals. However, there was an element of instrumentalism in the growth of public support for the arts. Its instrumental value was its autonomy. The autonomy of the arts, meaning here the support of art valued by its own professional constituency, was of political value. One front in the Cold War was for the hearts and minds of intellectuals. Western governments supported cultural activities designed to encourage the identification of intellectuals with liberal democracy. The State support of art that

displayed autonomy was one way in which the North Atlantic democracies differentiated themselves from the Communist countries. The ideologically multifarious character of the modern movement stood in contrast to the State-directed moralism of much Eastern block culture in general and of Soviet Socialist Realism in particular.

It might seem then that my proposed comparison is somewhat wilful. But if differentiation was a motive force for the West in the Cold War, the collapse of the Soviet Union opens up the possibility that in its absence Western states may come to resemble aspects of the departed polity. It should be remembered that the Soviet Union was the creation of Westernising intellectuals, attempting to build a rational modern society. It might now appear misconceived, but in some respects it may have been predictive.

When, in the early 1930s, Soviet Socialist Realism was promulgated, it did not set out stylistic requirements for the arts. It established the terms for social and political evaluation. C. Vaughan James in his book *Soviet Socialist Realism: Origins and Theory* identifies three basic principles of SSR: *naródnost*, art's relation to the people and the aspiration to a better future for all humanity; *klássovost'*, art's relation to the progressive struggle of the proletariat and its allies to overthrow the capitalist class; and *partíiost'*, the identification of art with the Communist party and its historic mission.[1] In the application

of these principles, art was required to be tendentious, to participate in the progressive struggles towards a classless society.

Naródnost: Art for Everyone

I will begin this exploration with *naródnost*, art for the people, and the current Government slogan of 'Art for Everyone'.

The Arts are central to the task of recreating the sense of community, identity and civic pride that should define our country.

Art must have its deepest roots in the very depth of the broad masses of the workers. It must be understood by those masses and loved by them. It must unite the feelings, thoughts and will of the masses and raise them up.

The first of these quotations comes from *New Labour: because Britain deserves better*, the 1997 Labour Party Manifesto,[2] the second comes from Lenin's *On Literature and Art*.[3]

John Rentoul, in his biography of Tony Blair, says that the latter's most distinctive theme as a politician is his idea of community.[4] Communitarianism is writ large in Blair's foreword to the Labour Party Manifesto. 'I want a Britain that is one nation, with shared values and purpose', he declares. 'New Labour is the political arm of none other than the British people as a whole. Our values are the same: the equal worth of all, with no-one cast aside; fairness and justice within strong communities.'

Tony Blair's communitarianism has its origins in the writing of Christian philosopher John Macmurray. 'If you really want to understand what I am all about', Tony Blair has said, 'you have to take a look at a guy called John Macmurray'.[5] Macmurray was born a Scottish Calvinist in 1891 and died a Quaker in 1976. He was, however, an unattached Christian for most of his life. Professor of philosophy first at University College, London, and then Edinburgh University, he gained considerable fame through his broadcasts for BBC in the 1930s, but disappeared from public and professional philosophical attention after the Second World War. Christian enthusiasts sustain his reputation now.

The post-war support for art in this country came out of the Kantian aesthetics of the Bloomsbury Group. Kant established the modern philosophical grounds for art as something that could not be evaluated properly by reason or by morality. The aesthetic was a distinct terrain. And so, for example, Maynard Keynes sought to build into the very structure of the Arts Council a degree of autonomy from political requirements.

John Macmurray's views were formed by his encounter, via Marx, with Hegel; from this he elaborated in the first instance a Christian Marxism in which art is evaluated against a political teleology. Similarly, Soviet Socialist Realism had much of its origin in the aesthetics of NG Chernyshevsky.[6] He translated into his materialism Hegel's idealist conception of art as the agent of history. The progressive aesthetics of both Chernyshevsky and Macmurray are anti-Kantian. They believed that art was subordinate to, and an instrument of, a social vision.

What characterises Macmurray's writing about art is the absence of an examination of its history, of past philosophical aesthetics or the particular work of any artist. Art is subordinated to his central idea of community. Universal community is to be realised by each person coming to a personal relationship to God. By coming to recognise in ourselves that of God in Everyman, we grow out of mere social relations into communal relations, which aspire to a model of mutually caring and disinterested friendship.

This idea of community is, then, an idea of both personal and social progress. For the individual, 'the practical function of art', writes Macmurray, 'is the refinement of sensibility. It is an education of emotion and a training in judgement'. However, a 'discipline that will produce a human result must succeed not merely in integrating the various capacities of the individual but in integrating individuals themselves in a community of free co-operation'.[7]

The Secretary of State for Culture, Media and Sport, Chris Smith, echoes in his collection of speeches, *Creative Britain*, Macmurray's valuation of art as an agent of personal development and of social cohesion. According to Smith, cultural creativity is important for what it can do for each of us as individual, sensitive, intelligent human beings: fulfilling ourselves and our potential. It is important for what it can do for society, because creativity is inherently a social and interactive process, and it helps to bind us together as people.[8]

What emerges from Smith's book is the tendentious vision of a common culture and that the arts should serve this vision. The requiring 'should' is encoded in apparently descriptive propositions that art 'is', or 'does' or 'can' in Smith's writing and other Labour Party pronouncements. This idea that art and social good should converge and serve the people and human progress is a principle of *naródnost* and a commonplace of Soviet cultural commentary.

For example, in an essay written in 1966, on 'Socialist Realism and the Artistic Development of Mankind', Vladimir Shcherbina, Nikolai Gei and Vladimir Piskunov write:

Socialist realistic aesthetics refuses to make a priori definitions of the essence of human personality and sets unlimited value on the originality of every man. It is concerned not only with the unique individual, but the integral spiritual life of all people and the psychology of the nation.[9]

Klássovost': Enemies and Victims
In the practice of Soviet Socialist Realism, *naródnost* did decline often into the argument that art that was not immediately accessible to a proletarian audience was intrinsically a reactionary product of bourgeois specialists. Such art was on the wrong side in terms of *klássovost'*, i.e. art's relation to the progressive role of the proletarian class. Progressive politics assumes a narrative in which there are victims and enemies. Lenin asserted that there were two cultures in any society, that of the exploiters and that of the exploited. The enemies are the exploiters and the victims are the exploited and the Party is the agent and saviour of the exploited. Likewise, Blair's preface to the Labour Party Manifesto uses a similar narrative, but here the enemy is an elite:

I want to renew faith in politics through a government that will govern in the interests of the many, the broad majority of people who work hard, play by the rules, pay their dues and feel let down by a political system that gives breaks to the few, to an elite at the top increasingly out of touch with the rest of us.

In an essay written in Paris and published before the fall of the Soviet Union, Milan Kundera observed that the words 'elitism' and 'elitist' did not appear in France until 1967/68. 'The very language threw a glare of negativity, even mistrust, on the notion of elite.' He goes on:

Official propaganda in the Communist countries began to pummel elitism and elitists at the same time. It used the terms to designate not captains of industry or famous athletes or politicians but only the cultural elite: philosophers, writers, professors, historians, figures in film and the theatre.
It seems that in the whole of Europe the cultural elite is yielding to other elites. Over there, to the elite of the police apparatus. Here, to the elite of the mass media apparatus.[10]

What I think Kundera is describing in the West is a convergence between the media and political elites. The media tends to be treated by politicians as the voice of the populace, presumably on the assumption that what they hear and read forms their minds. Any specialist or recondite cultural activity that falls outside the comprehension of political and media discourse can be condemned as elitist. Specialist cultures with a perceived beneficial aim such as science and technology largely escape censure as elitist. When art is seen as not serving social cohesion, then the specialist culture that values it is open to a charge of elitism; it becomes the enemy.

Chris Smith again:

perhaps most important is that the arts are for everyone. Things of quality must be available to the many, not just the few. Cultural activity is not some elitist exercise that takes place in reverential temples aimed at the predilections of the cognoscenti.

THE ARTS ARE CENTRAL TO THE TASK OF RECREATING THE SENSE OF COMMUNITY
IDENTITY AND CIVIC PRIDE
THAT SHOULD DEFINE OUR COUNTRY

BLAIR

ART MUST HAVE ITS DEEPEST ROOTS IN THE VERY DEPTH OF THE BROAD MASSES OF THE WORKERS
IT MUST BE UNDERSTOOD BY THOSE MASSES AND LOVED BY THEM
IT MUST UNITE THE FEELINGS, THOUGHTS AND WILL
OF THE MASSES AND RAISE THEM UP

LENIN

Note here the use of 'cognoscenti', knowledgeable people, as a term of disapprobation.

In October 1998, Gerry Robinson, the Chairman of Granada PLC, the media and catering group, in his new part-time capacity as Chairman of the Arts Council of England announced a new era for the arts. As part of the core policy of 'widening access', he proposed the abolition of the specialist art-form departments of the Arts Council in the name of 'flexibility'. It can be argued that each art form has its own political economy and body of knowledge and that these particular cultures of production and reception are essential to what an art is. What might motivate such an argument? Those who oppose ACE policies of 'taking the arts to a wider audience or crossing artform boundaries' may wish to 'preserve it for an elite', announces Robinson. And a charge to be taken seriously is that 'in parts of the arts establishment, access is still restricted to the elite'.[11]

In my opening remarks I said that, with the election of the Labour government, tendencies within the arts and the arts bureaucracy have conjoined with the political vision of the Government to initiate a reshaping of State support. There seems to have been a conjuncture between the Thatcher Government's attack on the power and ideology of the professions and the New Left's identification with alienated minorities. They agreed on who was the enemy if not on who were the victims.

It was in the 1980s that the Arts Council commenced direct support for art defined by social, ethnic or sexual orientation of the recipients. Some schemes set up were exclusively for artists belonging to one or other classification. However, the diversities recognised in these classifications were selective; they echoed the New Left roster of progressive victims. So, for instance, a classification neither used nor addressed was young, white, working-class men.

Towards a National Arts and Media Strategy was published in 1992.[12] It was the fruit of the National Arts and Media Strategy Monitoring Group set up by the then Arts Council of Great Britain, the British Film Institute, the Crafts Council and the Regional Arts Boards. It foreshadows the vocabulary and ideas of current government policy.

The report contains a section on 'Quality'. It lists various kinds of judgements of quality. The judgements of 'creators, producers and expert assessors and critics', in other words, people with professional expertise are described as 'essentially subjective'.

However, we are on firmer ground when considering something called 'Quality in Community': 'The arts can be powerful agents for bringing people together in communities defined by geography, ethnicity, gender, religion, or simply shared interests'. This apparently descriptive assertion shifts into a requirement for a kind of Social

Realism, that is, a realism in which, to employ a much-used SSR phrase, 'objective social conditions' are articulated. 'To the extent that they succeed in conveying a shared vision – giving voice to what had previously been silent – the arts may be considered to be of high quality.' In other words, this assessment requires these communities to reflect the role assigned them in a social classification. When the report summarises the grounds for judgements of quality, it includes the instrumental criteria of 'social innovation and significance'. This is the logic of *klássovost'*.

Partîinost': Party Goals
Partîinost' is a fully articulated awareness of the political function of art and allegiance to the Party and its policies and goals. What I have tried to show so far is the resemblance in principle and rhetoric of SSR and the Labour Government's cultural policies. What I want to turn to now is the implementation of Party goals.

The Soviet Union was a would-be rational state. The goals of Communism could be achieved by the application of reason in the form of Marxist-Leninism. This was a supposedly omni-competent regulative discourse capable of supervising and legislating for economic, scientific, juridical, social and cultural life. Rationality and a claim to competence, however, are not just the aspiration of Communist states. Amongst the distinguishing features of the modern state is the attack upon tradition and irrational

power in the name of justice, equality and economic efficiency.

While the Labour Government has abandoned the degree of public ownership and regulation of the economic sphere associated in the past with socialist governments, it is on the way to creating the mechanisms for a command culture in the public sector. In this endeavour, Marxist-Leninism was a crude instrument compared to the subtler omniscience now granted to management discourse. 'Performance indicators' and the like enable evaluation by people empowered by their managerial position rather than by their knowledge of a particular practice.

Public sector institutions are required to make themselves increasingly accountable. Whereas in the commercial sector the goal is ultimately profitability, in the public sector the goals are set by government policy. Having defined their aims and objectives in line with that policy and derived performance indicators from them, a public institution can be monitored against its targets.

In December 1997, Chris Smith announced the outcome of the Government's review of access to National Museums and Galleries: 'Access is a cornerstone of all this Government's cultural policies, including those for museums and galleries'. He went on to say:

I intend to invite museums and galleries to include access plans in their forward plans, and to set themselves clear targets against which progress can be measured. It is my intention that having an Access Plan based on the code of practice [on access] *will be a condition of grant-in-aid.*[13]

A priority is: 'Attracting those socio-economic groups that are under-represented amongst museum visitors'. In the draft Code of Practice on Access, a requirement is that museums must: 'Set out the measures being taken to extend access (such as research into visitor profiles, marketing and exhibition programmes)'.

The most salient predictor for arts audiences is not wealth, nor income, it is education. It is the relatively well-educated, teachers, academics and professionals, who constitute the dominant core of regular arts consumers. They constitute the cognoscenti, the elite audience for the arts. However, museums and galleries are now required to classify their visitors by class and ethnicity and then seek to mirror in their attendance the proportion of each of the designated groups within society as a whole.

An intensification of the means to monitor adherence to Government policy came a year after the announcement on access. In December 1998, Chris Smith announced the creation of a 'new watchdog for the cultural and sporting fields', QUEST, the Quality, Efficiency and Standards Team. At the news conference he said, 'We will give

direction; we set targets and chase progress, and where appropriate we will take direct action to make sure that our objectives are achieved'.[14]

In the job description for the Director of QUEST, all the requirements are for managerial skills and experience. 'A knowledge of and interest in the work of the DCMS sectors', might be thought to be an exception. However, the staffing of QUEST comes from the Civil Service, most of whom will already be in the DCMS, which is what is meant by knowledge of the sector.

Among the priorities of QUEST in the first two years is: 'A review of targets and indicators used within Funding Agreements between the DCMS and its first tier bodies'. And another is, 'A study of second-tier delegation and accountability'. What I have described are the Labour Government's specific requirements for museums and galleries and the means by which adherence to them is policed. The Arts Council and its clients are also subject to these requirements.

It must follow that institutions, curators and other cultural bureaucrats who pursue these targets will flourish. Listed amongst the activities to be monitored are gallery education and exhibitions. These, of course, affect what museums exhibit and buy. Consequently, artists whose work can be presented and interpreted as advancing the social goals of government policy will receive increased state support.

C. Vaughan James summarises the concept of *partîinost'* as follows:

It embodies, or 'demands from the artist', a threefold, conscious decision: (1) that art must fulfil a specific social function; (2) that function is to further the interests of the masses; (3) to further the interests of the masses, art must become part of the activity of the Communist Party.

What I have tried to show is that translated into the subtler hegemonic persuasions of a Western democracy we are looking at something pretty near to *partîinost'* as the determinate of public-sector arts support in this country.

The correlative of these policies is that there will be a diminution in funds for exhibitions, purchases and other forms of support for artists whose work cannot serve these ends. In other words, as Gerry Robinson seems to suggest, the days of those who fail to exhibit *partîinost'* are numbered:

Too often in the past, the arts have taken a patronising attitude to audiences. Too often artists and performers have continued to ply their trade to the same white, middle-class audience. In the back of their minds lurks the vague hope that one day enlightenment might descend semi-miraculously upon the rest, that the masses might get wise to their brilliance.

Conclusion

I will conclude by first pointing out some of things I have not said in this essay. I have not said that art is or should be apolitical. I have not said, for instance, that it cannot explore experiences of or be committed to ideas about ethnicity, gender or religion. I have not in any way implied a denigration of 'mass', 'popular' or 'low culture'. I have not set out to criticise Labour Government social policies in principle; I have only sought to demonstrate some of their implications for public-sector arts funding. I have used a comparison with Soviet Socialist Realism to demonstrate this and to imply a warning.

What seems to be implied and enacted by the present government's cultural policy is that certain social goals and political aims are so self-evidently good that subordinating much of publicly supported arts culture to them is justified. It seems we are seeing the tragedy of Soviet Socialist Realism replayed as a social democratic farce.

Is New Labour policy guided by misplaced social piety, unaware of the implications and precedents of its own assumptions and practice? Or is there a rather clever and theorised but undeclared strategy to moralise British culture? A strategy informed by right-wing critics of modernism but covered by left-wing rhetoric. The overt government demand on the arts is that they serve everyone and foster shared values in the name of social inclusion. The covert effect is to demote not just dissenting culture but also aesthetic integrity. As conservative and Christian critics have long argued, cultural modernism (past and post-) is an enemy of shared values. From FA Hayek to Daniel Bell and beyond, advocates of liberal economies have seen a conservative culture of shared moral values as a co-requirement of free markets. Ironically, it is the art market that has been, and is, the primary source of support for the tradition of the new that government policies now appear to oppose.

1 C. Vaughan James, *Soviet Socialist Realism: Origins & Theory*, Macmillan (London), 1973.

2 *New Labour: because Britain deserves better*, Foreword byTony Blair, Labour Party (London), 1997.

3 Vladimir Ilyanich Lenin, *On Literature and Art* (1967), Progress Publishers (Moscow), 1970.

4 John Rentoul, *Tony Blair*, Warner Books (London), 1997.

5 See Philip Conford (ed.), *The Personal World: John Macmurray on self and society*, Foreword by Tony Blair, Floris Books (Edinburgh), 1996.

6 See NG Chernyshevsky, *Selected Philosophical Essays*, Progress Publishers (Moscow), 1953.

7 John Macmurray, *The Philosophy of Communism*, Faber (London), 1933.

8 Chris Smith, *Creative Britain*, Faber & Faber (London), 1998. See also Department for Culture, Media and Sport, '"Museums Must be Energetic and Imaginative on Access", says Chris Smith', 10 November 1997; DCMS 119/97, '"Why Pay for Museums?" asks Arts Minister', 11 November 1997; DCMS 44/98, 'Chris Smith Announces £9 Million Package to Promote Access and Education in Museums', 17 March 1998; DCMS 167/98, 'Chris Smith Challenges Museums to Grasp an Historic Opportunity', 21 September, 1998.

9 *Socialist Realism in Literature and Art*, trans. CV James, Progress Publishers (Moscow), 1971.

10 Milan Kundera, *The Art of the Novel*, trans. Linda Asher, Faber & Faber (London), 1988.

11 Gerry Robinson, *An Arts Council for the Future*, Arts Council of England (London), 1998.

12 National Arts and Media Strategy Monitoring Group, *Towards a National Arts and Media Strategy*, Arts Council (London), 1992.

13 DCMS 155/97, 'Review of Access to National Museums and Galleries', 8 December 1997.

14 DCMS 19/99, 'Chris Smith Sets Out Next Steps in Setting Up QUEST: New watchdog will cover both arts and sports bodies', 28 January 1999.

Ben Gibson

The Art of the State, or Laisser-Faire Eats the Soul: British Film Policy

If there are things going wrong with British cinema, as a brand, as an economy, as an experience, a number of its key problems may come down to the fact that the most ill-founded ambitions and improbable fantasies of its makers are unquestioningly enshrined as goals of UK government policy. That is, if we're able to agree – and you may not – that it really matters what we say about our goals in creative endeavour, given the strange combination of freedom and slavery we have to live with: a mood of zealous laisser-faire when it comes to the funding and regulation of the audio-visual, combined with an agenda-setting ideological tone that we can describe, despite its lack of fiscal teeth, as 'dirigiste'.

The UK makes more films than ever, settling for the moment at around eighty a year after an unhealthy boom to 130 in 1996 and 1997. Many of these are well made and much more marketable than their equivalents of a decade ago. Strikingly, though, they include almost none – two or three in a good year – that could easily be recommended by Nicholas Serota or Susan Sontag, or attended by Harold Pinter without his having previously contributed a cameo role. For every *Ratcatcher* there are dozens of *Guest House Paradiso*s and so-called *Beautiful Creatures*. This isn't a question of art snobbery, but of the barest cultural visibility, of the building of a cultural asset base. British cinema's contributions to local debates about how we live, or to the advancement

of international film culture and its forms, are generally the result of great struggle and exceptional good luck combined. Range is something we have come not really to expect. The balance of these statistics is not accidental, given their relationship to a self-conscious national project. Much better make a populist flop than an ambitious movie in search of an emerging audience, is the first premise of our ruling orthodoxy.

Britain does make, amongst those eighty, some ambitious low-budget independent movies. It also makes some remarkable popular films and some bad specialist films. The point is that there are so few individual, provocative, quality films made, comparative to the overall output, and that very few escape either total rejection or a creative mauling at the hands of those who subscribe to the founding dichotomy of the enterprise: culture OR commerce. These observations are made, however provocatively, in favour of pragmatism rather than a new ideology to replace the current one.

British hit films are described on all sides as 'exceptions that prove rules'. Thus *The Full Monty*, a film financed entirely by a US Studio, is too low budget to fit into current arguments and isn't necessarily British anyway, but is shoehorned into the debate somehow because it made money. It 'shows what can be done'. Some other memorable films of the last few years actually carry industry messages, if we could only listen to them clearly enough. What about these few 'specialist' films?

Let's take some of the recent winners and runners-up in the Michael Powell Prize, Edinburgh's award for British film of the year, given by an international jury. Gary Oldman's *Nil By Mouth* (1997) was financed and produced by the French, who are keener on confessional writer-director debuts than us; Carine Adler's *Under the Skin* (1997) and John Maybury's *Love is the Devil* (1998), packaged by a hands-on specialist film agency, since abolished, both had trouble with the Lottery Fund – the first was rejected altogether and the second was assisted only after an appeal. This year's *The Last Resort* from Paul Pawlikowski was commissioned and made via a semi-documentary low-budget BBC scheme that most senior executives at the Corporation have never heard of.

In a climate where evidence of cultural success can't be read quite straight because everything is an exception, precedental law gives way to some kind of statute in our debate about film. Simple observations, such as the proviso that – filmmaking being an expensive activity – films with smaller audiences in view should be made and publicised much more cheaply, threaten to erode some unity of will to 'commerciality' that our leaders earnestly seek, and are discounted out of hand as the merest platitudes. The UK remains one of the most expensive places in the world to make a low-budget movie, much more expensive, within any kind of acceptable employment structure, than the US. This makes range, as

things are, something of a practical impossibility. By the way, the films above haven't made lots of money but they have and will all pay for themselves, develop extraordinary talents and build up interest in British film abroad that is quite disproportionate to their cost.

Film has not automatically, even usually, qualified as culture in Britain, as noted by François Truffaut in his legendary dismissal of British cinema. Intellectual tradition and government thinking have involved the theoretical separation of 'works of art' from 'entertainment products' on the page, before any film stock has been exposed. Taken to extremes, where does this lead our filmmaking?

The distinction creates a border to be policed. Culture is always the Other, defined by what it is not. Keeping things antiseptically clear implies, for the sake of symmetry, creating and then naming a very few films that technocrats can designate as 'culture-only cinema'. Since this is the opposite of the other kind, such an imaginary cinema must necessarily have an opposite intention: that of deterring and alienating audiences as much as possible. Far from being natural enemies to 'art cinema' defined in this exclusive way, British governments, their film quangos and powerful lobbyists can actually lay claim, in an Orwellian sense, to having invented it.

If those in control of cinema funding are opposed to the idea of cultural subsidy, which they are, they have a problem. Cultural subsidy in the end is what they do. They have only two possible courses of action. Resignation is dismissed as cowardly. What then? The remaining option is to launch a campaign to prove that cinema has nothing at all to do with culture. The sole disadvantage of the theory, as they say, is that it is not true. But if you are in control and can somehow get money from the Arts Council for True Blue, the true story of the Oxford and Cambridge boat race, then you can make it so, at least from film to film. The ugly side of the no-culture campaign is that it involves breaking the only big rule left in the arts and crafts: solidarity – that you mustn't attack your own. Such transgressions, rare in other film cultures, have been acceptable here for many years. American-connected producers and directors routinely attack local film-makers for what they might call 'Un-commercial Activities'. After a while, as the sinners move away and die out, this becomes less of a problem. The only unacceptable filmmaker Alan Parker can now think of to exclude publicly is a dead one. He's regularly quoted as saying that he has no money for Derek Jarman. I should think not; you've had your lot now, Derek.

Popularising a vocabulary of cultural prejudice is not the same thing as enabling creativity. What is being established with the official culture/commerce litmus test? The total equivalence of the good and the popular, even more than in so many other art forms here, has led to the right of individuals either entirely outside the market (the technocrats) or working exclusively for another market (the London-based international producers) routinely to exclude from consideration works that do not promise to reproduce in familiar terms experiences that large audiences have paid for in the past. In this highly polarised theoretical system, 'innovation' and 'audience' do not appear as parts of a single formulation.

This approach to local filmmaking inflects our support for broadcasters, their licensing and regulation, and the spending of the comparatively small amount of public cash available as investment to UK film producers. As in 'public service broadcasting', works whose budgets involve public funds are as much tied to 'intuitive' forecasts of short-term profitability as are those generated by the commercial sector alone. This is now the accepted norm for the support of the audiovisual in Britain.

Although the minuscule public and TV support for actual experiment in UK filmmaking is real money and welcome for itself – and in theory it is growing in the Film Council formula of funds – this few quid is also part of the splitting process, forever focusing attention on film's supposed duality and stiffening the sinews for what we are supposed to think of as the 'real game'.

The development of so-called niche markets as the key growth area of contemporary capitalism, we might suppose, will necessitate a new way of combining categories, destroying the validity of this careful splitting work. Within pure capitalism, where actual returns on real films form the empirical evidence for business realignments, this happens consistently: 'Classics Divisions' (specialising in lower-budget, 'riskier' films) proliferate in the major studios; the Sundance Festival of independent films, mobbed by the industry, is forced to impose a limit on the number of personnel accredited from each Hollywood talent agency; 'surprise breakthrough' are the watchwords of cash-hungry distributors. In government-assisted areas, however, where fairytale and rhetoric generally trump market evidence, the irrelevance of the categories to the actual process under examination has merely led to a more ferocious incantation of the original doctrine. 'Commercial, commercial, commercial' might have been the motto of successive government reports and keynote speeches over the last twenty years. Of course, this implies that we should be making money, but does it work and what else does it imply?

The first New Labour film report, 'The Bigger Picture', put aside funds for 'Commerciality Training'. Because the report was subsequently abandoned, we still don't know what this is exactly. In 2000, The Film Council has put aside a useful £5 million to 'improve the development process', but without so far mentioning the pragmatic issues: not every script, not more than 20% of scripts, is industrially far-ranging enough, or big enough, to need hordes of writers, 'script doctors', gag contributors, and dialogue polishers – most simply need to have their integrity respected and drawn out, and their risks taken at full value, or to be abandoned; there is no mention of the corporate poverty of low-budget film producers, or the implication that survival for them means producing 100% of what they develop, whereas in actual creativity, failure remains an option.

In practice, all this sounds implausible. How, it will be asked, can film professionals condemn themselves to the exclusion of their work from the 'cultural', an exclusion that also inhibits their potential to invent and to profit from new markets? Some possible answers: first, those whose successes have taken them into the arena of international cinema commissioned outside Britain, the people with the most influence at the top table, have grown accustomed to the openness to invention that characterises American independent film, and seem to think of it simply as a cultural difference rather than a defining, crucial asset for success. Our local way of talking needn't bother them because they are free, in the end, to travel. Second, and most powerful, is a thin but convenient alliance between two parties who have in common a deep-seated fear of art. In the left corner are those who believe that 'national identity' can be given coherence and expression by favouring certain genres taken as traditions, including those whose innate puritanism makes them define a trademark neo-realism not as a movement, but simply as an absence of any such pretentiousness. In the right corner of this unholy alliance are the aspirational producers of low-budget, local films, whose only target audience is the American mini-major buying community and their picks of last season. Their key, 'long-term' plan is to turn film history on its head by beating all the odds, taking the US box office by storm and in effect extending the local market for all their work from 6% of the world's audience to 71%. In 1998, only eight British movies grossed more than a million dollars in the US.

How does the alliance work? The first group clears the decks of complexity by declaring swathes of directors, from Powell and Pressburger and Hitchcock through to Derek Jarman and Terence Davies, to be interesting but in the end slightly foreign. They make art feel embarrassing for us all, regardless of any marginal return. The second team warns us repeatedly that we're going to have to focus doggedly on imitation and disguise if we're to capture a dream market in the manner of our wildest dreams. Invoking demand as their moving force, they make no apology for trading only in appropriately distorted reflections of their own realities.

The result of all this passionate caution, looking around at the development lists of the UK producers,

is a crucifying fear of marginality and of the long game – something akin to a neurotic football team in which there are only strikers and no offside rule: goal-hanging stops the game from really progressing at all, although many goals are let in. To summarise: the ritualised fear of 'art' serves its own cultural agenda, and also masks a fear amongst those currently in power that 'art' may paradoxically represent real audiences, which they are personally ill-equipped to serve.

Britain has little film support from either television or the public purse when compared with France or Germany (between five and fifteen times higher). In 1998, France spent three times as much in total as we did on film production, with Germany not far behind. Exceptionally, audiences for foreign (non-US) films here benefit from no distribution subsidy whatever. At least for now. All this is well rehearsed, and it is in any case widely accepted that we traditionally spend our local culture money on television, and not on cinema. After all, one cheap video diary says more about us than a half-dozen sleekly tongue-in-cheek East End thrillers.

A more telling comparison is this one: the new Film Council, which has the same cash resources as the organisations that were abolished to form it (around £30 million a year, including the BFI and the Lottery money), spends a tiny proportion of the figures per head for cinema in Australia, New Zealand or Canada. In those countries, it is

argued that local English-speaking cinema can easily be dwarfed by or subsumed into the American business and that their industries need extra support for an infrastructure equipped to survive this competition. What, then, is the UK's argument? Contrariwise, that because we speak the language of the Americans, we enjoy every opportunity of making our business viable based on their box office. Our lucky producers need 'soft' money like a fish needs a bicycle. A feature of low self-esteem, in culture as in the rest of life, is that it breeds confusion and, occasionally, shocking delusions of grandeur.

If some extraordinary films get made, why are they not seen more widely? One reason, beyond the almost-total foreign ownership of cinema chains and major distributors, is this: Britain's loyal film audience, in particular the emerging, youthful, indie crowd, tends to miss out on the best of our films, because a huge quantity of embarrassing, substandard and nondescript British pictures is sufficiently widely released to put that audience off this brand. Officially, such insulting of the critics' and audiences' intelligences is simply an accumulation of minor disagreements about 'taste'. In actual business, you learn most from the customers who complain.

In France, where *Guest House Paradiso*, *Elephant Juice* and *Beautiful Creatures* are simply not screened at all, audiences get to see a British Cinema without an

enforced diet of dismay and dissatisfaction, and the British brand can be protected from its own worst failures. Here, funders insist that no film can be financed without an up-front distribution deal, so that every turkey is displayed in public for as long as can be afforded. Those who had the misfortune to see the thirty-five or so films that turn up each year in the list as 'no distribution deal', might want better distribution for the good work, but will be under no illusions that anyone else wants to share the experience at £7 a shot and 100 minutes of their life gone.

The French, like the US studio distribution chiefs, call this write-off cinema the 'Devil's Share' (*le part du Diable*) and bury it for the sake of audience loyalty. At the very least, they avoid screening such films for the critics. But that doesn't fit with the UK Government's obsession with seeing culture in terms of 'access'. The other reason for the poor box-office showing of such critically successful local films is that UK distributors are not usually able to offset print and advertising costs for British films by making television sales. They don't have the time to wait for an audience or the cash to recruit it fast. The films, after all, are produced by and for television.

The current UK audience for British films represents up to around 6% of tickets sold in a year (with no Bond picture), compared to France with 38%. Expecting to recoup on UK films and their print and advertising costs locally is for the moment no basis for doing business. The real production market consists of people who, more and less intelligently, speculate on the US and other markets and cover their costs by supplying local prestige television. Our key producer, winner of the other Edinburgh prize of recent years for Tim Roth's *The War Game*, is Channel 4.

Channel 4 now makes its films via a commercial subsidiary, which vertically integrates production, world sales, theatrical distribution, video, cable and TV licensing. It is the closest thing we have to a studio. Channel 4 is promoting itself as purveyor of an unstuffy and attractive mid-Atlantic brand of independent-genre-fare-with-attitude, much more reminiscent of actual cinema than the old Film on Four. You might call it 'A girl and a gun, re-done'. This non-national independent cinema is constructed in montage by ads that blur the lines between Little Italy and Bermondsey so effectively that we can barely remember whether Film Four is American like *Frasier* or English like *Brookside*. It works. With this developing identity comes the realisation that such a business, a potential cash cow for the C4 brand, must invest primarily in films that will collaborate and compete on fairly equal terms with those from Miramax and the other US mini-majors and Classics Divisions. The stakes and the budgets for our most important local producer are higher than ever. What we might call our 'international range', the Valhalla, is expanded, but significantly, at the

expense of the old-fashioned films that used to be made based on someone's gut feeling of faith in an idea and some people.

Given that the vast majority of non-US films are not pre-sold in America, and categorised colourfully as 'execution dependent' (meaning too-much-of-a-risk-unless-we-see-it-work-on-screen-at-Toronto), Channel 4's capacity for funding risk can be calculated by factoring in: the lowest budgets allowable; the demands of corporate prestige; the personalities involved; and the strength of the business partnerships in Europe, where a bigger range of perhaps stranger films can be co-produced and even pre-sold. And at a moment when, if the risk formula can really be calculated, European partnership is the biggest factor of them all, there is really very little reciprocity on which to base a future of business collaboration.

In addition to the abolition this year of the small European Co-Production Fund and the UK's non-status (alongside Albania) outside Eurimages, Channel 4 itself shows foreign language films only very occasionally, and then almost always on its low-cost, low-paying cable channel. There's really no money going back into Europe. Although French and German companies are entering the English-language market increasingly via production and distribution bases in the UK, these are branch offices, not headquarters, and it is hard to see what they can really gain in

production finance from associations with British entities and their rigidly market-driven baselines. In fact, at present it is the American studios who are doing most in Europe, co-financing not just UK heritage cinema, but also an increasing share of German-language production.

In the case of Film Four, there is a complex mixture here of short- and long-term effects. In the short term, a well-marketed brand that rejects the cheesier aspects of the 'national' cinema culture in favour of a broad, relatively youthful audience of enthusiasts is building a strong internal structure for feeding audiences and generating value. Great. In the longer term, we have to forget, outside of the useful work of the 'Film Four Lab', eccentric, feisty films made on an enthusiastic whim. And on the day Film Four actually turns a net profit, the whole operation, with its prices and terms completely unregulated, becomes a traditionally British matter of trusting to the essential goodness of the dominant market leader rather than legally ensuring that they serve the industry or the public. Imagine a scenario in which Canal Plus, rather than being taxed and regulated by the French CNC, was simply given an indefinite franchise to vertically integrate and accumulate rights and equity from the other players at whatever prices the market would bear. Surely the sons and daughters of the *Soixant-huitard Nouvelle Vague* would take to the cafés and shut down French cinema immediately in protest.

It may be objected here that since 'Film Four Lab' exists, everything else can be left to progress in a Panglossian laisser-faire manner. Fine and good as far as it goes, but I refer you also to the objection that ghettoes imply exclusion as well as accommodation, and that since the films are not commissioned either on a fully independent basis or outside a profit-driven structure, we are trusting simply to our faith in a few individuals to ensure that it isn't all an alibi for the main Film Four brand, allowing their films to get bigger budget and more exclusively mid-Atlantic without attracting too much notice from low-budget filmmakers.

What, then, is the Film Council's proposed response to this conjuncture? Well, as we know, there is a low-budget cultural fund called the 'New Cinema Fund' based on resources previously spent by British Screen and the BFI Production Board, the development fund described, and the main fund, the 'Premiere Production Fund' aimed at 'commercial' films. This is in quotation marks because it does not, in the real world, mean that such films will recoup their costs easily. What it may mean, based on past experience, is that they will be over-budgeted for their stories and packages, anxiously and ingratiatingly populist in tone, and their stars will be the theme song, the clever twist and the ad copy. Direction will have brio and efficiency, but will be otherwise nondescript. Of course, I hope I'm wrong as much as the new gatekeepers do.

But let's consider first the future of the 'cultural fund', also in inverted commas. In relative terms, taken as a 'grown-up' BFI Production Board replacement, £5 million a year is a lot of money. Taken as regional film support, British Screen and the BFI, however, it's not so much. So let's see what it becomes.

One anxiety is that if it's a 'low-budget fund' or a 'classics division' based on experiment, it must shift its idea of a target market away from those endless coffee-bar discussions about reproducing the special worlds and moments of *Clerks* and *Blair Witch* – an obsession with trying for luck rather than judgement, which promises to render its output strikingly unoriginal, rather than refreshingly entrepreneurial. It must make and meld new audiences if it has a long-term point. But these are the right adjectives, and calling it 'cultural' would provide a pretext for other gatekeepers to develop a rhetoric within a public-funding body that loudly spurns cultural aspiration, and would send us down all the old dead-end roads again.

Another worry is that most of the good low-budget films have trouble financing themselves; in Wardour Street parlance, they 'can't get themselves arrested' before they turn out to be the good choices. Producers need someone to support their projects and packages absolutely without compromise for any of those projects to get started. So the risks must be affordable and almost total. Investments, most

crucially, will be in people before they are investments in 'ideas'.

Regional funding and funding for Black and Asian cinema need to be rethought entirely. The films we make in Britain are horrifyingly metrocentric and white, and this can't be responded to with half-hearted gestures, video pilots and do-nothing films of so-called 'local interest'. For a start, we have to accept that at least half the film-makers with something to say, well, in cinema, about the English regions or Wales are actually living in London and dreaming about their places of birth. A grown-up fund would specifically finance these people to go home with a project.

Short films can be a great part of the mix as long as we don't think of them as rehearsals for the legendary 'real thing'. They won't work unless they're entities in themselves. The great necessity in low-budget support is to make films by people who don't just need to make 'a film', but to find out the deepest relationships between people and material, so that we fund someone who 'must make this film'. This is often hard curatorial work, and while it certainly could be done entirely by the individual producers if they were paid to struggle in depth with such development, the simple fact is that they aren't and they must eat.

Last of all for this fund: pilots. Making lots of pilots will effectively convey mistrust, create anxiety and exacerbate a numbing corporate

fear of box-office failure, but will not make choices easy or more fruitful. The kinds of projects that need piloting usually aren't the personal, low-budget ones; they're the high concept, ideas-led ones. Taking the risk out of the process of commissioning can best be done, paradoxically, by investing total trust in certain people and asking them to talk about audience, in their very specific way.

The 'commercial' fund has £10 million a year to spend. It would be much more useful to call it a 'higher-budget' fund, not only because there is an obvious Dome-waiting-to-happen hostage to fortune in there, but also because, if the few hits of the last decade are anything to go by, the haul from cheap films may be better than from this slate. Crucially, those charged with guessing what might work at the box office will be politically charged with financing the biggest and spangliest packages on offer, and then their money may even be unwanted by the other financiers.

There's also the old but near-forgotten question of justifying the expenditure of public funds, even as so-called 'investment'. Cultural funding has taken on a let-the-business-do-the-business tone in the last ten years, but Alexander Walker, in his one-man crusade, is not actually the only one who finds the qualifications for support a little puzzling. Taken to its logical extreme – which is mostly where the Lottery fund's panel liked to

take it – in order to qualify for public money for UK filmmaking, you should first satisfy the funders and their advisors that you really have no need of the money. Neediness will be greatly distrusted. It will be taken to mean that rather than trying to feed an established audience, you have ambitions to either create a new one or expand some 'elitist' one of your own. Such ambitions, it is loudly argued, have no place in a healthy British industry, and tend to breed the 'self-indulgence' we should all fear so earnestly.

The people who generate a climate of fear around ambition, so well calculated to take the heat out of our creative endeavours, believe they know certain things for sure: the trends in the American marketplace (still a staggering 65% of the world market for an English-language film), and what will keep the funding flow running from government. The trouble, for all of us, is that these people usually fail to notice that the majority of cinema films made for less than $10 million are officially 'specialist' films in the US, and carry a definite market obligation to be somehow surprising. Second, they fail to consider that, whatever the populist anti-intellectual rhetoric of politicians, a local cinema producing a lot of work that loudly proclaims a passionate disdain for the culture of cinema or for the long term, may soon get cut off from government intervention on the perverse basis that they should be paying for themselves if they're so clever. Politicians use whatever arguments come to hand to rescue their careers by saving the Treasury money.

Finally, let's talk about how we attract good people to make cinema in Britain, what with everything else that's on their minds. American producers, because they have a hungry centre to their business and understand what it is to innovate at its rich periphery, are mostly better at making specialist cinema for themselves, and have a keen respect for artistic ambition in filmmaking hard to find amongst brow-beaten UK producers, tied up as they so often are in self-censoring aspirational knots about generating packages that sell. Given that in Britain, painting, sculpture, architecture, rock music, product design and the novel sustain peripheral spaces that pay returns and supply breakthrough innovation, and that these businesses see it as a key commercial imperative to invent new markets, there is very little to attract people with talent – often those in receipt of that generous, unfussy personal development funding you can get from the DHS – onto the leather sofas of the Soho film producers, rather than into these other fields of cultural expression. If the Film Council doesn't see itself as partly a talent agency, it remains part of the old problem.

Jeremy Deller

Unconvention: Artist's Statement

From 11 November 1999 to 16 January 2000 the exhibition 'Unconvention' was held at the newly opened, purpose-built Centre for Visual Arts in Cardiff. The exhibition was curated by the artist Jeremy Deller and organised by Bruce Haines of CVA, and attracted the largest audiences ever to visit the gallery.

Sadly, due to inadequate funds, on 5 November 2000, CVA closed after only 14 months of operation.

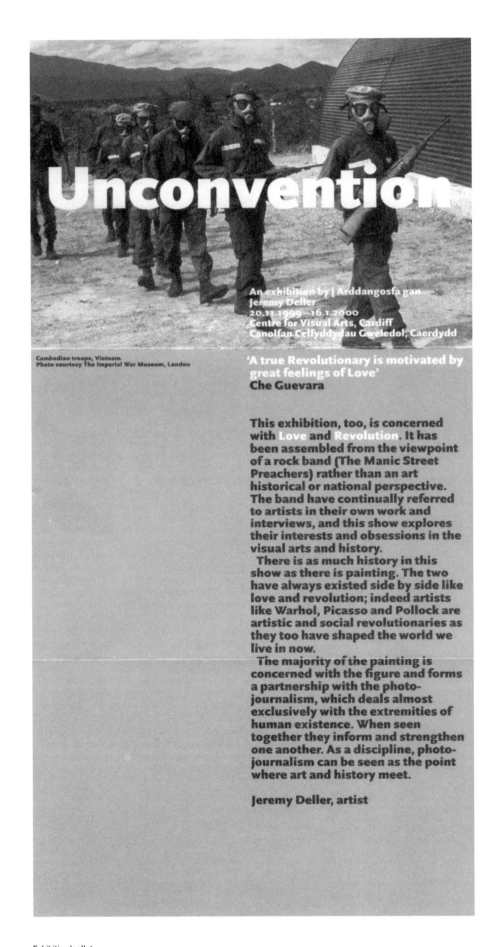

Cambodian troops, Vietnam.
Photo courtesy The Imperial War Museum, London

'A true Revolutionary is motivated by great feelings of Love'
Che Guevara

This exhibition, too, is concerned with Love and Revolution. It has been assembled from the viewpoint of a rock band (The Manic Street Preachers) rather than an art historical or national perspective. The band have continually referred to artists in their own work and interviews, and this show explores their interests and obsessions in the visual arts and history.

There is as much history in this show as there is painting. The two have always existed side by side like love and revolution; indeed artists like Warhol, Picasso and Pollock are artistic and social revolutionaries as they too have shaped the world we live in now.

The majority of the painting is concerned with the figure and forms a partnership with the photojournalism, which deals almost exclusively with the extremities of human existence. When seen together they inform and strengthen one another. As a discipline, photojournalism can be seen as the point where art and history meet.

Jeremy Deller, artist

Exhibition leaflet
'Unconvention', Centre for Visual Arts, Cardiff, 1999–2000

Matthew Higgs

Unconvention

Introduction to the publication for 'Unconvention', an exhibition and series of events curated by the artist Jeremy Deller, held at Cardiff Centre for Visual Arts, November 1999

Art is not a mirror to reflect the world, but a hammer with which to shape it.
Vladimir Mayakovsky

When asked to write a brief introduction for this publication, which commemorates, celebrates and documents Jeremy Deller's exhibition 'Unconvention' – a project inspired by the historical and cultural interests and obsessions of the Welsh rock band the Manic Street Preachers – I found myself in a quandary. How, if at all, would it be possible to describe an event that remains – without any doubt – the most challenging (and moving) experience I have ever witnessed in an art gallery? How could I hope to articulate in words – especially to someone who wasn't actually there – the complex range of emotions and possibilities that the situation engendered? (When was the last time you saw someone literally moved to tears in an art gallery?) How could I hope to describe the many pleasures, both visceral and intellectual, that went some way to reaffirming my own belief in art's potential both to illuminate and to transform our experience and expectations of life?

Short of an adequate answer or response, and by way of an apology, I can only offer here some brief observations of some of the events that took place on that bitterly cold November weekend in Cardiff. They are images and memories that will remain with me forever: a resplendent performance by the Pendyrus Male Choir, massed beneath Andy Warhol's funereal self portrait, singing songs of passion and resistance; Arthur Scargill – President of the National Union of Mineworkers – delivering an impassioned speech to an initially sceptical audience, an inspirational, humanitarian call-to-arms that insisted that only collectively can we challenge the orthodoxy of capitalism, that together we must accept the responsibility for our own destiny. It provided a graphic echo of Aneurin Bevan's earlier warning that 'we know what happens to people who stay in the middle of the road. They get run over'.

The exhibition itself: seminal works by artists as seemingly unrelated as Lawrence Weiner, Francis Bacon, Edvard Munch, Pablo Picasso, Jenny Saville, Jackson Pollock and Martin Kippenberger, displayed alongside documentary photographs by Robert Capa, Kevin Carter and Don McCullin, provided visual juxtapositions as unlikely as they were profound. Numerous organisations – contemporary points of resistance – from Amnesty International and the Campaign Against The Arms Trade to fanzines produced for and by the fans of Manic Street Preachers presented their activities in the gallery alongside archival material that charted the earlier struggles of the Welsh miners' fraternal involvement in the Spanish Civil War and the Situationist refutation of the 'Society of the Spectacle'. Each organisation, each artwork, each document, each individual was accorded an emotional equanimity, unburdened by the usual hierarchies, the usual distinctions between 'high' and 'low' cultural artefacts that art galleries so commonly reinforce.

Jeremy Deller's art is an art of democratisation; one that demystifies and liberates the construction of meaning, empowering both its audience and participants. 'Unconvention' was perhaps the most site-specific artwork I have ever encountered, in that it engaged explicitly and unashamedly with the social, cultural and political histories and legacies of its constituents – the people of South Wales, mediated through the agency of a local contemporary rock band who since their inception have sought to address the discrepancies and injustices that exist in society.

That some 4,000 people visited the exhibition during its opening weekend made it all the more remarkable, not only validating Deller's enterprise but vindicating his persistent belief that art does not and cannot exist in isolation. 'Unconvention' served to remind us that art can both challenge and engage with a broad and diverse public without pandering to the lowest common denominator.

I'm glad that I was there; I'm sorry if you weren't. It was an honour to be implicated in 'Unconvention'.

It is only with the heart that one can see rightly; what is essential is invisible to the eye.
Antoine de Saint-Exupéry

Arthur Scargill

Unconvention

Extract from an address given by Arthur Scargill, President of the National Union of Mineworkers, on the occasion of 'Unconvention', an exhibition and series of events curated by the artist Jeremy Deller, held at the Centre for Visual Arts, Cardiff, 20 November 1999

[...] There is a frequent misconception that working people, men and women, do not appreciate art, do not appreciate culture and, above all, do not realise the connection between culture, art and the resistance to those things in society that are so apparently wrong, whether it be hunger, lack of work, starvation, helplessness, hopelessness. Therefore, I thought the best way I could deal with this would be to talk about resistance, because the Manic Street Preachers, for example – a modern-day version of all those who've gone before them in South Wales and elsewhere – are actually preaching the politics of resistance to that which is wrong in our society. [...]

When you walk around the exhibition and you look at the paintings, photographs, poetry or imagery – read the books, read of the struggles, whether it be about the Spanish Civil War, the Vietnam War, the struggle against apartheid, or the ' strikes by mine workers in 1972–74 and 1984–85, or the struggle of the magnificent women at Greenham Common, or the struggles of the people at Critchley here in South Wales, or the struggles of the strikers of the Northeast, or the struggle that has been going on for five years at Hillingdon Hospital by Asian women who refused to bow the knee, no matter what was put in their way – you understand that this exhibition is a reflection of the kind of inspiration that has kept those people going. When I see the women of Hillingdon, no more than four-foot-eleven, five-feet tall – Asian women who refused to give in [...] I feel a pride in what they're doing. They are in the finest tradition of all this marvellous art that's around us, and this is a message for the new millennium: the faith that I have is as relevant in the twenty-first century as it was in the twentieth century and the nineteenth century. We are coming back to socialism because it's the only faith that can resolve the problems inherent in a capitalist society. If you agree with me, then you will undoubtedly take inspiration from this exhibition, and exhibitions like it. You will see the connection between art and culture and writing and the struggle of working men and women for true emancipation. You will understand the struggle of the Suffragettes, of the Levellers, of the Chartists and, above all, understand why we had to take action in the 1960s, the 70s, the 80s and still had to take action in the 90s. If you want to avoid having to take that type of action in the next century, then you have to take the inspiration you need to defeat the present system, and take inspiration from the exhibition around you and exhibitions like them that exist in this and other countries.

There is another way. You can either collaborate and accept what they dish out – whether it be unemployment and poverty and injustice and inequality or whether it be to destroy your faith in living itself [...], or, like me, you turn and say 'we're not prepared to accept this any longer'.

That's why I accepted the invitation to come here today. Because this exhibition, I believe, is part of me and I am part of it.

For some unknown reason, the 'Millennium Photographic Exhibition' have selected my arrest at Hargrieves as one of the images of the century. It is an image not of an arrest of a miners' leader, but of a State that sought to destroy the lives of ordinary men and women during the course of a struggle that produced connection between human beings on a national and international scale that had not been seen since the time of the Spanish Civil War. I, like many others, have been privileged to take part in that resistance. Privileged, as the French miners were to take part in their resistance. Privileged, as the mine workers and steel workers and workers throughout the world have been to take part in the struggles against injustice wherever it rears its ugly head.

I think this exhibition has a message, not just in political terms, but also in social and economic terms. It has a message that is relevant to your understanding of the world around you. If you look at these images in that way, then you'll understand that this is not some detached exhibition but an exhibition of all the struggles that have taken place in art over the years. And you can take from that the kind of inspiration that I get, and you will be fully equipped to resist just as hard as your parents and your grandparents. If you do that, it will be the kindest tribute not only to them, but to the artists who produced this work and, in doing so, made so many sacrifices. It's a privilege to be with you.

Centre for Visual Arts, Cardiff

Press Statement

The Pendyrus Male Voice Choir, CAV, Cardiff, 20 November 1999
photo: Kim Fielding

August 10, 2000

Centre | Canolfan
for | Celfyddydau
Visual Arts | Gweledol

Press Statement

for immediate use

The Trustees regret that the Centre for Visual Arts will have to close on the 5 November 2000 at the end of the British Art Show.

This decision has been forced upon them by the refusal of the officers of the Arts Council of Wales to work with the Trustees to explore the positive way forward recommended in the independent review of the Centre. The Trustees regret that the ACW has shown neither the strategic forethought nor the artistic vision to support the Centre on a comparable level with equivalent institutions across the British Isles.

The City and County of Cardiff have stated: *"We wish to continue working with the Trust to safeguard this major arts facility for the people of Cardiff and Wales."*

The independent report commends the high standards of education and exhibitions at the Centre for Visual Arts. The Trustees welcome the report's endorsement of the Trust's recommendations that free admission be introduced and that one gallery be dedicated permanently to the art and artists of Wales.

During the period before final closure the Trustees hope that the Chairman and Council of ACW will convince the National Assembly of the value of implementing the preferred option recommended by the independent report.

Ends

Please contact Jenny Brunsdon, Marketing Officer
Tel: direct line (029) 20 729 729 or (029) 20 388 922   Fax: (029) 20 388 924
Email: jen@cva.org.uk   www.cva.org.uk

Working Street, The Hayes, Cardiff, CF10 1GG
Tel (029) 20 388 922. Fax (029) 20 388 924. Email ad@cva.org.uk
www.cva.org.uk
The Cardiff Old Library Trust. A company limited by guarantee
Registered in Wales No. 2903071. Charity No. 1034079

Stryd Working, Yr Aes, Caerdydd, CF10 1GG
Ffôn (029) 20 388 922. Ffacs (029) 20 388 924. Ebost ad@cva.org.uk
www.cva.org.uk
Ymddiriedolaeth Hen Lyfrgell Caerdydd. Cwmni cyfyngedig trwy warant
Cofrestrwyd yng Nghymru Rhif 2903071. Rhif Elusen 1034079

Arts and Sport

The Earl of Clancarty: It is certainly time that the concept of 'social exclusion' was tackled in debate. The idea of social exclusion, whatever the term may mean – it may mean a number of things – seems to be one of the most crucial in current Government thinking. It is surprising that as a concept it has not yet been more widely discussed either in the media or in Parliament.

Just under two years ago, the noble Lord, Lord Bruce of Donington, asked the Government about the terms of reference of the newly established Social Exclusion Unit. In the course of a long Written Answer he was told:

Social exclusion is a shorthand label for what can happen when individuals or areas suffer from a combination of linked problems such as unemployment, poor skills, low incomes, poor housing, high crime environments, bad health and family breakdown. [Official Report, 9/12/97; col. WA20]

Does the Minister say that that is still a reasonable definition of 'social exclusion', or has the definition recently changed – perhaps it has shifted or broadened – in some way? I ask this because 'social exclusion' and 'access' together now appear to be the two concepts that most permeate thinking and policy in the Department of Culture, Media and Sport. If that is so, what is the association between these two ideas? If access is about a concern for broader and different audiences it is clear that we are also talking about social exclusion as something that may affect all classes or parts of society: exclusion by race, gender, disability and so on.

From the definition that I have quoted, social exclusion is characterised primarily by what are perceived to be the marginal or poorest parts of society. In this respect, the present Government has extremely laudable aims in combating what it perceives as social exclusion by funding government schemes or by indirectly encouraging smaller-scale projects at local community level. I mention a recent visit by me, at the suggestion of my noble friend Lord Listowel, along with my noble friend Lord Freyberg, to Buffy House, which is a hostel near Kensington, Olympia, run and funded by Centrepoint, where we were shown the art workshop organised by the remarkably energetic and enthusiastic Jaime Bautista. Each year it participates in an exhibition of work in the crypt at St Martin-in-the-Fields organised by the St Martin's Social Care Unit. Certainly, given the present level of homelessness, this is one of the very few such projects in London that need a real input from government in the form of finance.

Local projects are cited in Policy Action Team 10's report to the Social Exclusion Unit on arts and sport. One widely quoted project is a housing estate in the North West where the incidence of crime dropped from forty-four to six per month following the introduction of a community football scheme. There are many similar ongoing local community-based schemes across the country involving sport and different cultural activities. Such schemes that reduce crime can only be for the good.

I live on a council estate in north London where there are two playgrounds, one of which is used every night for football. It has never occurred to me that these playgrounds keep down crime, although in effect I suppose that they do. The playgrounds have always been there. They were built as part of the estate in the 1970s. I believe that I and other residents simply see them as normal, essential parts of the estate facilities. If they had been provided afterwards, the Government could probably have cited them on their list of schemes. That starts to raise in my mind questions about the degree to which initiatives should be, or should have been, an inherent part of the structure in the first place; or that new schemes become an organic part of the way a local community naturally develops according to its own requirements, according to the desires of the local residents, before the symptoms of frustration such as crime have set in; and how facilities once in place need to be maintained in good order by the community or by those immediately responsible for the local community such as the local councils.

In that respect, the most recent poor responses of councils to the desires and feelings of local people spring to mind easily. The actions of councils such as those of Westminster City Council this year in cutting community funding are examples of social exclusion. The current problems of the public library in Lewisham are another case in point. As with Camden, the feelings of the local communities are simply being ignored. It seems to me that that is as much a basic problem as any ultimate decisions over library closures – wrong indeed as such closures are.

In many ways, the central problem of the issue is the treatment of social exclusion in relation to the exclusive nature of society as a whole. It is of course classic socialist thinking to believe that the arts are primarily an instrument for curing society's ills, even though the Policy Action Team's report goes out of its way to insist also – I emphasise the word 'also' – on the independent significance of the arts. But that is not true either. The Government assume art and sport in a sense to be original agents: to treat them as though they have emerged from nowhere. Yet art and sport among other cultural effects are already entangled within society. Social exclusion is a dominant, perhaps the dominant, characteristic within our society and therefore within culture. Cultural activities themselves are already implicated in the process of exclusion. What perhaps we should be addressing, as well as the local symptoms, is the exclusionary nature of the tenets of our society as a whole.

To exemplify this, where I think that the Government seems to come unstuck in its thinking, or at least incomplete in its appraisal, is in the contradiction that exists between the desire for involving those at the margins of society in arts and sport and the encouragement of business at other levels – for example, the creative industries. In the Government's own thinking, there is a separation. In terms of sport we can, for instance, look at the now immense wealth of certain of the Premier League football clubs and the development at that end where the emphasis is on economic success rather than anything to do with community.

What effect, for example, does that have on the smaller local clubs where, from a governmental perspective, the moral emphasis is on shared community values, yet market forces will never be far away.

There is a parallel here with the star system in art, where a lot of money chases a relatively small number of known artists who are either kept in London or are sucked into London and away from the regions. In a sense, where the art stars tend now to win out, apart from financially, is that they escape the 'social' function of art operating at the local level: that is to say, the governmental policy towards the arts filtered down through the Regional Arts Boards' criteria for funding individual artists' projects. Increasingly, artists have to think their way around this situation to obtain the grants to do the projects that they want to do, or to continue the work that they are already engaged in, with whatever individual intentions that might exist behind that work. Such intentions may be extraordinarily diverse and that diversity is in itself a contribution to society. Yet despite that contribution, the effect of the system is that the great majority of artists work at or below the poverty line, which is in itself an example of social exclusion.

The principle at work here in society is the operation of the free market, which, to adapt the Government's own terms, excludes possibilities for the many in favour of the few. The Government instructs the local levels of cultural activity to take part in the curative process. Yet most money goes to the business end of those activities.

I asked at the beginning of the debate what was the relationship between social exclusion and access. This Government, perhaps society as a whole, sees access primarily in terms of the consumption of information as the key to knowledge – a trend very much embodied and supported by the information revolution with all the benefits that that supplies. That is 'external access'. But what remains, I think, largely unrecognised is the individual person as a primary source of knowledge, which comes from their being in the world. Individuals are producers as well as consumers of knowledge. Without considering the nature of this access, an access to an innate knowledge of the world, one can make only the crudest interpretations of how people visit museums, for instance, among many other activities. The denial of that as a possibility is in some ways the most significant form of social exclusion.

Lord Freyberg: My Lords, it gives me great pleasure to thank my noble friend Lord Clancarty for initiating this important and timely debate on the contribution that arts and sport can make towards social inclusion. Like my noble friend, I too look forward to the maiden speech of the noble Earl, Lord Shaftesbury.

On a personal note, I should like also to take the opportunity to thank my noble friend Lord Clancarty for the significant contribution he has made to debate in this House on the arts and in particular on museums and galleries. His passionate campaigning on these issues and others has been a great inspiration to me, and I am extremely sorry that this is the last debate in which we shall both be participating.

My noble friend has already told the House what the Social Exclusion Unit of the Cabinet Office defines as 'social exclusion'; I shall not repeat it. However, we have both been exercised on the subject of access to museums, particularly free access; and I think we both agree that museums have a useful part to play in tackling social issues, and that they must welcome every section of society.

On 12 October, the Secretary of State for Culture, Media and Sport confirmed in his speech to the Social Inclusion Conference that social inclusion is thought to be key across the whole of government and will be of increasing importance to his department. What I hope that he will enlarge on in future is the number of ways in which museums can be drawn upon to help the disadvantaged in our society.

There is a growing recognition of that in Government circles, but it has not always been so. The Policy Action Team 10, which reported earlier this year on arts and sport to the Social Exclusion Unit, made surprisingly little reference to the role of museums in creating social inclusion. I understand that this omission has been addressed and I hope that the group that has now been set up to advise the DCMS on this area of policy will be able to redress any previous imbalance.

Today, museums are no longer perceived merely to be repositories of valuable artefacts, although they of course hold a wealth of wonderful things and must continue to be bastions of scholarship. Nor is a visit to a museum considered to be the civilising ritual it was in Victorian England. Museums, however, play an important role in our communities. They give individuals knowledge of their cultural identity, an awareness of their traditions and, I hope, enormous pleasure and pride.

Walsall Museum and Art Gallery is an inspiring example of a museum that has successfully made the transition from Victorian municipal museum to paragon of contemporary best practice. Established in 1892, and about to open in a new, exciting building, the museum has gained a reputation over the past eight years for its pioneering new approaches to exhibition programming and interpretation of its collections. It aspires, in the words of its director, Peter Jenkinson, to be a 'national model of accessibility in the arts'. Walsall's recent education projects have ranged from the lowest technologies – jigsaw puzzles and 3-D construction models – through to the higher technologies of multi-media, video animation and video conferencing. Collections and exhibitions have been explored in a number of exciting and innovative ways, through commissioned music, dance and writing, as well as through the works of many visual artists. Such ground-breaking approaches must be built on and nurtured if our museums are to continue to inspire and attract new audiences.

But none of these new things can be done unless museums can afford to take risks. Museums have extremely limited financial resources and yet they need to be able to test out new and innovative ideas. This is why schemes such as the Heritage Lottery Fund's Museums and Galleries Access Fund are important. The fund exists: 'to support museums and galleries that are developing innovative, exciting and imaginative approaches in making their collections accessible to the widest possible audience'.

Through this scheme, the Heritage Lottery Fund is specifically encouraging museums to work with groups with which they are not traditionally associated, such as prisoners and victims of drug abuse. It is also aiming to fund projects that include groups such as the disabled and those from ethnic minorities. In addition, museums are able to apply for grants towards the cost of touring their collections to other venues, enabling audiences to look at works that they have had little opportunity to see before. Clearly, pioneering schemes such as these will have to be evaluated in order to make sure that the best ones continue and the least successful ones are dropped. It is hoped that other museums can then learn which projects might best suit them.

Museums can do much to ensure that they are equipped to provide the broadest possible access to the services they offer. They need to work in partnership with other organisations and, in particular, with specialist agencies, using a range of workshops and activities to engage people with their collections. Such agencies can act as a bridge with previously unknown audiences. In broad terms, I am encouraged by what has so far been achieved in this area. I hope that the Government will continue to support new ways of breaking down barriers between museums and the communities that they serve. [...]

Lord McIntosh of Haringey: My Lords, this is a sad as well as a happy occasion; sad because noble Lords who have taken part will no longer be with us, but happy because they have been able to do so and because the result has been such a constructive debate. It has been notable also for the maiden speech of the noble Earl, Lord Shaftesbury. Perhaps I may say immediately that anybody who names Jennie Lee has friends on these Benches. As the noble Earl probably remembers, she was in some ways an impossible woman. However, she was also remarkable for her involvement with the Open University and was probably the best Minister for the Arts this country has ever had. It was marvellous to hear the noble Earl paying tribute to her amidst his references to Keats, Voltaire, vegetable marrows and courgettes, which I very much enjoyed.

Let me say where I come from on this. I shall not say that everything in the garden is lovely, even though it is not a Westphalian garden. In the early 1970s, as a member of the Greater London Council, I was roped in to what was called The Spitalfields Project before Spitalfields became largely Bangladeshi. The theory behind that project was, 'What is wrong with deprived areas is the lack of co-ordination between departments and different levels of local authorities'. The Department of the Environment, the Greater London Council, the Inner London Education Authority and the London Borough of Tower Hamlets all got together and asked, 'Can we all act together in co-operation rather than separately?' That sounded fine. We had a small group of members surrounded by an enormous group of officials from various bodies, probably numbering fifty. We had meetings and a budget over a period of three years. At the end of that time, we had carried out some useful work. We had built children's playgrounds, converted buildings for community use, provided traffic-calming schemes and all sorts of good things.

At the public meeting held at the end of the project – we held our meetings in public – I was sitting at the table when an old lady came up and plonked a lump of mouldy bread in front of me. She said, 'It's all very well you lot tinkering around the edges. What's wrong with this place is that we do not have decent dry homes to live in, which is why my bread is mouldy, and we do not have proper jobs'. Fundamentally, that set me against pilot projects, demonstration projects and area projects that are and have been used by governments in the past as an excuse for not tackling the major issues.

The key to combating social exclusion is to make government programmes work more effectively to solve the basic problems faced by those who feel most excluded. That is why the main government strategy for social exclusion features health, crime, education and employment. I should add to that, from my own interest, housing. That does not represent a sidelining of the arts and sport but is a major opportunity for them to help on the ground: to get people fitter, improve their employment prospects and to divert those committing petty crime.

That is why social inclusion is a key initiative across government. It is remarkable that this is the first debate to be held in either House, not just on social exclusion and arts and sport but on social exclusion at all. There has been no proper debate in either House before today on this absolutely vital subject. I confirm that the early definition of social inclusion given by the noble Earl, Lord Clancarty, still applies. However, I do not place much faith in definitions. It is what we do with them that really matters.

The aim here is to address poverty and to give opportunities to everybody. I hope I can show in the limited time available that the way to achieve that is by the approaches being taken across government, in all departments, to ensure protection throughout life. We have mentioned child poverty. We have not talked much about pensioners, but we could have done, and everybody in between. Measures for families do not come under the category of social exclusion but perhaps they should. I refer to the working families' tax credit, which helps families get back to work; the National Child Care Strategy; Sure Start; education and initiatives to reduce truancy and exclusion; the education action zones and the commitment to nursery education of one kind or another for the under-fives, to which the noble Viscount, Lord Falkland, referred. I refer also to employment and the new deals to help people back into work. They start with the under-twenty-fives, go on to the over fifties and, as a result of announcements yesterday, are being extended beyond that.

The Social Exclusion Unit, set up by the Prime Minister on the initiative of No. 10 Downing Street, based in the Cabinet Office, is working on projects including the strategy for neighbourhood renewal, reducing teenage pregnancy and improving participation and achievement in learning by sixteen to eighteen year-olds. In the area of crime, there is the setting up of youth-offending teams. There is also the vital objective of reducing health inequalities and standards of care and, for all these departments, strengthening communities. I refer not to initiatives by one department but those that involve all departments in local partnerships, giving control of regeneration initiatives to local communities. I should refer to rough sleepers, mentioned by the noble Earl, Lord Listowel, who, as he knows, are a particular focus of one of the reports of the Social Exclusion Unit.

I turn to the role of arts and sport. The Policy Action Team 10 has been referred to by a number of speakers. It was set up by the Social Exclusion Unit and led by the Department for Culture, Media and Sport. I do not like to disagree with the noble Earl, Lord Clancarty, but he described it as a socialist theory of art that it should be there to cure society's ills. I should love to debate socialist aesthetics with him at some stage, from Engels to Luckacs to John Berger. However, that is not the way I see it and not the way I believe it is seen by modern democratic socialists. We see excellence in the arts as being their own objective. We do not see them as having their basis in social purpose. I am more of the Louis Dudebat school in 'The Doctor's Dilemma' than I am of curing society's ills.

Having said that, what we find already existing in government is that culture, leisure and heritage, in the broader sense, have a valuable role to play in neighbourhood renewal. There are numerous examples. I could take up an entire speech with examples. For instance, in relation to improved health we have the culture-sensitive provisions made by Hounslow Borough Council's Community Recreation Outreach team; in education we have the work of the Hartcliffe Boys' Dance Company in Bristol; in relation to reducing crime we have the education programme of the Galleries of Justice in Nottingham.

While I am on the subject of museums, I can advise the noble Lord, Lord Freyberg, whose examples of Walsall were welcome, that the Museums and Galleries Social Inclusion Group, which is due to report to Ministers by February of next year, had its first meeting at DCMS this morning. I am sure that the noble Lord will be interested in its conclusions after the study.

Participation in cultural and leisure activities, like amateur dramatics, playing a sport or visiting a library, can help to instil individual pride; it can raise expectations; it can raise community spirit; it can provide leadership capacity within communities. We want to see communities themselves having the power and taking the responsibility to make things better. From what I said at the outset it is clear that I agree with the noble Baroness, Lady Anelay, that we are not just talking of deprived communities; we are concerned with individuals, wherever they may be, who may be socially excluded and who should be included in the programmes.

The noble Earl, Lord Clancarty, questioned the relationship of access to social inclusion. Access is about providing convenient facilities for people to use. Social inclusion is about getting people involved and drawing them in. That is a link between them. There is no question of any conflict there.

The important point, which again relates to what I said at the beginning, is that we should not be tinkering with short-term projects; projects that will die after three years unless they fund themselves – the pattern in the past – pilots that will not exist in the long term. We want to see changes in the mainstream of how central and local government funding is spent. We want to see arts and sports bodies that receive public funds being accessible to everyone. That is not – I say this again to the noble Earl, Lord Clancarty – in conflict with business involvement. Indeed, if we look at the initiative of my noble friend Lord Hamlyn – the Hamlyn Week in the Royal National Theatre gives a whole week of cheap tickets to provide greater access – we see that business and charity can work together. However, it is true, as the noble Earl reminded us, that accessibility applies widely to people with disabilities, people of different ethnic origins, people with poor educational qualifications.

All the arts and sports bodies in receipt of public funding are being encouraged not to depart from quality, which is a prerequisite, and to work actively to engage those who have been excluded in the past. We want them to look outside their traditional, virtual funding patterns – this relates to what the noble Earl, Lord Shaftesbury, was saying – to provide the links between remedies for social exclusion and the arts and sport. Health spending on the arts can help treat mental health problems. Decent access to leisure facilities can reduce crime – the midnight football matches. Education spending on cultural leisure can reduce truancy. That is why the Policy Action Team was interdepartmental. It included the Cabinet Office, DETR, the Department for Education and Employment, the Treasury, the Department of Health, the Government Offices for the Regions and Number 10 Policy Unit.

We are embedding the social inclusion objectives throughout the Department for Culture, Media and Sport, and throughout government. We are setting up social inclusion groups to develop, advise and monitor social inclusion policy for libraries and museums. We are reviewing the funding arrangements that we have with our non-departmental public bodies. We are working – this relates to what my noble friends Lord Grantchester and Lord Faulkner said – with the Football Association, the FA Premier League and other interested parties, to develop a funding package for grassroots football, which is likely to be worth £50 million.

In all of that we must not underestimate the role of the Lottery distributors, who again are being encouraged, respecting their independence but within their agreed objectives, to look at the social exclusion element of the applications that come to them. [...]

Nicholas Murray

Culture and Accessibility

Essay based on Nicholas Murray's inaugural Gladys Krieble Delmas Fellowship Lecture at the British Library Centre for the Book, London, delivered on 11 September 1997, entitled 'After Arnold: Culture and Accessibility'

Whenever culture is discussed in England, Matthew Arnold is invariably called as a witness both for the prosecution and for the defence. One of the remarkable things about the author of *Culture and Anarchy* (1869) is the persistence of his influence on the debate about culture. Having weathered the storms of late twentieth-century cultural theory, he now seems to be sailing in more tranquil waters. Indicted variously in the past as a conservative, liberal, humanist, prig, lofty despiser of the masses, and subtle evader of the realities of class conflict, Arnold now seems to have stolen back into the affections of both Left and Right. But the author of a *Culture and Anarchy* for the early twenty-first century would look out onto a very different scene.

Current cultural discourse is far more fragmented than anything with which Arnold had to contend. There is not just a central tradition of liberal humanist criticism in the arts. There are specialised academic discourses. There is the continuing challenge of theory. There is postmodernism. Each of these ways of looking at, and talking about, the arts claims legitimacy, but how far these sub-discourses have penetrated the dominant ways of thinking and talking about aesthetic issues is moot.[1]

Arnold nearly called his famous work *Anarchy and Authority*, and looking out on the contemporary cultural scene I am tempted to argue that the current gold standard of aesthetic and critical value is

nearer the first than the second of these two poles. In a sense that postmodernist theorists, if no-one else, regard as exhilarating and liberating, there is no obvious centre of intellectual authority. Anything goes. Nonetheless, for those of us who think that culture matters, it is necessary to venture out onto these troubled waters and look critically at some recent examples of how the notion of culture is seen in contemporary Britain. In particular, I want to examine the currently fashionable concept of 'accessibility' and to ask if it is quite as benign a notion as it appears, and whether those who claim the ethical high ground in cultural politics are genuinely – as they would strenuously insist – on the side of the 'ordinary person' they so fondly evoke as the touchstone of the debate. Much of this argument turns on the distinction between populism and democracy.

That 'ordinary person', to whom the cultural mandarin pays such extravagant tribute (though a wide space of water remains between them), is much sought after by the 'culture industries', as they now call themselves – the language of marketing having displaced the language of aesthetics across swathes of contemporary British arts administration. Anxious about him or her finding opera too inaccessible, the English National Opera not long ago papered the London Underground with posters showing a semi-clad young woman whose charms were meant to render more accessible that notoriously difficult, obscure,

rebarbative, and unpopular opera, Bizet's *Carmen*. In 1995, a spokeswoman for BBC Radio 3 described a new daily morning show designed to win back listeners from its part-rival, Classic FM, which had twice as many weekly listeners. 'It is', she said, summoning up the image of the 'ordinary person' in her mind's eye, 'for those who do not want highbrow analysis – they can tune in and feel comfortable'.[2] We live in a political culture where a Prime Minister can address an adult electorate using the term 'the feel-good factor', so this new standard of value – feeling comfortable – shouldn't perhaps surprise. But what of those works of art that, far from inducing a pleasant interior glow, challenge and disturb, enacting what Aristotle called the emotions of pity and fear? Must art be toothless, bland, inoffensive, bowdlerised, placing no demands upon those who engage with it? What about the deep enrichment that can result from such challenges?

Staying with music a little longer, the 1995 Season of BBC Promenade Concerts at the Albert Hall was the occasion of a minor cultural scandal. With scant concern for the sensibilities of the ordinary person, the Last Night of the Proms scheduled a performance of a newly commissioned piece by Sir Harrison Birtwistle called *Panic*. Birtwistle, one of the most exciting and original contemporary composers, had returned to the world of Greek mythology, which has stimulated many of his works. The immediate trigger was a memory of some lines

of Elizabeth Barrett Browning about the god Pan: 'What was he doing, the great god Pan/Down in the reeds by the river?'. Half-human, half-goat, Pan, by shouting, overcame his enemies with an unreasoning fear or panic. It is a wild, alarming piece, which Birtwistle called a 'dithyramb' after the frenzied Greek choric hymn in praise of Dionysus, and it was played with wonderful energy by the saxophonist John Harle. It was aptly named, for no sooner had it been performed than the cultural thought-police of Middle England came clattering down Kensington Gore, their faces puffed and their helmets askew. That 'unreasoning fear or panic' did indeed grip the tabloid newspapers the next day. 'LAST FRIGHT OF THE PROMS', howled the *Daily Express*. 'LAST BLIGHT OF THE PROMS' whimpered *Today* newspaper. John Drummond, Controller of Radio 3 and the man responsible for visiting this music of the undead on an English audience at the Albert Hall had observed a couple of years earlier in a newspaper interview: 'The arts are not just instantaneous pleasure – if you don't like it, the artist is wrong. I belong to the generation that says if you don't like it, you don't understand and you ought to find out.'[3]

The ordinary person might well bridle at such comments – or would he or she? Does respect for an audience involve appealing to the lowest common denominator, the least demanding performance, the most untaxing pleasure, or does it mean crediting the common reader, the concert-goer, the civilised citizen, with some intelligence and appetite for invigorating artistic experience? Might it not be the case, indeed, that by proclaiming (without consulting the ordinary person himself) that he or she has no interest in anything other than Elgar's *Serenade for Strings*, the cultural power-brokers are in fact robbing him or her of potential aesthetic experience, patronising them, and confining the most interesting and innovative creative ventures in the arts to a small, knowing elite – what Arnold called 'the clique of the cultivated and the learned'. The person who enjoys both *Panic* and the *Serenade for Strings* has two kinds of aesthetic experience where the poor 'ordinary person' is judged fit only for one. Who is in control here? Who is exercising real choice? Who is in the driving seat?

The composer himself, Harrison Birtwistle, appeared puzzled and bemused by this outbreak of panic. Far from retreating to some ivory tower and pouring contempt on an uncomprehending public he said simply and honestly: 'People basically only want very little from music, and I want a lot from it. It's capable of amazing journeys and meanings. And if you understand that, the problem with the kind of music I write is no problem at all.'[4] Michael Berkeley, another contemporary composer, and one who in his broadcasting career has shown in an exemplary way how bridges of understanding can be built over the imaginary chasms of contemporary

musical taste, has said something similar: 'We learn to recognise a sequence that satisfies us, and if we don't get it we feel uncomfortable – yet the magic is that if you do allow it space, it's like unlocking the door of a secret garden.'[5] Amazing journeys. A secret garden. Why should I debar the ordinary person from this? Both composers are issuing not an anathema against the common man and woman but an invitation to join them. And in doing so they demonstrate that they respect the listener.

The suspicion that those in positions of power in the cultural world do not respect the listener, the reader, the viewer, and may only be professing to have the interests of the ordinary person close to their hearts, is confirmed by another example, this time from the world of publishing. In 1995, the French cinema director Bertrand Tavernier approached the publishers Faber & Faber with a proposal to publish a collection of his conversations with twenty-four great Hollywood directors and screenwriters called *Amis Americains*. It had already won the Prix de la Critique in France, but was turned down by the editor in charge of Faber's film list in the following terms:

I just don't think there is a large enough audience here. The majority of our readers are in their late twenties/early thirties, and for them the history of cinema begins with Taxi Driver. *Cinema before that is mainly those black and white films that appear on*

afternoon television – something about which they have no interest.

With commendable restraint, Tavernier described this as 'the most shocking, irresponsible letter I ever received'.[6] It is all these things, but it is also, I think, a *locus classicus* of contemporary cultural attitudes that repays closer textual analysis.

Firstly, there is the knowing, world-weary tone, the crocodile tears of regret at the smallness of the potential reading public. Then, the middle-aged cult of youth, awe-struck before a vision of its ignorance of the past, which is almost certainly a figment of the oldster's imagination and insulting to young people with a keen and intelligent interest in the cinema. Then come the confident generalisations about that public, which is judged to have a historical perspective on a medium scarcely a century old, that stretches back no further than 1976; that regards the classics of the cinema as beneath notice – 'in which they have no interest'. This, by the way, is the potential readership for a serious cinema list from a major publishing house – not the popcorn eaters in the multiplex foyer. Yet the man in charge of the list takes it for granted that his readers are grossly ignorant about the history and particular triumphs of their own medium. Starting with this contempt, what kind of job satisfaction can he derive? How can he manage, one wonders, to summon the energy to come in to his desk each morning?

Again and again in contemporary cultural debate one hears similar voices, the voices of those in commanding positions of power in the cultural institutions who take such a dim view of their potential audience, who confidently assert that it does not want any forms of art that are difficult, challenging, complex – not that the black and white cinema classics scorned by Faber & Faber could be construed as that. Purporting to be on the side of the public, they inform the world that it wants only pap. It seems proper to call these people culture's false friends for beneath their indulgent smiles for the perceived weakness of the public, they are viewing it with a barely concealed condescension. I for one will ignore their protests on my behalf.

In David Hare's recent play, *Amy's View*, there is a character called Dominic, a trendy television arts programme producer, who at one point defends himself irritably against attacks on the integrity of what he is doing:

I work in a medium on which you look down. You pretend it's not good. But in fact that's not your real reason. You really don't like it because television brings you bad news. Because actually, in some crude way, it does belong to the people.

He pits this television culture against the 'self-enclosed arty little world' of his mother-in-law, a famous stage actress.[7] It's a familiar, and somehow sterile, argument, that a popular medium carries some special entitlement to respect because it is a popular medium. Were the argument to be reversed, it would be dismissed as cultural snobbery. Truer, perhaps is the complaint of a well-known television scriptwriter, Paula Milne, commenting on the curious role of the Independent Television Network Centre, an obscure but powerful body that determines which of the programmes made by the various independent television companies viewers shall be allowed to see. Its operation since 1993, claims Milne, has resulted in a narrower, blander range of programmes being shown on screens. 'What appears now on ITV seems to have first been put through a populist computer', she complained. And as if to confirm her thesis, it was revealed that the Network Centre had rejected a further crime series from Scottish Television called *The Advocates* because – and I couldn't have made this up had I tried – it was 'too challenging'.[8]

Matthew Arnold – I confess I can't keep him out of the argument – claimed that: 'Plenty of people will try to give the masses, as they call them, an intellectual food prepared and adapted in the way they think proper for the actual condition of the masses'. Lord Reith, former Director-General of the BBC, said something similar: 'He who prides himself on giving what he thinks the public wants is often creating a fictitious demand for lower standards, which he will then satisfy'. Our false friends, in other words, may

be selling us short. It is our duty to complain of short measure.

My criticism of the term 'accessibility' is part of this critique of doubtful populism that tries to second-guess public preferences instead of providing real opportunities for choice as a dynamic democratic culture should. I hope it won't be thought that I am opposed to genuine attempts to boost audiences, to make performances more attractive, to remove cultural barriers, and the sorts of art-house rituals that are perceived as alienating by many people and which still deter them from participating fully in the arts. Highly educated people can often underestimate the extent to which those barriers exist. Let me give a simple example from my own experience.

As a sixteen year-old Liverpool schoolboy in the late 1960s, I took out of the public library a copy of Philip Larkin's *The Whitsun Weddings*. I remember being struck by a poem in that collection called 'Naturally the Foundation will Bear Your Expenses'. It was a satire on what we would now call 'the media don' and it contained a couplet: 'Perceiving Chatto darkly/Through the mirror of the Third'. I was haunted by these lines which nonetheless seemed to me wholly opaque. I had no idea what they meant. To my knowledge, there has never been an annotated edition of Larkin's poems, but today, thirty years on, simply as a result of the reading undertaken in between, one's growing familiarity with the literary

world, the mystery of those lines has vanished. I see now that they referred to the ambitious academic delivering a talk on the Third Programme, precursor of Radio 3, in the expectation of being noticed by the publishers Chatto and Windus, who at that time published Leavis, Hoggart, Williams, Empson, Davie – the sort of company an aspiring literary pundit would want to keep. It would have been helpful to me, as I sat puzzling at these lines in a squeaky vinyl chair in a north Liverpool library all those years ago, if someone had been at hand to point this out to me, if the poem had been rendered a little more 'accessible'. But that would have been an enabling assistance, drawing me into more direct contact with the real thing, one of the best poetry collections of the time.

Reviewing, not long ago, a BBC forward-planning document, the cultural critic Richard Hoggart reflected: 'Some of us have been saying for many years that we, the audiences, the customers, the voters, are not as daft as those who seek our support often seem to assume.'[9] It is in the interests of the cultural producers to have a large, docile, compliant class of consumers who will deliver economies of scale, and good advertising figures. Small print runs, specialist audiences and minority genres, are less easy to cater for than the best-selling products. As Jo Howard, Head of Books at the leading booksellers WH Smith, put it after media criticism of her firm's book-selling policies: 'Our customers are

looking for mainstream products. It would be no good Smith's having lots of interesting esoteric books and not the bestsellers ... Maybe the press doesn't like that populist approach.'[10]

Those who write and speak about culture often adopt a pessimistic, if not an apocalyptic tone. Matthew Arnold's work is the product of a particular historical epoch of expansion and a liberal belief in progress. I don't think of him as a prophet of doom, though he was mocked at the time as an 'elegant Jeremiah'. Perhaps today there are too many prophets of doom. It's too easy to strike attitudes of despair – although it has to be conceded that the temptations are strong. There is, for example, the much-discussed phenomenon of 'dumbing down', whose most articulate critic, George Steiner, wrote recently:

The great majority of us can no longer identify, let alone quote, even the central biblical or classical passages that not only are the underlying script of Western literature (from Caxton to Robert Lowell, poetry in English has carried inside it the implicit echo of previous poetry), but have been the alphabet of our laws and public institutions. The most elementary allusions to Greek mythology, to the Old and the New Testament, to the classics, to ancient and to European history, have become hermetic. Short bits of text now lead precarious lives on great stilts of footnotes. The identification of fauna and flora, of the principal constellations, of the liturgical hours and seasons on which, as CS Lewis showed, the barest understanding of Western poetry, drama and romance from Boccaccio to Tennyson intimately depends, is now specialised knowledge.[11]

As always, one feels that Steiner over-eggs the pudding but there is much that strikes a chord here.

With the spread of English as the language of global commerce and of the Internet, the British are becoming increasingly monoglot. While politicians issue endless declarations about their intentions to raise educational standards, it is my impression that the culture is losing its command of other tongues – a key means of 'accessibility' – and that the educated public reads less and less in other original languages. Perhaps it reads less overall in spite of the soaring annual figures for the total of books published. Not only is there competition from other media, largely electronic or visual, but the pace and texture of contemporary life may be becoming increasingly inimical to the habits of close reading, sustained attention, and strenuous reflection that a meaningful cultural life demands. Adult educators once worried that working men and women would be too exhausted by manual labour to spare time for education and self-improvement. But today, the middle classes, caught up in the cult of work and long hours, anxious and

insecure in workplaces that turn them into corporate drones, are as likely to be as exhausted at the end of a working day as a coal miner or worker in a chicken factory. The degree of leisure enjoyed by Lytton Strachey reading the sonnets of Petrarch on a Garsington lawn in the middle of a working day is increasingly unknown to the middle-class public. If there is any 'dumbing down' it is likely that it is showing itself in this section of society. The theatre director and playwright Peter Gill's recent remarks about what he calls the 'softening of the repertoire' at the National Theatre – the sudden outbreak of middlebrow musicals there – may be connected to this phenomenon: not widening the audience but easing the strain on the existing audience. A harried and exhausted professional class may not have the stamina on a Thursday night for *King Lear*.

I have a perhaps naive faith in the citizen's ability to resist and to challenge. As responsible members of an advanced industrial democracy, we don't have to take things lying down. I believe that we need to assert more vigorously our right not to be patronised, our right not to be told by those who control the levers of cultural power that we do not want access to 'the best which has been thought and said in the world'. One of the functions of the active intellectual in any society, as Edward Said has pointed out, is to 'tell truth to power'.[12] There is much that those in power in the world of culture need to hear.

I believe also that there is a need to defend such concepts as public-service broadcasting and State support for the arts, and to oppose the reduction of arts administration to accountancy. Politicians may be little help in this task. 'Every time I mention the bogey word "culture" to British politicians they just switch off', complained the architect and Labour peer Richard Rogers after his first taste of the House of Lords.[13] The Minister of Culture, Chris Smith, when asked to comment on the first hundred days of the New Labour Government declared: 'We have consigned the backward-looking Department of National Heritage to history and established a new Department for Culture, Media and Sport – signifying a new approach to Britain's 450 billion creative industries.'[14] Nothing, I think, to detain the man or woman of culture there.

In a spirit of Arnoldian 'returning upon oneself', I should perhaps say that there is another side to this argument. There are those – and they include to an extent Arnold, in an essay called 'Numbers', which I have chosen not to highlight – who say that there are limits to this process of democratisation of culture. And there are those who do not think it worth embarking on at all. TS Eliot had no interest whatsoever in Arnold's progressive meliorism, his social and political orientation. In a passage in *Notes Towards the Definition of Culture* (1948) that went on to sneer at 'equality of opportunity', he wrote that the apostles of equality (Arnold's term

for 'the men of culture') were barking up the wrong tree. 'A high average of general education is perhaps less necessary for a civil society than is a respect for learning', he sniffed.[15] Eliot believed in the necessity of an elite.

So did the critic FR Leavis, who wrote in a pamphlet published a decade earlier entitled 'Mass Civilisation, Minority Culture' (1930):

> *In any period it is upon a very small minority that the discerning appreciation of art and literature depends: it is (apart from cases of the simple and familiar) only a few who are capable of unprompted first-hand judgement. They are still a small minority, though a larger one, who are capable of endorsing such first-hand judgements by genuine personal response.*

He went on to say that:

> *The minority capable not only of appreciating Dante, Shakespeare, Donne, Baudelaire, Conrad (to take major instances) but of recognising their latest successors, constitute the consciousness of the race (or a branch of it) at a given time ... Upon this minority depends our power of profiting by the finest human experience of the past; they keep alive the most perishable parts of the tradition. Upon them depend the implicit standards that order the finer living of an age...*[16]

Let me say that, although I look on these issues as it were from the democratic camp, I can see that there is much that is valid in this. One has only to look at the fate of one of the literary arts, poetry, to see both how important it is and how few people in our culture are deeply engaged with it. Print-runs, readerships, rewards, are pitifully small and its survival really does depend on that small minority that cares about it and sustains it, not in the expectation of feeling themselves superior or members of a privileged caste but because they care *tout court*. It would be marvellous if the readership of poetry were much larger. It may become so. It ought to become so. But in the short-term a minority keeps it alive and that is a good thing.

I called just now for resistance to those trends in contemporary culture that seek to patronise the public and rob it of choice and provide it with an inferior fare while at the same time pretending to be offering people what they really want. A democratic culture will not be content until it has challenged this. Like Matthew Arnold, I am a democrat. But I am an exacting democrat. I believe that everyone should have access to a place-setting at the cultural feast, but I believe that the very best food should be served at that feast. I want culture to be as accessible as possible but I also want it to be real.

1 Postmodernism, for example, has not always won the hearts and minds of radical critics. See for example Terry Eagleton, 'The Crisis of Contemporary Culture', an Inaugural Lecture delivered before the University of Oxford on 27 November 1992: 'It is in the logic of late capitalism to breed a more fragmentary, eclectic, demotic, cosmopolitan culture than anything dreamt of by Matthew Arnold – a culture that is then a living scandal to its own firmly Arnoldian premises.' See also a further essay in Eagletonian disillusion, 'The Illusions of Postmodernism' (Oxford), 1996.

2 Quoted in *The Guardian*, 7 July 1995.

3 Quoted in *The Observer*, 12 July 1992.

4 Quoted in *The Independent on Sunday*, 7 April 1996.

5 Quoted in *The Independent on Sunday*, 7 September 1997.

6 Both the letter and Tavernier's reaction quoted in *The Observer*, 8 January 1995.

7 David Hare, *Amy's View*, 1997, pp. 67–68.

8 Quoted in *The Observer*, 16 January 1994.

9 *The Independent on Sunday*, 19 February 1995.

10 Quoted in *The Independent on Sunday*, 3 March 1996.

11 George Steiner, 'The Uncommon Reader', *No Passion Spent: Essays 1978–96*, pp. 14–15.

12 Edward Said, 'Representations of the Intellectual: the 1993 Reith Lectures', 1994.

13 Quoted in *The Guardian*, 25 January 1997.

14 Quoted in *The Independent*, 9 August 1997.

15 TS Eliot, *Notes Towards a Definition of Culture*, 1948, p. 100.

16 'Mass Civilisation, Minority Culture', reprinted in FR Leavis, *Education and the University*, 1943, pp. 141–71.

WE LIVE IN A POLITICAL CULTURE WHERE A PRIME MINISTER CAN ADDRESS AN ADULT ELECTORATE USING THE TERM 'THE FEEL-GOOD FACTOR', SO THIS NEW STANDARD OF VALUE – FEELING COMFORTABLE – SHOULDN'T PERHAPS SURPRISE. BUT WHAT OF THOSE WORKS OF ART THAT, FAR FROM INDUCING A PLEASANT INTERIOR GLOW, CHALLENGE AND DISTURB, ENACTING WHAT ARISTOTLE CALLED THE EMOTIONS OF

PITY AND FEAR

Adam Chodzko

MEETING
of
people with stammers
to
describe a fire

Here
Everyone Welcome

Adam Chodzko, *Meeting*, 2000
pigment on acid free paper, 59.3 x 41.7 cm

Richard Grayson

Greek

THE WOMAN HAS A SMILE ON HER FACE AND OTHERWISE IS
WEARING NOTHING. WE CAN SEE ONE OF HER BREASTS AND HER
NIPPLE IS TAUT AND ERECT. HER HAIR IS TIED UP AND
HER LEGS ARE BENT AND SPLAYED, AS IF SHE IS DANCING WITH
HER BACK TO US. IN HER LEFT HAND SHE HAS A
LARGE LEATHER DILDO WHICH MUST BE AT LEAST A FOOT AND
A HALF LONG. SHE IS HOLDING THIS UP TO HER MOUTH,
SMILING LASCIVIOUSLY AND IT LOOKS AS IF SHE IS ABOUT TO
WRAP HER LIPS AROUND ITS HEAD. HER OTHER HAND HOLDS AN
EQUALLY LARGE DILDO AND SHE IS POINTING IT BETWEEN HER LEGS,
AS IF SHE IS ABOUT TO FORCE IT INTO HERSELF. • THERE
ARE SEVEN MEN, SIX OF WHOM ARE NAKED AND ANOTHER WHO
IS WEARING A SHAWL OR A CLOAK AND NOTHING ELSE. PUZZLINGLY,
ONE OF THE MEN IS CARRYING A SMALL DEER IN HIS
ARMS AND ANOTHER, WHAT WOULD SEEM TO BE A TURKEY, BUT
CAN'T BE. THE MAN WITH THE TURKEY HAS A BIG ERECTION AND
HE'S LEANING FORWARD TO KISS THE MAN FACING HIM. THIS
MAN SEEMS TO BE PLAYING A LITTLE HARD TO GET. HE
ISN'T ERECT AND HE IS DRAWING HIS HEAD BACK A BIT.
THE MAN WITH THE TURKEY HAS HIS HAND OUT TO STROKE
THE OTHER MAN'S GROIN. THE GUY WITH THE CLOAK IS BEHIND
THEM AND ALTHOUGH HE SEEMS TO BE THE ODD MAN OUT
HE'S OBVIOUSLY PRETTY EXCITED BY WHAT'S GOING ON AROUND HIM AS
WE CAN SEE THROUGH THE FOLD OF THE CLOAK THAT HE'S
GOT A HARD ON. HE'S GOT ONE HAND THROWN HAPPILY UP
IN THE AIR AS IF HE'S DOING SOME SORT OF SCOTTISH
DANCING AND HE'S WATCHING THE COUPLE STANDING BEHIND HIS BACK.
ONE OF THESE IS HOLDING A SMALL HOOP AND SUPPORTING THE
WEIGHT OF THE OTHER MAN WHO IS SORT OF SLUMPED OVER
HIS SHOULDER. THEY BOTH HAVE REALLY STIFF PENISES AND THE
MAN WHO IS SLUMPING IS RUBBING HIS PENIS BETWEEN THE THIGHS
OF THE MAN WITH THE HOOP. BECAUSE HE'S LOWER DOWN
(OWING TO THE SLUMP) THE OTHER MAN'S PENIS IS RISING ABOVE
HIS. BEHIND THESE TWO IS THE MAN HOLDING THE SMALL DEER
IN HIS ARMS. HE IS DETUMESCENT BUT THE BLOKE BEHIND HIM,
WHO HAS JUST ATTRACTED THE DEER MAN'S ATTENTION, ISN'T. HE'S
TOTALLY NAKED, BENDING FORWARD IN HIS EAGERNESS, WITH HIS PENIS POINTING
ALERTLY AT THE BUTTOCKS AND UPPER THIGHS OF THE DEER MAN. •
THE MAN IS WEARING A BEARD AND HIS HAIR IS IN
RINGLETS, HIS KNEES ARE BENT AND HE IS SLIGHTLY CROUCHED, FACING
TO THE RIGHT. HE IS MAKING HIMSELF A LITTLE SHORTER SO
THAT HIS PENIS DOES NOT SLIP OUT OF THE WOMAN WHO
IS BENDING OVER, SORT OF SEMI CROUCHED ON THE FLOOR, HER
HANDS TOUCHING IT. THE FLOOR MUST BE CURVING, OTHERWISE SHE WOULD
FALL OVER. HER BACK IS TO THE MAN, HER FEET BETWEEN
HIS PARTED FEET AND HE HAS HIS ARM THROWN FORWARD IN
FRONT OF HIM, AS IF TO COUNTER BALANCE HIMSELF AGAINST
THE THRUSTS THAT SHE IS BRACED AGAINST. IT MAY OR MAY
NOT BE ANAL SEX IT IS HARD TO TELL IT LOOKS
PRETTY UNCOMFORTABLE FOR BOTH OF THEM BUT HE HAS A SLIGHT
SMILE PLAYING ON HIS LIPS ALTHOUGH SHE DOESN'T. • A MAN IS
STANDING BY THE DOOR OF THE BUILDING AND A YOUNGER MAN
IS LOOKING OUT OF ITS WINDOW. BOTH OF THEM ARE WATCHING
A MAN WHO IS SITTING DOWN IN A CHAIR, LEANING BACK,
LOOKING RELAXED AND EXPECTANT. HE HAS HIS HAIR UP IN A
BAND AND HAS HIS ARM FLUNG UP BEHIND HIS NECK LIKE
SOME HOLLYWOOD VAMP. HIS TUNIC IS LOOSE AND FALLING AWAY FROM
HIM TO REVEAL HIS ERECT PENIS STANDING UP PROUD FROM HIS
LAP. A YOUTH HAS ONE FOOT ON THE CHAIR THAT THIS
MAN IS SITTING ON. HE ALSO HAS HIS ARM REACHING FORWARD
AND ALTHOUGH WE CAN'T QUITE SEE IT, HIS HAND MUST BE
RESTING ON THE BACK OF THE CHAIR. THIS YOUTH IS TOTALLY
NAKED OTHER THAN SOME DECORATION AROUND HIS FOREHEAD. HE HAS A
STAFF IN HIS HAND HELD BEHIND HIM AND OBVIOUSLY HE IS
ABOUT TO HEAVE HIMSELF UP AND SETTLE HIS BUTTOCKS ON THE
SEATED MAN'S WAITING ERECTION. THE OLDER MAN WATCHING IS THE
MAN WHO OWNS THE BROTHEL WITH ANOTHER OF HIS BOYS. •

FOUR GREEK URNS IN LONDON MUSEUMS
1 LONDON E815, KYLIX BY THE NIKOSTHENES PAINTER, ARV 125 2 LONDON W39, AMPHORA, ABV 297, 16
3 LONDON E44, CUP BY THE PANAITIUS PAINTER, ARV 318-9 4 LONDON F65, KRATER BY DINOS PAINTER, ARV 1154, 35

Ken Worpole

When Worlds Collide

The funding of the arts from the public purse has always been a form of regressive taxation, transferring money from poorer and more disadvantaged communities and regions to fund the interests and enjoyment of metropolitan economic and cultural elites, a process further compounded by the advent of the National Lottery with its extraordinary social and geographical imbalance between where the ticket money comes from and where it is spent. Furthermore, most public arts funding remains devoted to supporting a portfolio of pre-twentieth century forms and institutions – classical music, opera, ballet, theatre, paintings and sculptures, all in dedicated and costly buildings. It is as if the 'age of mechanical reproduction' had not yet occurred. It is also as if the boundaries between 'high' and 'low' cultural forms had not been transversed on so many occasions in the twentieth-century that we now should regard them redundant, or superseded by new kinds of evaluation.

For these and other reasons I am therefore in favour of widening access to the arts, and the range of artistic practices worthy of consideration in cultural policy, especially those funded from public money. When I went to work for the GLC in 1984 with the brief to develop funding policies for these newer 'cultural industries', I was told that the 1983/4 season at the Royal Festival Hall had consisted of 420 concert performances, only sixteen of which featured music by living composers. This proportion between the old and the new seemed somewhat out of balance. More than that, in the early 1980s, the Royal Festival Hall programme, and even the building itself, had the atmosphere of a cultural mausoleum. In response, the GLC developed the 'Open Foyer Policy' – jazz and salsa in the bar at lunchtime or before the evening concert, gospel choirs, Irish music, and even jazz and African music on the main programme – and the place lightened up a bit, and one began to see a wider range of Londoners in and around the South Bank. The opening up of the South Bank to a wider programme made London seem a livelier place as a result, and gave many people a stronger sense of being a 'Londoner', happily complementing their other political and cultural identities.

The present Government, I understand, has sought to develop modest policies of access along similar lines, and while one has sympathy for anybody who has to fill in yet more forms, the principle of widening audiences and securing greater equity between where the money comes from and where it gets spent, seems reasonable, and long overdue.

Yet already there is a backlash. Access, according to some, has gone too far, even though the bulk of public arts funding still flows from taxes and Lottery ticket sales directly into the coffers of the old institutions, largely in response to the lobbying activities of the coteries that administer and defend them. Elsewhere in this collection, François Matarasso elegantly argues why it is reasonable for government to spend public money in securing the implementation of the policies upon which it was elected. Like him, I feel that the public funding of the arts should also be subject to forms of public negotiation and political settlement. But I'd like to go one step further. I want to insist that there is a necessary and crucial relationship between public arts policy and the political concern for securing greater social justice and equity, and that in the modern world, public arts policies and issues of social justice are interrelated.

It seems to me that the policies and principles that now govern public arts funding – from the election manifesto commitments of the government that administers it, the transparency and public accountability of the processes by which it is given, the terms under which it is given, and the negotiations that surround its legitimate uses – form a crucial part of developing that deliberative and proceduralist form of the democratic and public policy process that we badly need today in an era of large-scale disillusionment with the political process. More than that, in these unprecedented times of global economic, social and cultural change, in which historic national cultural identities are giving way to a multiplicity of emergent new affiliations and identities – and even competing moralities – procedure and transparent notions of fairness become more important.

The philosopher Stuart Hampshire adumbrated many of these issues some years ago in his long essay, 'Innocence and Experience' (1992). Hampshire was an interrogator of some of the defendants at the Nuremberg Trials, and knows enough of the wickedness and catastrophes of the world to appreciate how fragile and vulnerable even democracies can be. As a result, he says, he came to believe that respect for fairness and justice, and the development of forms of procedural justice, even when these are very limiting things, are far more important ultimately than the claims for liberty, even artistic freedom. For as he wrote in respect of the shocking way that seemingly civilised and stable societies rapidly collapsed into communal violence and other forms of barbarism: 'We have learnt that education and culture, scholarship and science, are paper barriers, which generally, and with a few exceptions, collapse more easily than the philosophers of the Enlightenment could have imagined'.

It is not that artistic freedom is not important, nor that the arts haven't played an invaluable role in developing new understandings of the possibility of human identity (the American literary critic Harold Bloom has recently gone so far as to suggest that Shakespeare invented humanity), but we should always pay equal attention to forms of procedural justice in the conduct of public affairs. In my opinion, this certainly includes the public funding of the arts, especially in a 'runaway world' of continuing and destabilising political and cultural upheaval and ferment.

This is bound to be a difficult terrain in public discourse, because it is on the border of two worlds, one of the artist and his or her right to untrammelled self-expression, and the other the world of the public administrator who has to work within the policies and procedural guidelines established by politicians. Put artists and administrators in the same room and two worlds collide. But we shouldn't be overly worried about this; indeed, we should expect it in a democracy, and this engagement at the border between the conflicting principles of freedom of expression and a civic concern for public accountability, fairness and greater social justice, is both healthy and necessary.

This engagement is part of a wider cultural dilemma of our times, notably in reconciling individual liberties and lifestyles (with their increasingly disruptive public externalities) with the need to retain some notion of a public domain of agreed common goods and procedures. The conflict between private choice and public goods can be seen, for example, in the debate about the survival of public service broadcasting in a global audio-visual marketplace, or the advocacy of public realm strategies to halt the flight from cities in Richard Rogers' recent report, 'Towards an Urban Renaissance'. It is most certainly there in the green movement's wish to reconcile private consumption with public environmental sustainability too. Developing procedures to arbitrate and adjudicate between collective interests and private choices is becoming more urgent.

So while I accept absolutely that artists and others have every right to the freedom of expression, and the development of their chosen cultural form in whatever directions they wish to take it, when public funding is involved, one expects a proper engagement with due public processes, accepting the likelihood that public funding will come with strings attached, most likely in the form of obligations to respect and meet both artistic criteria and certain public obligations as well.

We should welcome the opportunity to debate these rights and responsibilities, including the importance of due procedure, which public arts funding policies provide. Democracies need artists to push at the limits of the possible, but artists also need democracy and due process in order to flourish, as any issue of *INDEX ON CENSORSHIP* will testify, often in stories that will bring you to the edge of despair.

Helen Gould

Creative Exchange: The Forum for Cultural Rights and Development

The recent trend in arts policy is to embrace the role of arts in social inclusion and sustainable com-munity development. This move is not to be feared, and is greatly to be welcomed. In addition to their aesthetic and intellectual function, the arts play a powerful role in social transformation, in individual empowerment and community growth. This is an important dimension of the arts, which has been actively sidelined in the UK for at least the past decade.

This policy does not seek to replace existing aesthetic practice of the arts. However, it does seek to make the publicly funded arts more inclusive and accessible to a broader range of communities, which cannot be a retrograde step. It does not seek to make all artists community-development practitioners, but it recognises and supports an increasing number of artists who have or wish to develop specialist skills in this developmental use of the arts.

The arts and culture play an increasingly prominent role in social change, particularly internationally. Culture, more broadly, is an important foundation for living, and therefore cannot be ignored in enabling people to envision and change their lives. Increasingly, it has been noted that sustainable development programmes that ignore the cultural dimension tend to fail because they are not culturally sensitive.

Within this context, arts activities provided by specialist arts practitioners are used as powerful pro-cesses in conflict resolution and humanitarian relief (providing relief and support for rebuilding during and after the Kosovan conflict, for example) and in many different arenas of sustainable development such as health awareness and HIV/AIDS prevention; communication around water and sanitation; com-munity involvement in agriculture and forestry programmes; nutrition, particularly mother and child health; human rights and specifically the rights of women and children; and empowerment (there is a popular animation series in Africa and Southeast Asia promoting the rights of girl children to education); governance and democracy programmes — educating people about the right to vote, for example.

The change in policy is symptomatic of the UK's acknowledgement and recognition of this broader int-ernational trend and a desire to become part of it. We have a large body of specialist expertise in this field in the UK, which has been excluded from the arts funding system and arts policy until now. That this specialist expertise is going to find support and encouragement, even funding, and that it will be able to work towards improving people's lives in communities in Britain as well as some of the poorer countries in the world, is surely an important development.

A note of caution, however. It is important that both Government and the arts recognise that this is an area of specialist activity. Not all arts organisations and artists should be expected to deliver in this area, because unskilled practitioners and organisations can pose risks to the beneficiaries. My only concern about recent arts policy is that it has not attempted to resource specialist practitioners and agencies, but has concentrated on existing, regularly funded clients who in some cases do not have the right expertise.

I run a network of practitioners and organisations active in the field of culture and development. Our forum consists of eighty partners ranging from UN agencies to individual practitioners and community-based organisations in seventeen countries.

The forum includes organisations like UNICEF, the British Council, Tear Fund, Save the Children and Comic Relief. It includes Katha, which works using literature, drama and dance to build literacy and empowerment in a slum cluster of 16,000 families in Delhi; Street Symphony, which is working with street children using dance in Ethiopia; An Crann/The Tree, a project engendering cross-community dialogue and healing in Northern Ireland; Music For Change, which staged a music and carnival event with 20,000 football fans at Charlton Athletic recently as part of the process of improving race relations in football; and the UK's Centre for the Arts in Development Communications, a leading international training organisation in the field of Theatre for Development.

Together, we are developing knowledge and information systems that will enable us to learn and grow good practice in this area, and to enable us to pass on this knowledge to others. This network operates out of the UK, so this change in policy stands to benefit us, our users and their beneficiaries.

When we started trying to build this network five years ago, no-one in the arts funding system was prepared to listen. They called this use of the arts 'instrumental', and many still do. That we are seeing a change in policy is a clear and welcome indication that finally our voices are being heard.

To oppose a policy that allows our work and that of our partners, and all those working with the arts in community transformation, to be recognised and to flourish, is to deny all those people who stand to benefit from an opportunity to grow and change their lives in profound, creative ways. It also runs the risk of alienating a potentially vast new group of arts supporters.

François Matarasso

Freedom's Shadow

According to the artist and critic David Batchelor in his essay 'Unpopular Culture' of 1995, 'artists have a responsibility to art, not to anything or anyone else'.[1] If that were true, they would certainly be a unique class of citizen, truly a priestly caste, but such a position cannot be reconciled with any real understanding of democratic society. In fact, far from being detached from any social or moral ties to the rest of humanity, artists live within a complex network of responsibilities. Some of these – arising from personal relationships or the condition of citizenship itself – are common to us all, but other issues emerge from the responsibilities of the artist and the State to one another and the ethical framework within which artists work.

At one level, the artist can reject any particular responsibility to the State relating to her or his own work – unless it is paid for through the collective resources of taxation. The artist who accepts a commission or a wage from public fund, whether through the Arts Council, the National Lottery, a local authority or some other source, simultaneously accepts a relationship with the State that confers mutual rights, the first of which is to negotiate the terms of the contract and end it if they are not acceptable.

But what are the State's rights in that relationship? Principally, to assign resources to activities that it believes will advance its policies. There is nothing surprising in that: we elect governments to do things and the concept of a mandate rests on the right and duty of the government of the day to fulfil its electoral promises. Perhaps the quality of our democracy is not high enough; perhaps the electoral and political systems produce results that are less than fully representative. Personally, I would accept both propositions (though it is our responsibility to improve the situation), but that does not affect the basic premise that a properly elected government is entitled to pursue its social, economic, even political objectives through the way in which it allocates the public

resources in its custody. The Conservatives were entitled to seek business sponsorship and Labour is entitled to promote social inclusion. We may or may not agree with the policies – that depends on our own values – but we cannot deny government's right to pursue them.

There is no reason why the arts and cultural sectors should be exempt from this process, any more than education or health, where people are equally committed to their professional values and whose work has lifelong and life-affecting outcomes. Even if government were to adopt a wholly detached posture, allowing the arts world to spend public money on its own terms and priorities as it has sometimes in the past, that would be a political judgement that in itself would fundamentally affect the values and production of the arts. There can be no artistic independence – in the sense of adolescent irresponsibility – when the artist is paid by the State, any more than there is when he or she is financed by an aristocratic, religious or commercial patron. There is only a legitimate negotiation about values, duties, rights and benefits.

Uncomfortable as this might be to elements of an arts world now restless within public, commercial and political ties willingly accepted over decades, it is actually straightforward enough. More complex, and not much considered by society today, are the ethical responsibilities that artists have towards the rest of humanity. David Batchelor says they have none, beyond the making of art, whatever we accept that to be. But would we be content to say the same of scientists?

Like artists, scientists explore the boundaries of the possible, redefining reality in ways that may affect us all. They develop insights that not only lead to new medicines or weapons, but force us to question our most basic beliefs about the nature of existence, from the relative movements of the sun and the earth to the biological individuality of the person. Because this is so important, we have

developed a sophisticated philosophy of scientific ethics designed to give scientists the freedom to experiment and extend knowledge while securing some basic standards of practice and minimum guarantees of integrity.

It is striking that we have no comparable contemporary philosophy of the relationship between the artist and the rest of society, though artists maintain, and I agree, that their work is of critical importance. Since Beethoven redefined the role of the artist as a secular saint, independent of patronage and acting as unmediated conduit between ultimate truth and the rest of us, society has extended ever greater licence to its artists, with very little thought to the implications. It would be wrong and pointless to try to impose limits on artistic freedom, but responsibility is freedom's shadow, and we should be thinking much more about the implications of artistic practice.

The creation and consumption of art is a human act. As such, it exists inescapably in a moral environment within which it signifies an endless series of value judgements. There is no cultural gold standard, though there are many who would elevate their personal standards to that position. Artists who refuse to recognise any ethical, political and social ties of responsibility implicitly ally themselves with anti-democratic ideologies in which value, to say nothing of the rights accruing to those who control it, is determined by a self-selecting group and imposed on the rest. Such post-Romantic, Eurocentric and ahistorical perspectives cannot be reconciled with democracy or with liberty.

To Batchelor's view of the artist, I prefer Clive Bell's alternative analysis, put forward in his *Civilisation* of 1928: 'Only reason can convince us of those three fundamental truths without a recognition of which there can be no effective liberty: that what we believe is not necessarily true; that what we like is not necessarily good; and that all questions are open'.

Artists have a responsibility to art, not to anything or anyone else

David Batchelor

David Batchelor

A Brief Reply to François Matarasso

In an interview, the artist Don Judd once said: 'Of course artists should oppose US involvement in Nicaragua ... just as dentists should'. To my mind, this says pretty much everything that needs to be said on the subject of the political responsibilities of artists. It says everyone has responsibilities as a citizen, but that these are independent of one's responsibilities as an artist. It says that artists do not have a special relationship with politics that gives them greater or fewer responsibilities as citizens than anyone else. It also implies that a confusion of different responsibilities does nothing very much for art or politics.

At the same time ... The work of art can sometimes put a spanner in the works of culture. It can hinder, slow down, confuse and otherwise interrupt the relentless tides of habit – if only occasionally and then probably only for a moment. And under certain circumstances, this may acquire some political significance. But that will not be decided by the artist.

right David Batchelor, *Electric Colour Tower* (detail), 2000
Sadler's Wells Theatre, London
photo: The Artist

the artists dance
- to entertain -
pulling flowers
and stones from
their heads; they
offer both to the
people watching:
what the people
do next is their
choice

Roland Miller ©1990

Roland Miller

Extract from a Letter to Peer

Dear Peer

[…] I have been a self-employed performance artist for some thirty years, receiving, with my partner, Arts Council and British Council grants on a number of occasions in the 1970s and 80s. I was also a member of several Arts Council and Regional Arts Board committees. In the last four years, I have been an Arts Council Lottery grant assessor. Since 1994 I have been a full-time lecturer at the University of Huddersfield. This year I completed a part-time PhD in creative work (performance art) at De Montfort University, Leicester.

My perception of arts funding in the UK is that it has now become dependent on 'instru-mentality', which is to say that projects (and artists) are funded not for the art they produce, but for the societal, economic, educational or public health results of the work. […]

The current political agenda is one of 'addressing social exclusion'. This places on artists a burden that may interfere with their creativity. It may also be impossible to fulfil the funder's demands satisfactorily. […]

I was alarmed to discover, when I examined the A4E applications I was meant to assess, that sometimes the art content was minimal and that the main assessment criteria being applied by the Arts Council related to business plans, management structures and commercial viability. I found the whole process very unsatisfactory, and I would no longer undertake Lottery assessment.

Moreover, there appears to be no process of feedback of the results of Lottery applications to the assessors involved. I still do not know whether projects I recommended for funding two years ago have been granted money or not. […]

The original version of the drawing, *The Artist's Dance*, was one of my first recorded representations of the 'dilemma of creativity'. I made it in 1974, whilst my partner and I were working as performance artists in Portugal, immediately before the revolution in that country. I subsequently added the caption, and have shown the drawing in various art venues in many different countries.

I believe most strongly in the importance of art creation in all its forms […] Not only do I believe that art should be valued 'for art's sake', but, as my drawing shows, artists may create abjection (the stones) in response to their perception of life. Individual artists are responsible for their creations, and should be treated with respect for their responsibility. […]

Roland Miller, PhD

Richard Noble

Accessibility for All, Freedom for the Few

As part of its plan to 'modernise' Britain, the Government has decided to make 'accessibility' the cornerstone of its arts policy. It conceives its commitment to making the arts more accessible as part of a broader commitment to social equality, and what it takes to be its democratic responsibility to spend public money in ways that benefit all sections of the British nation, rather than the privileged few. The primary instruments of this project are funding agencies, most notably the Arts Council and its various Regional Arts Boards, which are charged with implementing the Government's broad policy on the arts. The relationship between the current Government and its funding agencies raises some serious questions about the freedom of artists and arts organisations to do their work. Traditionally, these agencies have maintained an 'arm's length' relationship to government, with the intent, if not always the practice, of protecting the arts from too much political interference. This freedom is crucial to their flourishing, and arguably more important to maintaining a healthy democratic culture than the Government's desire to justify its arts spending in terms of its overall social policy.

It is not so much the Government's access policy, but the Arts Council's enthusiasm for it that gives reason for disquiet. The Council's Cultural Diversity Action Plan outlines the extent of its commitment to improving access as part of the Government's broader goal of social equality: 'A concentration on access

tackles the bars to equality. It seeks to create an inclusive environment in which the creativity of all (whether as artists, audiences or managers) can flourish.' In addition, it wants to overcome inequalities that exist both inside and outside the arts communities it supports. Making the arts more accessible means bringing a broader audience to them, and establishing equal opportunities within the arts themselves. There is doubtless some overlap here, but roughly speaking, the Arts Council wants the artists and organisations it funds to produce art that is more broadly representative of (and hence accessible to) British society, and it wants the positions of those who work in the arts as artists, managers, curators and so on to be opened to a broader spectrum of people.

The principled justification for this policy is, I take it, relatively uncontroversial. If the arts are a public good worthy of government funding, there is little justification for a system of arts funding or an arts industry that, to use the Council's words, has 'a tendency, whether from ignorance, hostility or apathy, to marginalise groups and individuals'. Furthermore, it makes sense to argue that the arts need to be more accessible to a broader spectrum of the British population, that the people who actually work in the arts should more broadly reflect British society. The problem is not with the goals, but rather with what the Arts Council and its Regional Arts Boards should do to get artists and arts organisations to adopt them.

It might be helpful here to distinguish between two somewhat different aspirations embedded in the Government's policy. One is that the arts should be open to all and subject to the same equal opportunities policies as other public sector professions. The other is to make the arts into an effective instrument of the Government's social policy objectives. Should the arts be, as the Labour Party Manifesto puts it, 'central to the task of recreating the sense of community, identity and civic pride that should define our country'?

Both aspirations intrude upon the autonomy of artists and arts organisations to do their work. But whereas the former simply holds the arts to the same standards of equality, recognition of diversity, and accessibility to which other publicly funded institutions are held, the latter does something else. It turns the arts into an instrument of social policy, a means by which British society can be made more egalitarian, more tolerant, more at ease with its diversity and the social changes this engenders. Again, I want to stress that, personally, I support these goals. What I doubt is the utility of the arts as an instrument for achieving them, and what I fear is that any attempt to shape them to this purpose will destroy the already fragile freedoms they currently enjoy.

So why are the arts ineffective instruments of public policy? The most obvious reason for this is that artists cannot and should not be

trusted to make art that is in the relevant respects 'on message'. They are just as likely to sow the seeds of faction and intolerance in their audiences as they are to inspire a sense of community or inclusiveness. Whatever their intentions, artists can hardly be held responsible for how audiences interpret their work. Lots of art work is political, or deals with political subjects, but it is very difficult to say, even in retrospect, what its political effects actually are. There is very little historical evidence to suggest that turning art to political purposes can effect the predictable and sustainable political change sought by democratic governments. In fact, art is probably at its most politically effective when it articulates compelling forms of dissent against prevailing political orthodoxies and policies. This is a valuable political role in any democracy, but it is not one easily put in the service of public policy initiatives.

Furthermore, there is a great deal of historical evidence to suggest that forcing art to specific political purposes undermines creativity and innovation. Think of the Socialist Realists, or Nazi art, or for that matter the vast majority of public sculpture celebrating the achievements of British imperialism. Interesting political art usually has a hostile or at least oppositional relationship to power; and this is true even when power is being directed to laudable ends. Of course, no one is suggesting that the Arts Council is attempting to impose a monolithic ideology on the British arts community. But what are we to make of the following statement?

Vigilance and action are needed to combat exclusion and to ensure that the full talents of society as a whole are given outlets. The proper application of Equal Opportunities principles – and attainment of access – involves constant re-assessment, a conscious awareness of old mindsets and previously unquestioned assumptions. This ... calls for inspiring, persistent and principled leadership from the top.

Inspiring to whom? Not, I would guess, to those who actually make art or programme the institutions through which the public have access to it. To say that arts organisations should be open to a broader spectrum of people is one thing; it is quite another to say that they must be ready and able to respond to the 'full talents of society as a whole'. The former calls for guidelines requiring arts organisations to comply with equal opportunities hiring, that their programming reflects the cultural and class diversity of Britain, that their buildings and facilities are such that the public enjoys and is able to visit or attend them. There is already widespread support for this in the professional arts community.

The latter, on the other hand, calls for direct bureaucratic intervention in the content of what artists and arts organisations produce and select. It means subordinating the professional aesthetic and intell-

ectual criteria used in funding artists and arts organisations to criteria based on the public policy goal of making society more equal by improving access. The Council states that it intends to 'devise and put into operation a system whereby the extent to which Cultural Diversity is becoming integrated into mainstream programming could be monitored'. Faced with such monitoring, institutions will feel the pressure to give 'access experts' more input into programming, to divert their already scarce resources into making their programmes accessible, and to shape their programmes according to the Council's imperatives. All of this restricts the freedom of artists, curators, artistic directors and so on to innovate, experiment and challenge the public.

There is a real danger that this sort of 'top-down' bureaucratic leadership will achieve the opposite of what it intends. Instead of inspiring a lasting and substantial diversity that truly reflects the reality of Britain, it will promote banal and patronising programming that will alienate the public and artists alike. Arts organisations should meet the same equality of opportunity standards as other public sector institutions. They should also be open and welcoming to the whole range of British society. But in meeting these targets, they must protect the freedom of artists and those who facilitate them to make art that in no way corresponds to the political goals of governments. It's worth remembering that access

to the arts is only a public good because what artists produce is so valuable. To erode the freedom of artists and arts organisations in the name of access is simply self-defeating.

Ian Breakwell

The Caller

10.2.1990, Perth, Western Australia

The searing late-morning sun is reflected from the concrete paving stones of the plaza, in the middle of which is an 11-foot-high bronze statue of a man in medieval robes who stands with feet planted firmly apart, his head tilted back, his upstretched hands cupped on either side of his mouth, which is open in a soundless shout directed into the clear blue sky. He is *The Caller* and for twenty years he has stood rooted to his spot while skyscraper office blocks have risen on the skyline all around him, heedless of his call, and now a spider has woven a web between his hands.

12.2.1990, Perth, Western Australia

Now that *The Caller*'s once vehement cry is no longer strong enough to break the gossamer shroud in front of his face, the spider has become more bold and has woven another web between his teeth, sealing up the gaping mouth with silken threads.

14.2.1990, Perth, Western Australia

The spider has woven a web over *The Caller*'s left eye, and now crawls along the edge of his right eyelid, spinning a matching net.

The Caller, Perth, Australia, sculptor unknown
photo: Ian Breakwell, 1990

Ian Breakwell   79

Antony Gormley

Total Strangers

Extract from an interview with Udo Kittelmann for the catalogue *Total Strangers*, Kölnischer Kunstverein (Cologne). 1998.

These images document a work executed in Cologne, 1996, by Antony Gormley, titled *Total Strangers*. The work comprised six identical life-sized solid-iron body forms. One was placed inside the Kölnischer Kunstverein; the other five were situated outdoors, integrated into the urban environment.
photos: Benjamin Katz

AG: It's interesting that you [Kittel-man] equate baring the body with baring the soul; this question of openness is about art's ability to communicate. If you are not pre-pared to expose yourself, you will have nothing to communicate. I don't want the work to be rhetorical or dominating. I want it to be direct. The body is a reviver, and acceptor of conditions. It can also transmit a sense of internal condition. The piece in Cologne, of all the work that I've made in iron, is the most vulnerable and pathetic. This is a body lost in space, in some way a victim of its context, but also a medium by which the space inside the body is connected to feelings inside the viewer. [...]

I am interested in the body because it is the place where emotions are most directly registered. When you feel frightened, when you feel excited, happy, depressed, some-how the body immediately registers it. One of the problems of bringing the naked male body back into sculpture is that it seems to infer idealised universals. I reject the ideal, but I am interested in uni-versality. The body is the collective subjective and the only means to convey common human experience, in a commonly understood way ...

David Bartholemew

The proposed sculpture

The proposed sculpture has been the subject of a sixteen-month Consultation Exercise.

The proposed sculpture is destined for a prestigious city centre site.

The proposed sculpture will be paid for by a National Lottery grant of £122,650.

The proposed sculpture is nearing completion in a warehouse somewhere in Belgium.

The proposed sculpture was the winner of a competition.

The proposed sculpture was judged to be the best of the entries by a panel of judges
    judging the proposals on artistic merit.

The proposed sculpture aroused the interest of the local newspapers.
    Artists' impressions were printed.

The proposed sculpture generated 6,359 letters to the local newspapers.

The proposed sculpture was exhibited in 1/8 scale model in a perspex box in the foyer
    of the Town Hall. It was attacked with glue.

The proposed sculpture complied with the relevant standards and was approved by the
    Planning Dept.

The proposed sculpture was derided as elitist and alienating by some local socialists.

The proposed sculpture was described as a boon for the city centre by the
    City Centre Manager.

The proposed sculpture will be 4 metres high at its highest point.

The proposed sculpture is to be made of steel. It will be mostly grey.

The proposed sculpture was criticised for being made by a Belgian.

The proposed sculpture was admired for its solidity.

The proposed sculpture will have public seating in the vicinity. There will also be litter bins. The seating
    will be paid for by the Sponsors' Forum of local businesses on the condition that each seat bears a
    plaque listing their names. The bins will be paid for by the council.

The proposed sculpture was denounced as passé socialist romanticism by Sister Charlotte of the nuns
    of St. Bernard.

The proposed sculpture aroused indifference in most of the population of the city.

The proposed sculpture was welcomed in 472 of the letters received by local newspapers. In 3,858
    no opinion was expressed. 122 people wrote in to say they were bewildered.

The proposed sculpture was criticised by Councillor Potts because he thought the money would be
    better spent elsewhere. When pressed, most people thought the money would be better spent
    elsewhere.

The proposed sculpture is being prepared in seventeen parts which are due to be welded together on site by the artist, two of her colleagues and a one-time shipbuilder from Sunderland.

The proposed sculpture was so disliked by Mr G. Hutton of 67 Lime avenue that he threatened to boycott the city centre if the proposal ever came to fruition. Mr Banks, address withheld, said the city centre would be a better place without him.

The proposed sculpture was described as flippant by Melanie Croft from the Regional Arts Board.

The proposed sculpture was described as hideous by a local business leader.

The proposed sculpture was commissioned, and contractual obligations entered into on both sides, two years before the launch of the Public Consultation Exercise.

The proposed sculpture should be melted down and used to make a ramp for disabled access to the front of the Town Hall in the opinion of an office worker interviewed by a local newspaper.

The proposed sculpture was supported with enthusiasm by Dawn Petch of the City Arts Collective. She said the city needed bold artistic statements if it wasn't to be thought of as a cultural backwater.

The proposed sculpture might teach children the importance of diligence.

The proposed sculpture would be welcomed by the city authorities in Barcelona.

The proposed sculpture was hailed as a major attraction by the Environment, Leisure and Tourism Department.

The proposed sculpture has become the subject of a fiction by a local writer.

The proposed sculpture has featured in national newspapers and on local TV.

The proposed sculpture was described by the artist as symbolising the resistance of the individual to dehumanising power structures.It was an optimistic statement.

The proposed sculpture has been the subject of arguments in council chambers.

The proposed sculpture was too frightening, according to three people who attended the Public Consultation meetings.

The proposed sculpture could be neither inclusive nor exclusive, according to a professor of philosophy at the city university.

The proposed sculpture has been discussed on nineteen occasions by a committee of interested parties. To date, no agreement has been reached, though plans for the seating and the bins are well advanced.

The proposed sculpture has a name, though it is referred to as the proposed sculpture, so it is largely unknown.

The proposed sculpture weighs 3 1/2 tons and is encircled by a band of mirrors.

The proposed sculpture will be accessible to be touched or felt by anyone.

The proposed sculpture remains a proposed sculpture to everyone but the artist.

HACKNEY WICK

SINGLE REGENERATION BUDGET

COMMUNITY CHEST APPLICATION

Please ensure you read the guidance notes enclosed before completing your application form.

SECTION A

YOUR ORGANISATION

1. Name of organisation or implementing agency

    THE HACKNEY HISTORIC BUILDINGS TRUST

2. Address of organisation or implementing agency

3. Telephone/facsimile/e-mail

4. Name of contact person

SECTION B

YOUR PROJECT

5. Project Title

    THE PORTICO PROJECT

6. Project Location if different to 2 above.

    LINSCOTT ROAD, HACKNEY, E5

7. Give a brief description of the project or purchase for which you require a Community Chest Grant.

This project will commission a contemporary artist to make an art work for an important historical and architectural site known as The Portico. Martin Creed has designed a large (9 meters long) neon sign to be installed on the entablature which will dramatically illuminate the structure which is located in this area of urban regeneration. The sign will read EVERYTHING IS GOING TO BE ALRIGHT. The HHBT are working closely with Groundwork Hackney and Clapton School to develop a project with 30 to 60 pupils based on The Portico. This project will encompass local history with art and IT. This project will culminate in an exhibition of the pupils' work at the Round Chapel to which teachers from Hackney Wick schools as well as parents and friends will be invited. The Portico is just outside the Hackney Wick boundary, but many visitors and significant numbers of pupils directly involved in the project will be residents of the Hackney Wick neighbourhood.

8. To which Community Chest Criteria does your project best apply and why?

Children and Young People will particularly benefit through their participation in an educational and creative project carried out by Groundwork Hackney. Self confidence and pride will result from the presentation of their work in an exhibition at The Round Chapel. The **Cultural Development** of this area of urban regeneration will be enhanced through the presentation of a high quality work by a young British artists with an increasing international profile.

9. Will the project contribute to the producing of any SRB outputs? Yes/No
If yes, please give details (see guidance notes).

SRB Code	SRB Output	Quantity
I K ii	students involved	30 - 60
7 A ii	access to new cultural opportunities	200 +
7 A vi	number of new cultural facilities	1
13 A i	Art Commissions	1

10. Which client groups and communities will directly benefit from this project, e.g. Black and Ethnic Minorities, Women, People with Disabilities, The Elderly, Children, Youth etc.

Client groups to benefit will be communities in the immediate area around the site, including Hackney Wick. Because of the nature of this project it will be available to all sections of the community including Black and Ethnic Minorities, Women, People with Disabilities. It may have particular resonance for the Elderly who have lived in the area for some time and have a memories of it prior to demolition. Young people will be specifically targeted through the workshops organised by Groundwork Hackney.

11. How will this project benefit the above defined group?

These groups will benefit from the opportunity to experience a high quality work of art in their community which celebrates the architectural grandeur and historical richness of a local landmark. It is intended that this work will instill a sense of pride and provoke interest in the local history of the area. Specifically, the pupils who take part in the workshops and exhibition will benefit both educationally and creatively as well as providing an exciting opportunity to work on an integrated project outside of school.

SECTION C

FINANCE

12. What is the total cost of this project?   £10,400

13. Please provide details of all other sources of funding relevant to this project.

Martin Creed, Work No. 203, 1999, Linscott Road, London E5, commissioned by Ingrid Swenson
photo: Hugo Glendinning

Joan Key

Statement

There is an assumption underlying State policy-making regarding arts funding that there is a universal need for art, and a further assumption that it will be regarded as a benevolent act to satisfy that need on the democratic basis of universal inclusivity of provision. None of this takes into account the fact that there is nothing essentially benevolent or democratic about either the work of the artist or the work of art, and this remains the case even if benevolent or democratic causes are claimed for the work.

A current example of institutional benevolence is the performing of music in art galleries during exhibitions. Not only is a self-sufficient exhibition provided, but there is an additional offering of pleasure in the same space. This represents 'an appeal to new audiences', 'an educational initiative', 'a symbol of cultural diversity', and a 'cross-boundary hybridity'. The feel-good factor of 'creative exchanges and artistic liveliness' accrues to the corporate institutional identities that can commission the work of artists, musicians and composers to fit their programme, but hardly impinges on the artists' own practice.

Arts organisers express the generosity of their cultural ideals in a rhetoric that is far removed from the concerns of the visual artists and musicians involved, whose own dialogue is managed by, rather than supported by, such discourse. In a sense, Peer's publication is complicit with this managerial position even while seeking to give voice to the possibility of objections 'from those who care about the arts'.

Calls for 'cultural diversity' suggest avoidance of the narrowing effect of cultural exclusion, and the State arts establishment reviews its own performance in this respect. The aim must be greater democracy in availability of the arts, but the question for the artist must be 'how is that to be achieved?' Is the judgement a structural one about the form of art that is appropriate to a democratic environment, taking into account the values that inform its means of production, its authorship and ascription, and its availability in presentation or representation? Or is it a numerical question about how many people were involved and who they were, eventually a publicly accountable monitoring of popularity?

Modern history shows that promoting popularity does not necessarily lead to democratic developments. However, there remains the question of finding structures that open up the ways in which art can resonate with meanings to a wider audience, and this may require unexpected cross-boundary strategies, support for which is the strongest role that an interventionist organisation such as Peer can play.

I am submitting a piece of music – on which I have worked with the cellist Christopher Mansell – to this dialogue precisely because music is not the language that has been asked for. I am interested in positioning it in relation to the texts about arts policy because it cannot be read in those terms, and cannot be read at all in any literal sense. It can be read as music, though only in a round-about kind of way because the text has been modified to be viewed as a visual work. The composer is the musician, who wishes to leave this notation as open as possible to reinterpretation in further performance.

I hope that reading this music suggests the immediacy and responsiveness of playing.

Christopher Mansell

8 + 3 = 11, 6 + 5 = 11

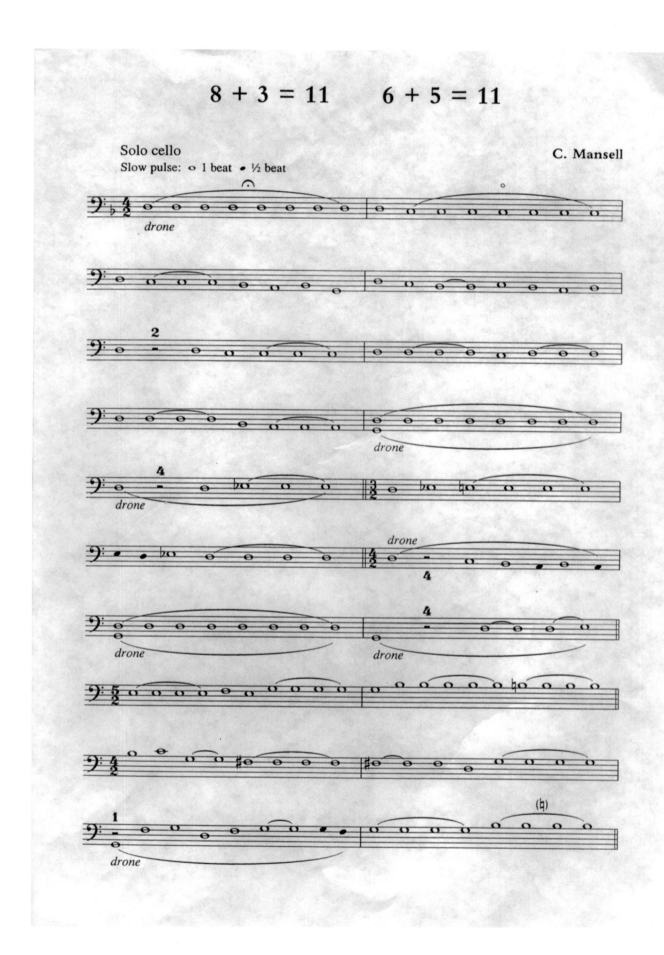

ATTENDANCE

AGES 18-35

12 WHITE MALES

2 BLACK MALES

12 WHITE FEMALES

7 BLACK FEMALES

South London Art Gallery

Attendance Chart

Southwark Council

SOUTHWARK arts

DAILY TOTAL OF ATTENDANCE FIGURES

Please record these figures on a daily basis and transfer onto weekly table for submission to Southwark Arts Marketing Department by midday every Monday. Please submit weekly total by fax or e-mail.

'Domestic Bliss.'

	MEN										WOMEN									
	'WHITE'					'BLACK'					'WHITE'					'BLACK'				
	-10	10-18	18-35	35-50	50+	-10	10-18	18-35	35-50	50+	-10	10-18	18-35	35-50	50+	-10	10-18	18-35	35-50	50+
			✓✓✓	✓✓				✓					✓✓✓	✓✓			✓✓✓	✓✓✓		

DATE: S Ser 200

SOUTHWARK ARTS VENUE: SLG

Charles Saumarez Smith

Museum as Memory Bank

Extract, first printed in *Prospect*, July 1998, from a talk delivered at a conference hosted by the Victoria & Albert Museum and the Royal College of Art, London

One of the most memorable lectures I heard when I was on the staff of the Victoria & Albert Museum was a training talk given by Valerie Mendes about her experiences of collecting examples of contemporary dress for the museum. She brought along a rail of twentieth-century frocks. To look at, they did not seem particularly interesting, rather like items of salvage from an expensive West End Oxfam shop. But as she talked about each in turn and how she had acquired them, they became intellectually engaging. Each item ceased to be a piece of old fabric wrapped in tissue paper and stored in the vaults of the museum, and was transformed into something that had not only been made by a particular designer, but had also been bought by a particular person, used, loved, cared for and sufficiently valued for it to be considered worthy of presentation to a public collection.

I remember being struck by the contrast between the private life of the curator in a world concerned with the history of past experience, and his or her public obligations – documentation, classification, attribution and systematic record. This combination lies at the heart of the modern museum.

Many museums were founded as instruments of enlightenment thinking. Objects, pictures, coins, bones, were removed from the private world of an individual's collection and placed in the public world of a museum, where they were stripped of their previous associations and made available for public inspection as an item in a series, as an object type or an example of an artist's oeuvre.

If museums are collections of artefacts, they are also research institutions. Once you have a comprehensive set of objects – the bones of a dinosaur or the portraits of eighteenth-century worthies – then you need people who will be responsible for further acquisitions, who are sufficiently knowledgeable about the subject area to make sensible choices, and to describe and record those acquisitions in a scholarly manner. This is the aspect of museums that has been most subject to attack in the last two decades, partly because issues of classification and taxonomy have become unfashionable in the human, as well as in the biological, sciences.

In the past two decades, the two original purposes of museums – as collections of artefacts and as research institutions – have either been at war with, or been replaced by, two new purposes.

The first one is the museum as educational resource. This is where most political capital is to be gained, as I know from the experience, as Director of the National Portrait Gallery, of our annual visitation from members of the Department for Culture, Media and Sport, when half a dozen men in grey suits troop through the Gallery looking bored until they come to the areas devoted to educational activities; their eyes light up as they see something of which they think their ministers will approve.

The truth is that much of what museums and galleries do is not in any straightforward way educational. If children want to learn about dinosaurs, then they are more inclined to do so from books and CD-ROMs, to which a large proportion of the population now has access. They will visit the Natural History Museum not in order to learn about dinosaurs, although they may do this in passing, but in order to authenticate the reality of the existence of dinosaurs, to see and experience, so far as is possible, what dinosaurs looked like. (Sadly, the Natural History Museum, in its anxiety to be seen as a modern institution, has abolished dinosaurs and replaced them with computer terminals, which children can just as well consult at home). I am not convinced that people come to the National Portrait Gallery in order to learn about history in a conventional sense. Do they want to know when Sir Alec Douglas-Home was prime minister when they look at his portrait? No. They are looking for a different experience of the past from that which they can obtain by conventional methods of learning. Museums may be educational, but they are essentially an experiential, rather than an academic, form of learning.

The second new purpose is the museum as leisure attraction. When the history of the post-war museum comes to be written, this will be seen as the key *modus operandi* of museums in the 1980s – when the Natural History Museum sent its staff to be trained at Disney University, when the ticket gates were installed, and the V&A advertised itself as 'An ace caff with not a bad museum attached'. All of this now has a dated feel to it; museum directors no longer want their museums to look like motorway service stations at off-peak hours. The problem is that if we want to treat museums simply as leisure attractions, then the private sector is almost certainly better at providing them and the argument for public subsidy disappears.

I am not convinced that members of the public want museums to provide the same experience as they receive elsewhere, as is evident from the widespread public unease about the levels of investment going into the Millennium Dome. What is the point of spending more than the cost of the British Library on a structure whose contents consist, so far as we can tell, of superficial simulation?

It is more useful to consider the metaphor of museum as memory bank. Memory is an essential attribute of the human psyche: the way we think about and order the experience of the past is not just as history, which is systematic and sequential, but as memory, which is more personal, more concerned with the experience of the past.

The idea of museum as memory bank encapsulates the public roles and responsibilities of museums. It connects museums to their seventeenth-century origins as cabinets of curiosities. In their origins, museums were not places of enlightenment order, but places of wonder, where you might expect to find an elephant's tusk next to a portrait. The museums that have the greatest grip on the popular imagination are not those that are most modern and systematic, but often those that are the most disorderly and individual, like Sir John Soane's Museum in Lincoln's Inn Fields or the Pitt Rivers Museum in Oxford. The experience in these places is not of history, ordered and systematic, but of memory, provocative and strange.

Thinking about museums as memory banks is also in line with recent developments in museums internationally. The obvious examples are the growing number of museums devoted to the record of the Holocaust. Less obvious are the experiments in connecting the world of popular taste and collecting through local 'People's Shows', pioneered in Britain by the Walsall Museum and Art Gallery.

Thinking of museums in this way also provides the best explanation as to why people are visiting them in greater numbers. At the National Portrait Gallery, I have always felt it to be inadequate to think of one million visitors coming to see a '1066 and All That' account of British history. Nor do people necessarily come to look at portraiture as an art form. They come because the images prompt the creation of an individualised recollection of people in the past that operates in the realm not of narrative history, but of public and private memory.

Finally, thinking about museums as memory banks provides a weapon for public advocacy. My experience of the public funding of culture is that simplicity is essential in the arguments about the allocation of national resources. Thinking about museums as memory banks provides a simple and memorable metaphor. It also connects museums back to the world of complex intellectual and aesthetic experience, the exploration of public and institutional memory. It takes them away from the superficial and ephemeral worlds of simple learning machines or simulated experience. It gives them back their historic identity.

B E W A R E
THE INFLUENCE OF
PUBLIC OPINION

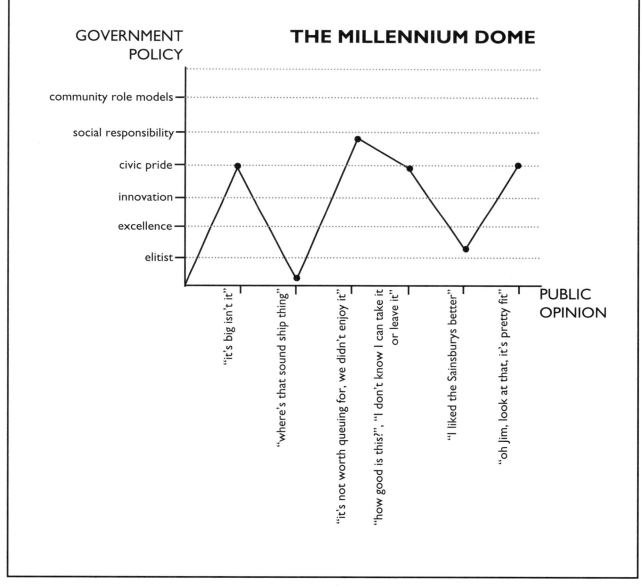

This graph represents comments overheard while visiting the Millennium Dome measured against Government arts policy objectives.

Roger Cook

Pierre Bourdieu, William Blake and the Battle for the Autonomy of the Arts

... it is only at the end of the nineteenth century that the system of characteristics constitutive of an autonomous field is found assembled together (without ever excluding completely the possibility of regressions to heteronomy, such as the one starting today, thanks to a return to new forms of patronage, public or private, and because of the encroachment of journalism).
Pierre Bourdieu, *The Rules of Art*

As the foremost sociologist of culture in Europe, Pierre Bourdieu has shown in his book of 1992 (translated as *The Rules of Art* in 1996) that the tradition of the avant garde is the tradition of hard-won autonomy. Its relationship to the State is inevitably one of struggle, a struggle that has its origins in the nineteenth century, when avant-garde artists broke free from academic regulation. According to Bourdieu, this autonomy is at present seriously threatened by the rise of the political neo-liberalism of the Right and Left, which can only conceive of the development of culture in crudely rational economic terms. As we know, art of a certain sort – the easily assimilated, vulgarly seductive sort associated with the heteronomous end of the culture spectrum – has always been a powerful agent in the triumph of totalitarian regimes.

If Bourdieu is right, the present situation is serious and those who work in the institutions of the art world need to be vigilant with regard to what Bourdieu has called in the title of a recent article 'the cunning of imperialist reason', which he sees as increasingly dominating the international field of cultural production, through the heteronomous agency of television and journalism. Bourdieu shows that the field of cultural production is stretched between two ends: the autonomous end of the restricted field – the small group of avant-gardists whose work is motivated by symbolic rewards, the pure pleasure, of competitive experimentation, without thought of economic profit – and the heteronomous end of the large-scale field of commercial production, which seeks to please. If a government is to be, rather than merely appear to be, truly progressive, then it must be seen to support difficult and experimental research in the arts. A current problem, which haunts the present popularity of the new British art, is that the very notion of the avant garde has become vulgarised through its popular misrepresentation in the media: only too often equated with the obviously transgressive, spectacular or bizarre. What is truly advanced in the experimental research of the arts is not always obvious to those who are not specialists in the field.

Art, then, must not be controlled by that 'ratio' that threatens to destroy what William Blake called the 'lineaments of gratified desire' (the primacy of embodied experimentation with new forms of gratification), emblematised in his 1826 engraving of the Laocoön, on which he wrote: 'Where any view of Money exists, Art cannot be carried on but War only'.

Blake knew that art could only develop within the autonomy of its own circuits of pleasure and desire. This was his objection to the Academy of Joshua Reynolds and his 'cunning band of hired knaves'.

According to Bourdieu, the field of cultural production is, like all fields, a battleground in which various factions are engaged in internal struggles for the legitimation of intellectual and artistic culture. Bourdieu also recognises that the field of intellectual and artistic culture has always been engaged in external struggles with the field of power. Speaking of the present in his 1997 Ernst Bloch Prize speech, Bourdieu acknowledged

the fact that we are currently in a period of neo-conservative reconstruction [that] ratifies and glorifies the rule of what we call the financial markets, a return to a sort of radical capitalism answering to no law except that of maximum profit; an undisguised, unrestrained capitalism, but one that has been rationalised, tuned to the limit of its economic efficiency through the introduction of modern forms of domination ('management') and manipulative techniques like market research, marketing and advertising.

And in his recent book *On Television and Journalism* he complained that:

Wherever you look, people are thinking in terms of market success. Only thirty years ago, and since the middle of the nineteenth century ... immediate market success was suspect. It was taken as a sign of compromise with the times, with money ... Today, on the contrary, the market is accepted more and more as a legitimate means of legitimation ... It is very disturbing to see this ... because it jeopardises works that may not necessarily meet audience expectations but, in time, can create their own audience.

Hopefully, there are those in the established field who do not inevitably submit to the symbolic violence of economic capital. As Bourdieu writes in his postscript to *The Rules of Art*:

The threats to autonomy result from the increasingly greater interpenetration between the world of art and the world of money. I am thinking of new forms of sponsorship, of new alliances being established between certain economic enterprises ... and cultural producers ... But the grip or empire of the economy over artistic or scientific research is also exercised inside the field itself, through the control of the means of cultural production and distribution, and even of the instances of consecration. Producers attached to the major cultural bureaucracies (newspapers, radio, television) are increasingly forced to accept and adopt norms and constraints linked to the requirements of the market and, especially, to pressure exerted more or less strongly and directly by advertisers; and they tend more or less unconsciously to constitute as a universal measure of intellectual accomplishment those forms of intellectual activity to which they are condemned by their conditions of work (I am thinking, for example of fast writing and fast reading, which are often the rule in journalistic production and criticism).

THE RULES OF ART

THE THREATS TO AUTONOMY RESULT FROM THE INCREASINGLY GREATER INTERPENETRATION BETWEEN THE WORLD OF ART AND THE WORLD OF MONEY. I AM THINKING OF NEW FORMS OF SPONSORSHIP, OF NEW ALLIANCES BEING ESTABLISHED BETWEEN CERTAIN ECONOMIC ENTERPRISES ... AND CULTURAL PRODUCERS ... BUT THE GRIP OR EMPIRE OF THE ECONOMY OVER ARTISTIC OR SCIENTIFIC RESEARCH IS ALSO EXERCISED INSIDE THE FIELD ITSELF, THROUGH THE CONTROL OF THE MEANS OF CULTURAL PRODUCTION AND DISTRIBUTION AND EVEN OF THE INSTANCES OF CONSECRATION. PRODUCERS ATTACHED TO THE MAJOR CULTURAL BUREAUCRACIES (NEWSPAPERS, RADIO, TELEVISION) ARE INCREASINGLY FORCED TO ACCEPT AND ADOPT NORMS AND CONSTRAINTS LINKED TO THE REQUIREMENTS OF THE MARKET AND, ESPECIALLY, TO PRESSURE EXERTED MORE OR LESS STRONGLY AND DIRECTLY BY ADVERTISERS; AND THEY TEND MORE OR LESS UNCONSCIOUSLY TO CONSTITUTE AS A UNIVERSAL MEASURE OF INTELLECTUAL ACCOMPLISHMENT THOSE FORMS OF INTELLEC-TUAL ACTIVITY TO WHICH THEY ARE CONDEMNED BY THEIR CONDITIONS OF WORK (I AM THINKING, FOR EXAMPLE OF FAST WRITING AND FAST READING WHICH ARE OFTEN THE RULE IN JOURNALISTIC PRODUCTION AND CRITICISM)

PIERRE BOURDIEU

Lord Freyberg and Baroness Blackstone

Art Colleges

Extract from House of Lords Debate. Hansard (London). 12 October 1999

Art Colleges

Lord Freyberg: My Lords, it gives me great pleasure to introduce this debate on the Government's plans for the funding and role of art colleges in the United Kingdom. I wish to spell out the enormous changes that have taken place in art colleges in the past decade; the effect of those changes, and the likely consequences if certain aspects of funding are not re-thought.

The case for art colleges is an unusual one. Their importance lies not only in the obvious end results – painting and sculpture – but in the atmosphere of creativity engendered and encouraged. Over the years, that has borne fruit in the work of the creative industries, which range from product design and fashion and furniture-making to graphic design, the film world and the theatre. In other words, our colleges make a major contribution to Britain's economy, although many of the most profitable movers and shakers in the design world start off studying fine arts before turning to more practical applications. That is because creativity has to be properly nurtured before any quantifiable results appear. Britain's imaginative art school courses have in the past been excellent at doing that, winning admiration worldwide. However, with their emphasis on employability, governments sometimes seem to confuse education with training. For example, recent Conservative governments attempted to boost vocational art courses at the expense of non-vocational ones, not realising their interdependence.

In the past decade, art colleges have been forced to run themselves as commercial enterprises. While there is nothing particularly sinister in modernising institutions or putting professional practices in place, the cost-cutting has gone too far. Every year since 1989, governments have demanded an annual efficiency rate of at least 1%, and sometimes up to 3%, in real terms. The practice continues under the current Labour Government. While there was room for improvement initially, the continuing chipping away at funding throughout the 1990s has had a detrimental effect. Instead of putting their energy into maintaining excellence, art colleges have had to concentrate on fundraising, while course heads have been overwhelmed with paperwork. The pressure has eroded core teaching and damaged a precious ethos. It is a running battle that staff feel they are losing. Students and their work suffer as a result, while tutors are frustrated at being diverted from what they were hired to do. The policy is short-termism at its worst.

Of particular concern are two practices that art colleges have been forced to adopt. These were reasonable in their initial stages but have been taken to damaging extremes. First, since the late 1980s, colleges have been obliged to take on more and more students in order to maintain their original level of funding, but without a corresponding increase in facilities, working space or tutors. For example, in 1989, I was one of around 100 students on the foundation course at Camberwell College of Arts; today,

there are 324. Extra students may keep up figures – and thus funding – but teachers have less time for individual tuition, and students find that there are simply not enough kilns, video-editing suites or materials to go round. Surveys at the London Institute all indicate that students are dissatisfied with the amount of equipment, studio space and resources available.

The second cause for concern is the explosion of overseas art students in the UK, up from 3,316 in 1994-5 to 6,654 in 1997-8. In theory, that development should be exciting and enriching; in practice, such students are encouraged chiefly for the extra income their fees provide. In 1998-9, 2,143 students from eighty-eight different countries contributed fees of £12.2 million to the London Institute, which consists of Camberwell College of Arts, Central St Martin's, Chelsea College of Art, the London College of Printing and the London College of Fashion. It would not survive without that extra income. Is it right to depend on overseas students to that extent?

Colleges are free to set their own level of fees for students from outside the European Union – depending on what the market can bear. Thus, the Ruskin in Oxford charges £6,684 a year; the Slade £11,435; and the Royal College of Art £15,670 a year. By comparison, Eton College, with longer terms and full board, costs £15,660 per year. Without such fees, these institutions would go to the wall. They are therefore obliged to take as many foreign students as possible. There is no set limit. Inevitably, the quality of those students' work is less important than their ability to pay. Too often, overseas students cannot speak much English – in spite of their course involving written work.

That naturally lowers the morale of other students who have to fight harder for their own places. But everyone's credibility is affected. The overseas students feel that they have been seduced to British art colleges as cash cows and that, thanks to over-extended courses, the back-up and facilities they were promised simply do not exist. There are several cases pending in London where overseas students are suing the college they attend for delivering poor value for money.

In addition, there are stories of art colleges touting for business abroad, vying in an unsightly manner with each other for desirable potential students. Is it really desirable that rich foreign students alone – rather than talented ones – should have access to British art colleges? Rather than making further education more accessible, such a policy diminishes diversity. That is an iniquitous double standard. Moreover, it is extremely difficult for institutions to voice their concerns without fear of being penalised.

Worse still, by cramming in students and accepting some of dubious standard, Britain risks losing its reputation for excellent art education – the very reason why overseas students are prepared to pay over the odds. So far, people are still willing to pay, but if the current situation continues we shall kill the goose that lays the golden eggs.

Art colleges should not be penalised for practices that have been forced on them. However, that could well happen once there is regulation of the recruitment of overseas students, the level of their fees, and so on, and the findings are published, as should properly happen. Instead, the Government should accept that they have pushed the situation too far, show that they are prepared to get to grips with the problem, and allow otherwise efficient organisations to operate at a less pressurised level in the best interests of students and staff alike.

There are other financial problems, in particular the lack of postgraduate funding, which is the responsibility of the Arts and Humanities Research Board, set up in 1998. Postgraduate bursaries for arts and design are far fewer than in other subjects and the competition steeper. At Ph.D level, students of English and history are eligible to apply for funds, but arts and design graduates are not.

With that scenario, the brightest and most promising students are likely to be deterred from continuing their studies because they cannot face further debt. So, while the UK's invisible earnings in music, art and film are mammoth, and the Government makes a lot of mileage out of Britain's creative industries, the funding to develop those skills largely runs out at undergraduate level. Where is the logic in that?

All these concerns would not matter if students were getting a better education, but they are not. The academic base of art colleges is being constantly eroded. Sadly, the reason is financial – the commodification of art education. By placing too many financial and managerial constraints, you blight standards and morale.

What we have in our art colleges is very special. It is the driving force behind the creative economy. That is why colleges deserve sustained funding to continue in the most robust manner possible. The Government must act soon or they will destroy – however unintentionally – one of Britain's best resources. [...]

The Minister of State, Department for Education and Employment (Baroness Blackstone): My Lords, I too am very grateful to the noble Lord, Lord Freyberg, for giving me this opportunity to speak about the role and funding of art and design colleges. Art and design is central to society and to our sense of ourselves, enriching ourselves in every way. It is inextricably linked with our culture and heritage. I very much agree with the remarks of the noble Lord and the noble Earl, Lord Clancarty. We should value the fine arts for their own sake. But art and design and its associated activities make a very large and growing contribution to the economy, and that is not something that we should ignore.

Before I turn to education in art and design, I should say a brief word about general government support for the arts and perhaps respond to some of the points raised by the noble Viscount. Following the Comprehensive Spending Review, the Government has put in place a three-year funding settlement, which involves an increase of £125 million for the arts and £99 million for museums and galleries. This is the biggest-ever increase in funding for cultural activity by central government and

is something of which we can be proud. It will help to create stability, fund new productions, support key arts organisations and increase access, we hope, for many thousands of people.

We have taken other measures. We have established a special fund – the noble Baroness, Lady Blatch, referred to this – to enable dance and drama students to obtain proper grants and assistance to undertake courses at accredited colleges. We are ensuring that the provisions of the New Deal are appropriate to the needs of young musicians who wish to follow that career path. We have insisted that art, music and drama must remain a statutory part of the national curriculum in our schools. I think that issue was raised by more than one speaker. We have also established NESTA (the National Endowment for Science, Technology and the Arts) to provide a national fund for talent.

The arts provide their own justification by what they do for us all. As I think the noble Baroness, Lady Blatch, has already said, they also have an increasing economic importance in our national life, in commercial music, film, architecture, design, publishing, broadcasting, multimedia, and fashion. Growing at twice the rate of the economy as a whole, these industries are worth over £60 billion per year. I am not sure that I completely understood what the noble Earl was saying in his comments on creative industry, but I think it is reasonable to consider these collectively as a creative industry because they rest ultimately for their economic value on the creativity of individuals, and the intellectual property that is created by them. Economically, artists and designers are categorised as part of the creative industry sector. Recent work by the Department for Culture, Media and Sport attempted to measure, for the first time, the extent of this sector. The estimate was that it generated added value of about £25 billion, with export earnings of nearly £7 billion. These industries are growing at a rapid rate – a 34% increase in employment over the ten-year period of the census compared with only a slight increase throughout the economy as a whole. Of course, many of these industries take in graduates from our art and design colleges. At a rate of growth between 4 and 5% per annum, which is less than the current rate of growth, within ten years they could be employing 1.5 million people and generating revenue of £80 billion.

The Government is committed to supporting art and design colleges and to underpinning the provision of the broad range of teaching and training that it offers to students. Students enrol on art and design courses with many different aspirations: to progress to higher education; with a wish, often long held, to fulfil a talent; as a leisure interest, or with a very determined career intention. The range of college provision is extraordinarily diverse. Art and design includes the traditional artistic disciplines – painting, drawing, sculpture, print-making and the full range of design specialisms. Although the disciplines encompassed are various, underlying them is a shared emphasis on personal creativity. [...]

THE SECOND CAUSE FOR CONCERN IS THE **EXPLOSION** OF OVERSEAS ART STUDENTS IN THE UK, UP FROM 3,316 IN 1994–5 TO **6,654** IN 1997–8. IN THEORY, THAT DEVELOPMENT SHOULD BE EXCITING AND ENRICHING; IN PRACTICE, SUCH STUDENTS ARE ENCOURAGED CHIEFLY FOR THE EXTRA INCOME THEIR FEES PROVIDE IN 1998–9, 2,143 STUDENTS FROM EIGHTY-EIGHT DIFFERENT COUNTRIES **CONTRIBUTED FEES OF £12.2 MILLION** TO THE LONDON INSTITUTE, WHICH CONSISTS OF CAMBERWELL COLLEGE OF ARTS, CENTRAL ST MARTIN'S, CHELSEA COLLEGE OF ART, THE LONDON COLLEGE OF PRINTING AND THE LONDON COLLEGE OF FASHION. IT WOULD NOT SURVIVE WITHOUT THAT EXTRA INCOME. **IS IT RIGHT TO DEPEND ON OVERSEAS STUDENTS TO THAT EXTENT?**

Surveys of employment available in the area of art and design often use overlapping definitions, but its importance is often underestimated. It makes an enormous contribution to the economy, bigger than perhaps many people imagine. *The Financial Times* has made an assessment that this sector employs more people than the high street banks and building societies combined. We are looking at something approaching 800,000 people, with a turnover to match.

The importance of art and design in the arts industries is a consequence of the very high standing in the world enjoyed by British designers and creative technicians. They include household names such as the artist David Hockney, designers such as Sir Terence Conran and James Dyson, and fashion designers such as John Galliano and Zandra Rhodes. Of course, we could mention many others. Most practitioners who contribute to the vigorous national culture for which this country is renowned began their careers in further and higher education courses in art and design. As well as preparing them for employment, these courses educate students to become enlightened consumers of the arts and the media, something we should not forget.

Chris Smith has recently said that the present 50% of the population who enjoy or take part in the arts should be increased to two-thirds within the next ten years. I hope that his prediction proves to be right. Also, we know that the arts, when taken together with sport and leisure, can contribute to neighbourhood renewal, urban regeneration, and can help to counter social exclusion.

Perhaps I may advise the noble Viscount that I do not think there is any evidence that fewer people want to go into the arts. There are fifteen specialist art and design colleges – seven are in the further education sector and eight are in higher education. Although HEFCE does not technically regard it as a specialist art and design college, there is the London Institute, covering the Camberwell College of Arts, which counts among its past students the noble Lord, Lord Freyberg, and there are the other well-known colleges that comprise the London Institute, such as St. Martin's, which I think is now known as Central St. Martin's; Chelsea; the London College of Fashion, and the London College of Printing.

There are about 5,000 students studying art and design in the seven FE colleges and 8,000 in HE in its eight specialist colleges. Around 14% of those students are postgraduates. The London Institute, through its five colleges, adds a further 6,000 art and design students, again with around 14% being postgraduates. We must not forget that this is only a part, albeit a very central part, of the much wider picture. Some 330,000 students are studying art and design in other colleges in the FE sector and over 80,000 students are studying art and design at other HE institutions. Overall, there are around 430,000 students on art and design courses.

Incidentally, I am not sure that I really agree with the implied criticisms of the noble Earl, Lord Clancarty, about the merger of some of the former art colleges with the polytechnics, which happened under the previous administration. I believe that those new universities, as they have subsequently become, are providing very good courses in art and design for many of the students to whom I have just referred.

I turn now to the issue of funding. I do not want to get into arguments about what the previous administration did. I do not want to dwell on the fact that there was a 40% reduction in per capita funding for students in higher education; nor do I want to dwell on the collapse in funding for further education colleges when the demand-led expansion was introduced. What I do want to say, however, is that this Government has acted to restore funding in both further and higher education and that, of course, the art colleges will have benefited very substantially from that. The settlement following the Comprehensive Spending Review was excellent news for both FE and HE. For further education, another £725 million is being made available over the next two years with another £776 million for HE.

I cannot answer the precise questions of the noble Baroness about the art colleges' share in these overall figures, but we shall certainly write to her. What I can say is that specialist FE colleges receive over £12 million per annum. The number of students is expected to rise by 8% over the next three years and the number of students studying art and design is expected to rise by 12%. Again, I think that that adds to what I said to the noble Viscount earlier.

In higher education, the specialist art and design institutions are getting over £30 million in the current academic year that has just started. That is over 11% more than last year. Again, the somewhat downbeat assessment by the noble Lord, Lord Freyberg, was not entirely accurate. However, I think that he was referring to some of the cuts that had taken place earlier.

Unfortunately, I have run out of time and I shall not be able to pick up on all the other questions including those that related to funding of overseas students. However, I wish to say briefly that international students bring great benefits to the UK – financial, commercial and artistic. It is a very good business. But those students also bring with them a lot of talent. I do not accept that we are simply taking in rich students from abroad at the expense of able students. Nor would I accept that the art institutions are overcharging those students. As the noble Viscount said, the provision of art and design is expensive. They charge full-cost fees, but they are not above the actual cost of provision. I conclude by saying that the specialist colleges and courses in art and design play a vital part both in our society and our economy. I can give my assurance to noble Lords who have spoken in the debate that the Government will continue to give their full commitment and support to our art and design colleges.

Government pronouncements on the arts are dutifully uninspired. They are full of intentions, good only from the perspective of Downing Street. The Government would like to see smiling artists trained to produce inspired culture, to be consumed by a happily educated and busily employed work force. Perhaps the Dome has Disneyfied Downing Street.

Before their careers begin, art students face the financial burden of paying for their education, an expense shared by other students but with one exception: art students have a less than 1 in 300 chance of earning their living as artists. Perhaps they would be better off reading business studies, to help them understand that their commodity is unsaleable.

Unemployed artists are not natural allies of a government for whom the arts exist in one of two modes: they glitter or they are invisible. Unfortunately, from the Government's point of view, financially successful artists are just as likely to cause trouble; witness their financial contribution to Ken Livingstone's mayoral campaign.

Visual artists find in the Government, and in Tony Blair in particular, dedicated and steadfast opponents. This is because the Government, and Tony Blair in person, have systematically thwarted any attempt to allow artists the benefit of resale royalties. Europe has legislated for a comprehensive umbrella of benefits to artists, which Blair has successfully scuttled as far as Britain is concerned, on the grounds that these measures would harm the trade (in artists).

Government wants an intelligentsia but not intellectuals, and certainly not of the creative variety. The message to artists from New Labour, 'community, identity, civic pride, access, innovation, excellence', reduces art to therapy, to collaboration, to passivity. How about 'reflexive criticism, agitation, opposition, empowerment'?

Jean Fisher

The 'Proletarianisation' of Art

Throughout the twentieth century, the least formalist movements in art tried to bridge the divide between artistic practice and the politics of the everyday. Since the critical debates in the 1980s of the so-called postmodern condition, the notion that there could be a transcendent category called 'everyday reality' has become suspect: the everyday is the artifice of MTV or TV soaps. Thus it is not art that becomes like real life but 'real life' that encroaches on the territory of art. Where does this 'aestheticisation of everyday life', as some commentators have called it, place art?

There seems to be little doubt that the rapid expansion of communications technology and corporate forms of visual culture in the postwar decades have contributed to this crisis in art in the West. Art could not compete with the proliferation of consumer culture and the seductive realities it projected, nor reach a fraction of its audiences. Part of the crisis of art has therefore been to redefine what kind of object or image it is in a world of rapidly expanding objects and images, and what and whom it might be addressing. Historically, art has addressed and represented the needs and interests of the sector of society that patronises it. However, throughout the modernist period, art became progressively dissociated from its patronage, while its radical gestures found little sympathy among the traditionally under-represented classes. Furthermore, representations of a unified national identity and homogenised reality were (and are) not sustainable in pluralist societies like those of post-industrial metropolitan Britain. The massive migrations and demographic shifts in populations throughout the twentieth century of both class and race, together with shifts in sexual and gender definitions, have changed the pattern of culture in the metropolis. In fact, the postmodern metropolis emerges as a conglomerate of sub-cultures, many of which (groups concerned with sexual politics, ethnic and religious affiliations, green politics, specific forms of popular music, the club scene and so on) interlink, traverse and transgress the traditional boundaries of British society. New social constituencies are generated, all of which demand some form of public representation.

Mass media has served a paradoxical or even conflictual function in these processes. On the one hand, it has been instrumental in the dissemination of alternative political agendas and lifestyles, while on the other hand it has tended towards a homogenisation of social attitudes and opinions. By contrast, art has come to seem of little relevance to general cultural life except as occasional entertainment – take, for example, the annual Channel Four sponsorship of the Tate Gallery's Turner Prize. In any case, the less privileged sectors of society (not trained to recognise the value of visual arts thanks to a state-education system in which art has low priority in the curriculum) have always invented their own idioms of pop culture to represent themselves. From these perspectives, art of the late twentieth century, to some extent, has been art in search of an audience.

Mass-media technologies, appropriated and controlled by ideologies of power, tend to marginalise or commodify both art and pop culture. Perhaps there is a case for arguing that one characteristic distinguishing some recent British work from that of the 1980s is its desire to form alliances with popular or subcultural forms as opposed to international postmodernism. However, because such forms arise from local traditions and lean on autobiographical codes, the work reflects a kind of provincial or domestic aesthetic that lends itself to appropriation by spurious nationalistic agendas. What can be packaged as British art, according to certain stereotypical institutional definitions, is what gets promoted, and a great deal of what constitutes the diversity of British culture gets excluded.

Among the many factors that might have contributed to this particular trajectory of art in the UK, aside from the ubiquitousness of mass media itself, one might include the way in which art in higher education evolved during the 1980s. Change occurred not only by way of the new technologies available in colleges, thereby expanding material possibilities beyond the studio-based traditions of painting and sculpture, but also through the introduction of a new theoretical landscape.

By the mid-1980s, the conventional academic art-history courses that had been the classical adjunct to fine-art studio teaching were being replaced, or supplemented in the more progressive schools, by 'complementary studies'. Taking their cue from US-style education, these provided elective courses addressing less programmatic and more broadly based cultural issues. To some extent, 'complementary studies' paralleled the development of 'cultural studies' – an interdisciplinary approach to cultural analysis and production that drew variously on perspectives developed from film and literary studies, anthropology and ethnography, psychoanalysis, sociology and political theory. Under this developing field of 'cultural studies', questions of subjectivity and social context, which the more formalist and conservative art history programmes were slower to accommodate, were taken into account.

From its inception, cultural studies addressed the politics of class, race and gender. Theorists in women's studies and those from the post-colonial diaspora expanded critical analysis into a form of socio-cultural anthropology whose objective was the forensic dissection of British society itself rather than the ethnic 'other'. The raw material of these 'sciences' – statistical analyses, photo-documentation, personal anecdotes and testimonies – had already been incorporated into the anti-formalist practices of both black and women artists on both sides of the Atlantic in their critiques of Western culture's universalist versions of history and contemporary social reality. This autobiographical testimony, or the bearing witness to 'other', hitherto unrepresented cultural histories, identities and realities, has since slipped into British art practice in general, albeit in an often depoliticised form.

However, what was lost in the shift towards cultural studies was art history itself. Emerging generations of artists are frighteningly ignorant of the histories and languages of their own practice beyond their immediate predecessors. As a result, we find a repetition of gestures already performed in the 1960s and 70s, but without the frisson of irony. If we acknowledge that fine art is a professional practice, we should not accept such ignorance. This is not to say that I am advocating a return to the old classicist education of art history, but rather the development of a more appropriate balance between disciplines that provide education in the history of art and those that more generally contextualise cultural practices.

With the slippage of cultural studies into art education, the traditional alliance between the academy and the 'cultured' object of study – conventionally the classics of literature, music or fine art – was broken down. As a result, any expression of popular or mass culture could become the object of critical analysis. On the one hand, this 'proletarianisation' of theoretical enquiry served to legitimise all forms of mass-cultural production, from pop music to TV soaps, pulp fiction and advertising. On the other hand, the solemn institutionalisation of critical theory was perceived to have distanced artists from the pleasures and contradictions of the everyday.

Thus, a levelling of culture began to take place in the 1980s. In the process, local or provincial values became legitimised and students moving to London from elsewhere no longer had to feel pressured to adopt the values of the metropolitan cultural elite. A delight in kitsch and the banality of the everyday became as central to the work of this generation (educated in the atmosphere of Thatcherite populism) as the critical distance (admittedly sometimes bordering on the censorial and puritanical) achieved through semiotic analyses of commodified forms of representation and presentation was for the previous generation.

If this trend has helped to blur distinctions between the avant-garde and kitsch, or 'high' and 'low' forms of cultural production, it has given fuel to those advocates of an 'art that is closer to life'. Thus, a rather confused notion keys into the apparent naturalism offered by the indexical nature of photographic and televisual media, about which more needs to be said.

Michael Madden
A Warning from a Trade Unionist

Being Secretary of a Trade Union at the Natural History Museum, as well as a lifelong artist who paints murals, puts me in an unusual situation, which I could never have conceived as a self-employed artist. I make public artwork but am also involved in discussions about terms and conditions of employment.

As we all know, the Thatcher Government deregulated all public bodies and the Civil Service in general. Management numbers grew in many cultural establishments, and in-house technicians (many from arts backgrounds) were scaled down. 'Flexible' employment came in, with less favourable terms and conditions. Charging for culture was encouraged, which divided museums and turned visitors into customers, while a campaign of the most virulent anti-Trade Union legislation was being implemented. This led to arrogance in management. At the same time, student grants were being phased out and manufacturing and heavy industries were suffering from a deliberate lack of support, and have not recovered since. Under New Labour, we have seen the will to fund huge capital building projects but without proper staffing. This is leading to further job threats throughout the cultural sector, and continues one of the biggest mistakes under the Tories: the concentration on appearance and accountancy without proper understanding of basic practicalities.

It concerns me to see New Labour embracing the fundamental error made under the Tories: the mixing of the cultural and commercial sectors. This is uncharted territory and to use terms such as 'creative industries' is dangerous. Industries, as we know them today, evolved in the Industrial Revolution, and soon became highly unionised because the workforce realised that they would starve to death if they failed to organise. During the nineteenth and twentieth centuries, these industries made our wealth. The arts were left alone and not considered an industry in the same sense. Artists are still considered separate from the rest of the skilled workforce, and are generally self-employed – whether this is beneficial or not. There have been few attempts to change this situation, but they have been unable to withstand the competitive nature of capitalism. If anything, the modern era merely strengthened the idea of the artist as an isolated, inspired individual on the fringes of commercial society.

The worry therefore is that what appear to be populist ideas may be another way to suck the best from a fragmented and non-unionised workforce. The carrot is fame, yet how many artists achieve it or even make a good living solely out of their art? How can a group of completely separate, highly individualised artists deliver the access, excellence, innovation and educational opportunity that Chris Smith asks of them in his 1998 statement? They cannot begin to try unless a very prescriptive structure is designed for them to follow, and it is precisely here that the danger lies. In effect, they would become public servants, but in a land where there is only commerce. Dumbing down will follow.

Maybe it is fortunate that we are obliged to engage in this debate, as discussion of many of these questions is long overdue. It is vital to keep in mind that the Latin root of our word 'art' is 'skill', and that there are all sorts of skills available that are excluded from the present idea of 'art' and which are being neglected. Neither Damien Hirst nor Jeff Koons possess the skills required to make their valuable works. Their skills are intellectual and managerial, and they are both shrewd. So the danger in the present British art scene is that we may be seeing creative spin masking a living lie. After all, access to an art education is now for those with well-off parents. Where does this leave skilled or aspiring working people who wish to lead more creative lives? The best way to improve access is still to have free museums and free education. The best way to achieve excellence and innovation is to allow creativity throughout society. Anything else is fudging the issue. As far as the creative industries are concerned, artists should beware of glittering opportunities that are not underwritten by tight contracts, and should beware of arts managers in general as they rarely possess the skills they manage. The Museums and Galleries division of DCMS, for instance, is not run by professionals, but by twenty-six staff who are mainly career administrators.

Is it really a government's job to make creative industries after the old ones have been folded or allowed to die? Why trust them? If they want to make us public servants, we will have to unionise. Otherwise, what will be in it for artists as we serve our 'customers'? Not much, judging by the way the Government treats other public servants. In the words of the great art historian, Ananda Coomaraswamy, speaking in 1937:

> *What the trade union should require of its members is a master's accomplishment. What the class thinker who is not merely an underdog, but also a man, has a right to demand is neither to have less work to do, nor to be engaged in a different kind of work, nor to have a larger share of the crumbs that fall from the rich man's table, but the opportunity to take as great a pleasure in doing whatever he does for hire, as he takes in his own garden or family life; what he should demand, in other words, is the opportunity to be an artist.*

Artists should not fool themselves that originality or 'genius' will carry them through to riches in the new marketplace. We may end up merely feeding the creative industries with 'new' ideas, but with no security and no future. We may end up famous for fifteen minutes, but this will hardly bring us nearer to a creative life.

Graham Higgin
Lotting the Lottery

Though everywhere in evidence, the bureaucracy is obliged to be a class imperceptible to consciousness, thus making the whole of social life unfathomable and insane.
Guy Debord, *The Society of the Spectacle*

Art, in the era of the commodity's rampant triumph, can no longer be conceived as an autonomous sphere. The liberation of artists, and hence of art, depends on the general liberation of society and the revolutionary abolition of commodity relations. Hence, artists should not be treated as a breed apart, deserving of state subsidies and special treatment, which is always a cause for suspicion. Rather, artists should disown their snooty self-importance and accept their chances along with everyone else in the generalised lottery of capitalist existence.

I propose, therefore, that all subsidies to the arts be replaced by a lottery system in which everyone is a potential beneficiary. Instead of bureaucrats deciding what projects are worthy of gifts (i.e. those that further the interests of State power and bourgeois society), the lottery treasure chest should be added to the tax-revenues detailed for 'cultural projects' and then divided up into equal £20,000 parts. Each week, these will be distributed by lots, drawn randomly from a comprehensive list of UK nationals or, under a more desirable European-wide lottery, EU citizens. Artists can hope for luck individually, or can show an unwonted foresight and group together into co-operative cartels, sharing out whatever lots fall their way under consensual arrangements worked out by the group. The expenditure of those deliriously expectant people who buy lottery tickets will no longer fund projects from which they are estranged, but will flow back towards them in a manner that will encourage them to form themselves into societies of mutual aid. By allocating the proceeds of the lottery by lot, the dispensations of change will further the project of rational co-operation.

Whether 'art' as it is currently constituted between the devil of the commodity and the spectacle's deep blue sea will remain intact as concept and product will remain to be seen. It is expected that the arts of living, however, will undergo a revolutionary overhaul. Through stretching to its extreme the principle of the lottery, a barbaric institution may by a dialectical quirk give rise to a civilised society of common enterprise where life and art may be put back together again.

Alex Sainsbury
The Total Quality Culture

In business, selling is increasingly theorised and sophisticated. In the USA, the impulse to understand the flogging of product as a rare art requiring arcane description has exercised corporations since the 1970s. The service industry has become bloated with management consultancies who tout strategies for winning. In politics, the Labour Party has set a precedent by so successfully appropriating business theory to sell itself to voters that we can't imagine a party winning a general election now without a squadron of sales strategists to dictate its manifesto. The terminology of the business theorist has become the language of the political back room, which seems appropriate for an age in which the market is becoming the culture. Business models are being adopted across all government departments. In education, schools are being burdened with the capitalist paradox of having to demonstrate 'continuous improvement'. And in the arts, a shift in government policy reflects this new business-like scheme more than it demonstrates change in attitudes to art.

Jargon is stacking up, not only with reference to sales, but also to efficiency. 'Joined-up thinking' is a form of process management appropriated from business theory, where all policies are conceived as a totality. This is not totalitarian, but is rational, and indeed efficient. Education is connected to child care, to hospital-bed vacancies, to housing, to community policing, to education, to art. Arts funding can be brought into the whole circle of government policy so that its cost may bolster other areas: education, social regeneration, etc. How else could Chris Smith have sold the high cost of free museum access to the Treasury?

A political party must project itself, through the media, as a strong and singular brand; it must have a uniquely persuasive 'offer'; it must have a good USP – a Unique Selling Point. All of Government policy must be seen to represent the party's brand of democracy. Funding art that appeals only to elite audiences would be confusingly 'off-message'. The Government must be seen to support arts that might appeal to everyone. This is how it will project its strongest offer – the UP with the best S: that it can fix the country with the best social glue. An art must be located that all can be for. That way, social incoherence can be postponed, perhaps, and values might be shared, and the political party that is seen to foster such art will greatly strengthen its brand.

Big business attends to its 'front-end', that is, its customers. It wants to know exactly what they want to buy, and how they want to buy it. Voters are theorised as 'customers', and focus groups are assembled to chase – conjure – that phantasm: capricious, spooky 'public opinion'. Political parties must have an undistracted focus on their core business purpose, re-election, and know what the voters want to buy next time around. Opinions about every small subject need to be coaxed out of well-chosen samples of voters. The least informed of these opinions are those generated by the subjects of least interest, such as art.

So manifestos will be forever reactive to focus groups; and forever reactionary. But to rule by public opinion is, after all, a rational form of democracy. And to believe that the media tell people what to think is as weak a conspiracy theory as any the media foists. Perhaps it is the increased independent-mindedness of a more educated population that rejects the imposition of marginal art using money from tax (although if they could see where else their money is spent, people might worry less about the trickle that goes to the ballet). Arts funding is bound to be shunted by expediency when handled by politicians, whose concerns we cannot blame for being too materialist, utilitarian even, to grasp art's uncertain appeal. This particular government's arts policy could be understood as merely a gesture from its front bench to its back bench, a misplaced sop to old-style interventionism, sticking a big paddle into the thin soup of the arts as a poor substitute for the implementation of command economics.

We should sympathise with government politicians, such poor malnourished things, starving themselves of the chance to be visionary or even particular. We can see that even the would-be visionary talk of the current government is monitored for its sanction by 'public opinion', for its brand-strengthening pitch. The Secretary of State would certainly not have been allowed to publish his – no doubt earnestly intended – book about art's place in society's bounty, unless his views fitted the party's business plan. Art's role is explained as a means to cultural identification, which would allow it to secure the party's best 'offer': that it provides the ingredients for a new social glue. So a new direction in government arts funding is argued as a means to cementing community in godless times (as well as earning money for brand Britain, now that sales of the Queen have dipped). This might be a moral vision, but I think the party's sales strategists have more influence than its philosophical wing: providing access (to shared values), education (about shared values), social regeneration (of shared values), and economic importance is the right aim for art because it is 'on-message'. Arts can be funded provided they fit with the government's offer on the definition of art as a purveyor of shared values. Art's status needs to be elevated and popularised because voters identify it with a new brand of Britain created by a new brand of Labour Party. Furthermore, there will be no waste in the budget as all government policies can be advertised as pulling together, pulling us in the direction of 'better'.

For those who want art to be pleasure and commentary autonomous of policy, who would like it to stand outside the government's 'joined-up' circle of policy, I suggest we persuade the party strategists to heed a focus group we could assemble: the Arts Utility Focus Group. The aim of the group would be to establish 'public opinion' on the use for art in our society, and on the vote-winning possibilities of the Secretary of State's ideas. The group would consist of an average cross-section of regular-type people (who would wear government-issue, strong-fibre, multi-coloured polonecks). They would be locked in a room and serenaded with art: a little fist-fucking from Robert Mapplethorpe, some cacophony from John Cage, a rape from Howard Brenton. And they could be asked questions such as 'have you ever seen a picture as pretty as a tree?', 'How do you think art can demonstrate "continuous improvement"?' After the group shows its fair disgust, after it falls about arguing, the strategists could reassure themselves that, outside the sturdy arms of commerce, art serves no useful or vote-winning purpose. An artist's fantasy is not necessarily moral, nor are its values best shared, and in the cajoling of social unity, the last century's art is useless. Then art could be left alone and treated like any other minority sport. And if it can't sustain itself independently as a revelation of fantasies within this society, which has this brand of politics and this brand of market culture, we won't worry if it shudders and disappears, unsupported.

Arts Council of England Christmas Card, 1999

Photo: Richard H Smith

The Arts Council of England's Chrisi Bailey Award is a unique national photography award. It promotes exploration of photography and digital imaging by primary school-age children. Chrisi Bailey explored photographic education with young children until her death in 1986.

This year's award was presented to children from Hempshill Hall Primary School in Nottingham by Professor Andrew Motion, Poet Laureate and member of the Arts Council. The children took photographs with a digital camera and a microscope, using plants and flowers found in the school grounds. The resulting work combines the children's beautiful pictures with their poetic responses to the images.

The images are at: **www.chrisibaileyaward1999.ndirect.co.uk**

Front image:
by Hempshill Hall Primary School in Nottingham, winners of the 1999 Chrisi Bailey Award
(see back page for more details)

Arts Council of England
14 Great Peter Street
London SW1P 3NQ

Tel: 0171 333 0100
Fax: 0171 973 6590

www.artscouncil.org.uk

Charity registration number: 1036733

sherbert
iceberg
reflected
in ice cold
shimmering
waters

Season's Greetings

THE **ARTS COUNCIL** OF ENGLAND

John Pick

The Two Faces of Chris Smith

The practice of putting an economic value, and nothing else, upon heritage and the arts was well established when Dr Smith assumed office. The Lottery had already wrought its destructive ends, and the importance of 'mapping' the cultural and creative industries (so targets could be set and controls established) was already well understood in Whitehall. What was quite distinctively New Labour, however, was the adoption of a coarse, foreign method of cultural control, which came, not from the Kremlin, but from Australia. It happened because a year before he was elected, Tony Blair (while mouthing the usual stuff about the importance of the arts), felt it important to fly to Australia to do a deal with Rupert Murdoch over the direction New Labour would take in office. While there, he became enamoured of a broad, crude (and short-lived, as it turned out) cultural blueprint being touted by the Keating Labour government. It was called 'Creative Nation'. This 'cultural vision' was emphatic about two things – its size, and its economic significance: 'This cultural policy is also an economic policy. Culture creates wealth. Broadly defined, our cultural industries create 13 billion dollars a year. Culture employs. Around 336,000 Australians are employed in culture-related industries.'[1]

This 'broadly defined' cultural survey had been underpinned by a detailed statistical 'mapping' of the Australian 'industries', undertaken by an Australian business organisation called Cultural Concern,

working to the Statistical Advisory Group of the Cultural Ministers Council. Work on it had begun in 1986 – two years before the much less ambitious Economic Importance of the Arts in Britain was published here. 'Creative Nation' was less a cultural policy than an economic smokescreen to hide the fact that the government did not want to think about culture in general, or the arts in particular.

Mr Blair was mightily impressed by the Murdoch-friendly approach and the bigness of the Australian vision, and when he returned home he ordered his shadow Heritage Minister, Jack Cunningham, to scrap the detailed arts policies that had been painstakingly prepared in opposition, and instead to draw up something wide-ranging and big, fashioned on the Australian model. As a result, New Labour came to power ready not just to adopt the Australian terminology, but also to adopt its techniques. When the new Culture Ministry put out its 'mapping document', it was largely cribbed from the work of Cultural Concern.[2]

At that strangely macho time, Dr Smith came to office to find himself heading a politicised bureaucracy whose crude but determined beliefs must have offended his academic self. He was working under a Prime Minister who had called for a 'big' cultural vision, and who believed he had found it in the crude generalities of the Australian Labour Party, and alongside cabinet colleagues and ministry officials who still secretly admired Mrs Thatcher's way

with the cultural sector: her refusal to engage in debate except on her own mercantile terms, her determination to view 'heritage' and the arts world as just parts of Great Britain PLC, and her love of simple solutions to complex problems. With the establishment of the Lottery was spawned a massive bureaucracy of consultants and assessors; in the process, the relationships of artists with their audiences was distorted, and the arts were relentlessly undermined by the powerful government-backed promotion of its own short-term, tawdry satisfactions.

Meanwhile, the practice of recording artistic activity by economic outcomes was well begun, and was proving a nice little earner for another army of cultural number-crunchers. So Dr Smith had to find a way of reconciling his fastidious recoil from these horrors with his loyalty to the cultural diktats of his Labour leadership. So 'Chris' was born, and Chris spoke a strange polygabble that tried to bind together eternal truths about the arts with the Ozziebabble of New Labour cant:

The Department's interests cover the spectrum of life in Britain, from the popular culture of music, television and the drama of the Lottery draw, to those areas of the arts that, in Matthew Arnold's classic definition of culture are a 'pursuit of total perfection by means of getting to know ... the best which has been thought and said in the world'.[3]

The surprise here is not that all cultural activities should be seen to belong to one continuum, but that the Lottery draw should now take its place alongside music in the popular culture.

But then, New Labour's redefinition of the 'creative industries' for the purposes of 'Creative Britain' was equally eclectic. In them, the arts are set alongside activities that not very long ago were regarded as the very opposite of 'the best which has been thought and said'. Components of the new 'industries', such as advertising, the antiques business, TV and radio, computer games and the fashion world would, like gambling, once have been thought of as belonging to quite another realm. Now, they are all lumped together for the purposes of government accounting, in one 'industry', with a currently estimated combined wealth of some £50 billion. All semblance of critical judgement has been dropped; Boy George and Simon Rattle are fellow workers in the 'music industry'; Jeffrey Archer's works take their place alongside the novels of Jane Austen, and Mr Murdoch's *Sun* newspaper, in the 'publishing industry'. On the grounds of their real historical, cultural or artistic value, most of the goods included in the 'creative industries' should not be there. But plainly that is no longer an issue. The only thing that matters is how well things sell. In Chris's loyally Blairite words: 'The continuing strength of our "creative industries" opens up the prospect of Britain enjoying immense competitive advantage, as economic activity becomes even more global and ever more competitive'.[4]

Yet if competitive economic advantage is the sole or chief point of these creative activities, then one is bound to ask why the Government does not include profitable segments of the porn or drug industries in its calculations. They make plenty of money. Or, if the point is partly to 'rebrand' the British way of life, why is domestic gardening, a briskly profitable domestic sector, involving one way and another all of our diverse ethnic communities, and a cause of delight to tourists, not included?

Yet to ask such questions is to miss the point. The true objection to New Labour's culture actions is not to the minutiae of their policies, but to the system itself. The new Ministry of Culture, and the gabbling pile of self-important quangos that now speak for British culture, are themselves an important cause of the cultural catastrophe we face, and for three reasons. First, because they are collectively wasteful of resources – of the tens of millions spent on them, of the time and space they consume, and of the critical language that they take over and destroy. Second, because in treating the heritage and the arts as saleable goods, useful only for lining the national coffers, they strip them of their true meaning and value, and so make our futures bleaker. Third, because they inhabit a closed world, and talk only in their own private language, and so are

determinedly blind to the realities of cultural power. Their 'cultural policies' are the aggrandised posturings of the defeated Führer in the underground bunker. They concentrate upon imposing a flabby, self-destructing political correctness on their own remaining subordinates, while ignoring the enemies circling all about.

Anybody who takes any interest at all in contemporary events is bound to be struck by the huge gulf between the great events that are really shaping our futures and actually reinforcing or changing the way in which Britain is perceived abroad, and the small-scale, semi-secret gestures of the cultural bureaucrats who claim to be 'redefining the present by the future' or 'rebranding Britain'. Above ground, Britain is still selling arms profitably all over the world, and at home, still turning away asylum-seekers, still trying to eradicate institutionalised racism from some of its public services, and still attempting to tame its racist thugs. Meanwhile, in the bunker, an Arts Council of England initiative called 'The Wider Picture' is planning for 'Cultural Diversity' in Britain. It is going to achieve this by giving grants only to those whose work, in the opinion of its bureaucrats, 'reflects the cultural mix of society'.

Now there is of course nothing wrong with the intention (though one might wish to see the participating groups being asked to do something rather more challenging than simply reflecting what the Arts

Council thinks of as a correct cultural mix). What is wrong is its midget scale, allied to its faint note of self-congratulation as it proposes another gesture in lieu of action. A real policy of cultural diversity would tackle the gutter press, the dreadful inequalities of the education system, the racist bile on the Internet, the bias at all levels in employment, and the slack law-making that allows so many private clubs (of all kinds) in Britain to practice racial exclusion. But then, a real cultural policy would confront the threats from dumbed-down television, from porn on the Internet, from the greed promoted by the Lottery, from the self-interested materialism of the global corporations, and from the amoral head-line-grabbing of modern academia, instead of joining them in their headlong rush towards a society where wealth is the sole criterion of value. Above all, a real cultural policy would surely be set up in opposition to Rupert Murdoch, not to appease the mercantile forces he so obviously represents.

Is it too late for Dr Smith to avoid the dreadful trap he has helped to dig? Is it yet possible that he might acknowledge the fact that cultural life is given vitality and meaning by the past, not by government plans for the future? I dare to think that hope has not been extinguished. And I base my belief partly on the fact that in recent months he seems to have disowned his book and has spoken rarely of his cultural vision, but largely because, as Minister for Culture, he has said practically

nothing about the shambolic cultural mess that is the State-created Greenwich Dome. That which was to reveal to us both the glorious future, and the way in which the present is being shaped by it, that which was to draw more than twelve million souls to gaze and wonder, has of course turned out to be meaningless and garish, as culturally void as a Las Vegas hotel, and an entirely suitable venue for Miss World 2000, which it is shortly to host. It may seem over-optimistic to put my trust in a significant silence, but I rather suspect that there is a spiritual reawakening within Dr Smith. The political scales may have fallen from his eyes. He has now seen the cultural future, and he knows it doesn't work.

1   'Creative Nation', 1994.
2   *The National Culture – Leisure Industry Statistical Framework*, Corporate Concern, 1989.
3   *The Times* (London), 15 July 1997.
4   *Ibid.*

David Heathcoat Amory, MP

The British Art Market

Extract from *A Market Under Threat: How the European Union could Destroy the British Art Market* (Chapter 2), Centre for Policy Studies (London), 1998

The total British Art market is comprised of about 10,000 businesses with an annual turnover of just over £2.2 billion.[1] The Bond Street and St James' area of London contains the world's greatest concentration of auctioneers and dealers. Outside London is a huge network of similar but smaller businesses. Then there are the support services, such as conservation, restoration, the organisation of fairs and exhibitions, and shipping, insurance and freight. When all these ancillary business are taken into account, the economic impact of the British art and antiques market is larger than the music business and comparable to the book industry. Total employment is estimated at just under 51,000.

For many years, the British art market fed largely off domestically generated business, such as country house sales. Much less business is now available from these sources and the consequence has been a growing dependence on trade from abroad. The big auction houses rely on works of art being sent to London for sale. This attracts foreign customers who not only buy at auction but are also vital to the trade through specialist dealers. Businesses outside London also often sell works originally sent from abroad, or are dependent on foreign buyers at some point in the chain.

The large number of foreign visitors coming to Britain to buy and sell art is itself a source of foreign exchange earnings. For 1995, this is estimated at some £2.8 billion. As well as being spent directly on art and antiques, it benefits hotels, restaurants, shops, taxis and the tourist trade generally.

The prominent position of London in the art trade illustrates a truth about the United Kingdom's place in the world and the unusual position that it holds in the European union.

Throughout our history, two forces have exerted their influence upon us: the Continental and the Atlantic. On the one hand, Continental Europe has always exerted a pull natural to its proximity; our membership of the EU and the Single Market reinforces it. On the other hand, Britain is also a global trader. This 'Atlantic' side to our national character explains the extraordinary spread of the English language, the huge size of our overseas investments,[2] and the fact that over half of our total foreign earnings still come from countries outside the EU.[3] This dual nature explains how Britain has built up very strong positions in a number of financial and trading sectors. The international art market is one of them, rather similar to the position of the City of London in the financial sector.

But it is vulnerable. Art is a totally mobile commodity. A picture can just as easily be sold in Geneva, Tokyo or New York as in London. Competition in this global marketplace is fierce and unrelenting. The decision regarding where to sell is highly sensitive to comparative costs. If one art centre faces the imposition of an additional tax or regulatory levy, business simply moves away to the others.

The British art market faces exactly this threat. It comes from two taxes proposed and promoted by the European Union. Like a nutcracker, these taxes hold the British art market between them. If the nutcracker closes, it will do irreparable harm to an important British industry, and prove beyond doubt that the internal politics of the EU count for more than the economic wellbeing of a member state of European success in the wider world.

1   The figures are taken from the MTI report, *The British Art Market* (1997), prepared for the British Art Market Federation.

2   Direct and portfolio assets totalled £731.7 billion in 1996 – more than any other G7 country (source: *Pink Book*, 1997).

3   51.1% of current credits were from non-EU countries in 1996 (*ibid.*).

DEMOLISH
SERIOUS
CULTURE!

Stewart Home

Why Public Subsidy and Private Sponsorship Can't Save Art from Complete and Utter Irrelevance

To say that the current system of funding the arts is inequitable is to state the obvious, although many of those involved in the cultural industries are unable to understand this. These convenient mental lapses cannot simply be put down to a confusion over terminology. 'Art' and 'culture' are sometimes used interchangeably, while at other times 'art' is used to differentiate allegedly superior cultural forms from light entertainment (the music of Stockhausen, for example, being identified as 'art' and thus as somehow inherently superior to the work of Jim Reeves). Misunderstandings stem not just from terminological sloppiness but also from the fact that in order to function effectively, the hierarchical and highly commodified culture industry requires a good number of those ensnared in its activities to be thoroughly mystified about exactly what it is they are doing.

In class societies, culture is stratified on class lines (this is a bald statement but some of the ways in which it can be elaborated will be evident to anyone who has made a close reading of *Caste, Class & Race: a study in social dynamics* by Oliver C. Cox). Thus, what I am saying is not that culture is irrelevant to most people, but that the way in which it is integrated into everyday life is haphazard and uneven. Precisely because it rarely receives direct subsidies, popular culture is forced to make itself relevant to a broad audience. Popular culture takes on board the social longings of its audience, and while those selling it deliberately confuse the notion of community with that of consumption

(which is not even an impoverishment of community but rather its antithesis), popular culture must at least address the wants and desires (albeit in a distorted fashion) of those it sets out to seduce into a purchase. Musicians playing in Afro-American idioms are looking for a response to what they do; they don't expect their audience to sit silently contemplating the notes they are hearing. They want their audience to get down, make a noise, shuffle and shout – in short, to join in and express themselves as a community. While the relationship between audience and pop performers leaves much to be desired, it is infinitely preferable to the way in which much so-called 'serious' culture is consumed. In the gallery or the concert hall, the audience is supposed to contemplate works of 'genius'. There is no room for spontaneity, for improvisation, for truly human contact and meaningful human relationships. The audience for classical music is supposed to focus on artistic intentions, as if the composer can exist independently of both the musicians playing his works (successful classical composers are usually both white and male, and the blatant institutional discrimination that underlies this provides yet another reason why 'serious' music should not be subsidised), and the broader audience listening to them. The classical concert replicates industrial society with audience, musicians, conductor and composer occupying specialist roles. In 'serious' culture, quick-witted, improvised elaborations of human community are abandoned in favour of brutal and numbing celebrations of human alienation.

The consumption of art is supposed to be improving and this is generally the basis on which it is subsidised, but in reality, for most people contact with 'serious' culture is largely a negative experience. However, even if it were feasible to judge objectively the intrinsic merits of cultural productions (which is actually quite impossible since what really matters is the human relationships that produce cultures and which are simultaneously mediated and redefined by them), the bureaucratic ways in which grants and sponsorships are awarded would still result in the subsidy of the most boring, alienating and mediocre 'work'. Like the artists they subsidise, many arts administrators are unsure as to whether what they are involved in has any value at all. It is therefore important that it is made clear to those involved with 'serious' culture that not only are they failing to contribute anything positive to the world, they are actually doing a great deal of harm. The culture industry, and in particular the subsidised end of the culture industry, likes to portray itself as at loggerheads with business interests, but subsidised opera seats are still snapped up by business to help oil the wheels of commerce. Factions within the bourgeoisie may bicker between themselves over how to divide the spoils of the capitalist system, but at the end of the day, it is in the interest of all those involved in these arguments to defend capitalist exploitation. When cultural bureaucrats call for more money to be spent on the arts, what they really mean is that they want to feather their own nest. Since art subsidies are largely squandered on a useless bureaucracy,

it is imperative that while this money remains up for grabs, those making critiques of capitalist bureaucracy do all they can to expropriate these resources for deployment in the elaboration of a truly human culture.

What's actually required if culture is to serve human needs freely is the abolition of money (which would necessarily coincide with the abolition of classes and art as a separate sphere of human activity). While our lives remain distorted by the cash-nexus, a more creative and combative culture would emerge if all arts subsidies were cut and the money that presently funds a bloated bureaucracy were pumped into a comprehensive welfare system – or, at the very least, facilitated a return to 1960s/70s levels of unemployment benefits, since this would enable those who wanted to take time out from work and/or poverty to get their shit together, while simultaneously avoiding the absurd biases that characterise current arts funding. It is repugnant that vast sectors of the population are excluded from access to arts money on the utterly spurious grounds that they aren't 'artists', when being 'unproductive' can be a very 'productive' experience for anyone. Likewise, the abolition of all immigration laws and ultimately all national boundaries is essential if culture is to play its proper role in the development of free human communities.

DEMOLISH SERIOUS CULTURE!

Terry Atkinson

Eurostar Avant-Gardism Secured in Both Directions by Dumbing Down from London and Wising Up from Paris

Certain artworks initiated in the mid-1960s left a legacy that made both the epistemology and the ontology of art practice, the matter of how art was made and what it was made of and from, more complex. This complexity rendered the position of the established models of artistic subjectivity less secure. Or rather, it should have done. That mid-60s moment seems a world away from the present art climate of populism,[1] socially decorative, careerist networking as a substitute for intellectual exchange, and audience-access mania. Under the present populist flags of various hues, the contrary has happened. The old models of artistic subjectivity have not just been reinforced, but hyper-inflated, and none more so than the avant-garde model of the artistic subject.

This loss of security of the well-established models was treated in the mid-1960s by the practice of which I was a contributor, Art & Language, as an opening rather than a closure of possibilities; as an opportunity rather than a threat. The impact of this particular mid-60s work raised a number of questions. One of the most important was centred on the notion that the interrogation of the established models of the artistic subject might offer more possibilities of what that artistic subject might become than the ones originally on offer. Under this was subsumed the entire range of issues concerning the character and status of the art object.[2] The matter of what an artist might or might not become necessarily also

raised the matter of what an artist ought to become. In the mid-60s, it was the various communities of the art milieu, not least the art school community, that seemed especially worried by the matter of what an artist ought to be. In the common or garden art school equation, this *ought* reduced to what kind of objects/events an artist *ought* to produce in order to be counted an artist. To put it less than elegantly: an artist was recognised as an artist by the type of work that he or she produced, rather than through the work being recognised by the cognitive performance of the given person. At best, first the person (producer) had to be recognised as an artist via the objects of that person's production before any criteria were brought to bear to evaluate the cognitive performance of the potential artist.

In the day-to-day business of producing/teaching[3] art, this 'ought' panned out as a great many people having a pretty clear idea of what art objects *ought* to look like and *ought* to continue to look like, which simply meant: to enjoy the status of 'artist', a person ought to produce such and such a range of objects. Hence, the widely held view that a person could be detected as an artist by the type of objects they produced. Or, to put the equation in its opposite form – a person who produced objects/events that did not look like art was not an artist.[4] What this view entailed in the longer historical run was that the art of the future would look very much like the art of the past. Contrary to its rhetorical bluster that the practice was 'radical' –

and just as much today as in the mid-60s – the practice is seemingly a very conservative one when it is dominated by such a prescriptive view. But if the art of the future was to look very much like the art of the past, then a counter proposal at least tiptoes into the margins of the scene – namely, could the art of the future, whilst looking very much like that art of the past, at the same time, not *be* like the art of the past? What, then, is separated here, is looking from *being*. What is tentatively suggested is that the function of art being, may not reside, solely at least, in the function of how art *looks*. This has been the sphinx-like riddle of the legacy of the most unyiedling Conceptualist[5] practices of the 1960s. Such a line of questioning raises the matter of tradition, of the respective cognitive strategies of continuity and breach. For the moment, let us leave this as a moot point, and approach the matter from another direction.

Amongst the most embedded models of the artistic subject today is the avant-garde model. It is the conventional model *par excellence*. This model embraces many kinds of production from painting and sculpture to performance and installation. The latter term, 'installation', is a kind of catch-all word that may embrace any, some, or all of the other three. And performance itself may also embrace any number of these and also cross into other art areas – say, theatre with a significant sound-based component, or music with a singular sound-based function. The categories of installation and

performance are typical indexes of the complexity of the practice, not only internally, but also externally, at the practice's boundaries with other arts. This has been part of the complexity of practice since the mid-60s. The categories of performance and installation have been coined to try and help structure the range of objects that contemporary art produces. We can savour the range: paintings, sculptures, bottle-racks, snow-shovels, texts, preserved sharks, soiled beds, etc. – it is a familiar catechism. It is the list of the objects of art, the ontology of art production. But the list as list is cognitively insignificant because the avant-garde model of the artistic subject is currently little more than an automated and cyclical expansion of the list. In this form, it is not so much an expansion as a reproduction, and the thing it also reproduces is the model of the avant-garde artistic subject. It is not so much that the list should be continually reproduced – and the market and the so-called art-critical community asks little more than that it be reproduced – it is the epistemological complexity that produced the ideological space for the ontological items in the first place that needs taking up, that needs to be at the centre of the inquiry, that needs an ongoing interrogation. The reproducing list generates an ontological zoo in which, seemingly, there is less and less critical purchase.

The smart old American philosopher Willar Van Orman Quine[6] has stated that what gets singled out is a result of how one does one's singling out. What, at the start of these remarks, I termed 'epistemological complexity', is the move to interrogating the singling out processes themselves, rather than the objects that get singled out as the result of any given process. This latter is the ontology. By late 1967, the centre of the Art & Language inquiry had moved from what we might call 'object production' to an examination of how objects get constructed, from what they are constructed, what kinds of objects there may be – in short, to how intriguing and troublesome the notion of an object is.[7] By this time, any objects that Art & Language did produce (mostly texts or text-based production) were in the service of interrogating the singling out process. Inside this inquiry, no object was secure, and no established model of artistic subject was granted privilege.

This seems to be in contradistinction to the current conditions of production in the art world. The YBAs, for example, seem totally secure in their subscription to the avant-garde model of the artistic subject. No model has a more settled outlook and cognitively self-satisfied programme than that which persistently congratulates itself on being 'radical' and 'advanced'. The avant-garde model, with its now long-acquired mechanical recipes for being 'advanced' and its unquestioned convention for treating itself as 'unconventional', is now a self-congratulationary historical repository. The YBAs, with their caravan of backers, theorisers and

camp followers, are a current exemplification of the congealment of the avant-garde model. This paradigm of the artist as a self-confirming centre of truth – and the avant-garde model is just that – means a proliferation of object production within a fixed and rigid epistemological band. It means all kinds of object production reinforcing the same kind of subject production.

The term 'dumbing down' is a sound-bite standing for the climate of anti-intellectualism that is now so widespread in the art world. So-called theory in the art world/art schools is more or less literary and more or less bad (not least in the prolific effusions of what I might call here 'French Theory', which have been so characteristic in the milieu over the last twenty years or more),[8] and has been set to the service of prescribing, reinforcing and hyper-inflating these overlearned models of the avant-garde subject. My own view is that whilst one can sympathise with an outlook that is critical of and rejects such theorising, it is, nevertheless, a rich historical paradox that both the theorisers and the artists who have rejected them, embrace the same model of the artistic subject – the avant-garde model. The pro-theory people learn the model by, so to speak, 'French' rote; the anti-theory people slot comfortably into one of the most conditioned reflexes of the avant-garde model: the theory, often lumpen, of anti-theory. It is in this sense of the embrace of both theory-of-theory adherents and theory-of-anti-theory adherents that the

regime of the avant-garde model of the artistic subject is a totalitarian one – both pro and con, it aims to populate the world with endless, cyclical avant-garde subjects.

1   Art talk is plagued by terms used in such a general and unspecific way as to be rendered near-enough useless. 'Populism' is one of these terms (so is 'Conceptualism', see note 5 below). This being the case, I had better try and write a bit more about how I intend to use the word here. I have one specific context in mind, but this, I guess inevitably, overlaps with others. This is the increasingly widely consumed avant-garde notion of the artist as a popular stereotype. The historical pathways that have led to the formation of this stereotype have provided a number of components. Again, I have one particular component in mind here.

I am thinking of the telescoped and caricatured Freudian interpretations that increasingly infiltrated popular culture throughout the last century, not least the notion of the artist as a hysterical type. Or perhaps, working to a tighter historical specification, a view that believes the possession of a hysterical nature to be a necessary condition in the constitution of an artistic temperament. At the end of the nineteenth century, conservative art critics held hysteria to be a sign of artistic degeneration. By the end of the twentieth century, the possession of such a hysterical condition as a necessary condition for producing profound work had become a conservative stereotype in itself. For example, Picasso, Warhol and Bacon might all have been comfortably fitted into this wide-ranging stereotype. Perhaps more spookily, both Warhol and Bacon may have actively sought to promote such a view of the artist. But this populist stereotype rests not

so much on whether an artist can be clinically diagnosed as hysterical, as on them being believed to be hysterical, both by themselves and by the art milieu at large – and this needn't depend on an explicit acknowledgement, the naming, of hysteria.

One of the clearest examples of the popular consumption of this stereotype of artistic temperament is an anthem, written in the early 1970s, to Vincent Van Gogh by the American popular songwriter Don Mclean, unsurprisingly entitled, *Vincent*. It is a eulogy to the 'misjudged and mistreated'. Van Gogh is perhaps the exemplar of the popularly conceived and consumed model of artist as supersensitised because hysterical. It now seems to be confirmed that Van Gogh suffered (if indeed this is the right way of characterising the matter) from temple-lobe epilepsy. This very week, I heard Susan Greenfield describe the result of Van Gogh's condition as 'awesome creativity' (*Brain Story*, BBC 1, 18 July 2000). I'm not exactly sure what follows from this – that all artists who are considered to have produced profound work have some such condition, or whether there is a prescriptive tone somewhere behind the evaluation, that artists need, or even ought, to have such a condition.

The ontological zoo – the wide range of objects of art production – is taken to be symptomatic of the alleged hysterical artistic condition. Not only are the bottleracks, the Cubist images of women, piles of bricks as sculpture, texts as art, butchered cows, soiled beds etc., taken to be the necessary hysterical outbursts of the artistic temperament, but the fact that Charles Saatchi is willing to pay £150,000 for the soiled bed is seen as a necessary addendum to the hysterical condition. This populist stereotype is, then, an undiscriminating one. (For a series of intriguing arguments and a telling, wide-ranging gathering of historical information on the notion of hysteria, see

Hystories: Hysterical Epidemics and Modern Culture, Elaine Showalter, Picador, 1997; on related matters, Rewriting the Soul: Multiple Personality and the Sciences of Memory, Ian Hacking, Princeton University Press, 1995.)

2   One of the prominent controversies in mid-1960s practice concerned what could and could not be counted as an art object. Duchamp was a central historical figure in this controversy. The text or conversation was widely seen in the art milieu as a typical kind of Art & Language 'object'. We spent some considerable time and energy protesting that such a characterisation of our work was likely to misrepresent us. Despite this, the characterisation endured. Under this characterisation, 'reading' was subsumed as some kind of (fancy) looking. Whilst it is clear that looking is a necessary condition of reading in sighted persons, it is also clear that most forms of looking are not reading; therefore, though looking may be a necessary condition of reading, it is not a sufficient condition. The widespread view of Art & Language texts as 'visual' objects turned text into a specious kind of pictorialism, a pictorialism of the text . Mostly, the response was something like: 'if they expect us to read it then it's not art, it's literature, philosophy or something!' Art & Language was always interested in text as reading, not text as visual. Text as reading was an important part of the epistemological methodology. We bitterly resisted attempts to treat our texts as one more readymade. Hence the Art & Language critiques of the Duchampian tradition began right here, at this point. What we were interested in was interrogating the artistic subject. Any production and interrogation of objects rested on this. A characteristic problem in the inquiry was a 'chicken-egg' one: whilst the object produced was a symptom of the condition of the subject (one important condition governing the kind of object produced being the view of the

artistic subject that the producer had of him or herself), the reverse was also the case: the object produced also frequently tended to reinforce the view of the artistic subject, which had been a primary condition of the kind of object produced. In most cases, the production was a reinforcement mechanism of the presently held model, and even when it wasn't, a move from a presently held model of artistic subject would be, invariably, a move to an equally well-established model of artistic subject. We are back, again, to the matter of breach and continuity – an essay in itself of far larger extent than these remarks.

3   It tends to be forgotten these days, perhaps, that the first formation of Art & Language was founded as a teaching formation at Coventry and Hull Colleges of Art, and since teaching was practice, then teaching was part of Art & Language's production. Teaching was producing. There was no divide, ontological or epistemological, between teaching and producing, as there is in most art teaching today.

4   The business of producing work that does not look like art of either the past or the present might be taken as a kind of epiphany of at least the conceits of the avant-garde model. But clearly, everything will depend on what we mean by 'looks like'. There is clearly a sense in which Cubist paintings looked like paintings; they were 'advanced' in respect of their resources of representation as painting. This again, is the matter of continuity and breach of a given tradition. Dumchamp's readymades/found objects strategy put the whole universe of objects, including the object of the universe itself, within range of being granted art status by virtue of an act of declaration. But the resources of expression of the declaration device were applied to the visual – thus everything that could be discerned through the faculty of vision was within range. Whilst the bottlerack may not have looked like art, it clearly had a look – it

looked like a bottlerack, for example. The range of questions that Art & Language tried to raise was to produce work, the representational resources of which were not dependant on how they looked as object, but how they read (looked) as symbolic system. There is, then, a sense in which we do read a Cubist painting or a Duchampian readymade, and in this very broad sense, Art & Language productions were very much like the art of the past. Nevertheless, it was widely argued, in say 1967, that Art & Language texts did not look like the art of the past or the present. The story is a long one and requires some considerable attention, but this brief sketch may, hopefully, provide some picture of what I mean by the increase in epistemological and ontological complexity.

5   'Conceptualism' is a bucket term that catches many kinds of practice of the past thirty years or more. As such, it is a more or less useless term. One finds oneself using it only because it is so widely employed – which is a poor excuse. Perhaps if we were to find a serviceable term that would pick out the characteristics of Art & Language works, it would not be 'Conceptualism'. A clear example of the term rendered useless was the panoply of intra-contradictory work caught under its currency at the exhibition 'Live in Your Head' at the Whitechapel Art Gallery in February–March 2000.

6   One of the doyens of twentieth century Anglo-American philosophy, much of whose work was a prominent beacon in Art & Language labour 1967–70. We were intrigued by such Quinean sorties as the arguments to naturalise epistemology, that we might well dispense with the notion of mind, etc. Since I left Art & Language in 1974, I have persistently consulted Quine's work in my practices.

7   Michael Baldwin and myself devised a number of projects in 1966–68 particularly, inquiring into a number of kinds of objects – mental objects, intensional objects, abstract

objects, objects from the realm of quantum physics, etc. Amongst the many intriguing things that these projects raised, at least for us, was a notion of the limits or otherwise of representation. Bertrand Russell's philosophical work in the first half of the twentieth century is awash with ingenious stabs at positing and defining a whole range of objects, many of which ideas, following the strictures of his analytical method, he moved on to discard.

8   Russell too, is some use here. What he terms, in his History of Western Philosophy (George Allen and Unwin, 1945), 'literary philosophers', Nietzsche and Heidegger for example, have been the dominant model for French theorising in the art schools. Russell's attack on Nietzsche's concept of the artist-tyrant, in the book cited above, is a keen attack on the Romantic roots of the model of the avant garde. As is his critique of Byron in the same book. Paradoxically, Russell seems to have been susceptible to more liberal versions of the same model. (See the essay 'The English Verb to Russell' in my Fragments of a Career, Silkeborg Museum , Denmark, 2000). The alleged 'Death of the Enlightenment Grand Narratives' scenario, beloved of Lyotarde et al., has been a significant element in fuelling the anti-science sentiments of many current cultural cadres, and the fall back into superstition, theological heavy breathing, and nature fetishes so characteristic of many of these cadres.

Gerry Robinson

The Creativity Imperative: Investing in the Arts in the Twenty-first Century

Extract from 'The Creativity Imperative: Investing in the Arts in the Twenty-first Century', *New Statesman* Lecture, Banqueting House, Whitehall, 27 June 2000

I'd like to go back to when I took up my role at the Arts Council two years ago. I was very quickly branded as someone who was simply there to close it down or, at best, to slim it down. [...] But what interested me, what I saw as the prize, was the opportunity to achieve a real change in the arts.

I wanted to put the creator and creativity right back at the centre – something that I sensed very early on had been lost by the Arts Council and by parts of the arts community. I wanted to help provide every person, regardless of class, age, economic status, race and social background, with a chance to enjoy the arts. I wanted to embed the arts in education and to embed education in the arts.

I wanted to be part of making our arts the best in the world, to promote the intrinsic value of the arts, as that which gives meaning to our lives, the thing that makes the essential difference between existing and living. These were the real goals. That was the prize. [...]

A word now about the current debate – in my view a false debate – about the intrinsic versus the instrumental value of the arts; a false dichotomy between art for art's sake, as opposed to art and its social and economic impact. A number of commentators have characterised us as only interested in the arts as social engineers. My own position on this, and the position of the Arts Council, is very clear. Not even the most self-professed philistine can imagine life entirely without stories, pictures, plays, poems, songs or dancing. And those stories, pictures, plays, poems, songs and dancing must first and foremost delight, fascinate, disturb, question, inspire, enchant and amuse people as human beings. They may also have relevance to economic regeneration, to health, social inclusion and so on, but only if they first have meaning to us as people.

The Arts Council's job is to support those art that provide meaning. Where there is that meaning, there is no question of the power and the relevance of the arts in terms of regeneration; special educational needs; enhancing racial understanding and tolerance; social inclusion; and economic development.

We should be proud of what the arts can do in these ways. We should celebrate their achievements whenever we can.

Sacha Craddock

Art between Politics and Glamour

Extract from an article first published in *tema celeste* (English edition), No. 81, July – September 2000.

What's happened? There has been an incredible shift in the attention the media pay to visual art in this country, and more often than not it's directed towards a few artists and institutions. You can hardly open a newspaper or magazine without a profile about an artist's lifestyle, designs or fashion jumping out. There's been a complete shift in audience attention too. Queues have formed outside the old Tate and the huge Tate Modern is already full. Is art easier to understand now? Have people become more sophisticated? Or is this about something else?

Avoiding the simple insistence that anything written on the subject is better than nothing, it would be good to look at where this change comes from – at the way artists, media and the main institutions bend towards each other like flowers to the sun. [...] Attitudes towards the way in which work is displayed at Tate Modern are indicative of this change. In the first three days that the building was open to the public, 123,000 people walked through the doors. The quiet relationship between artwork and individual is fast being replaced by 'been there', 'done that', and quickly grasping what the work is about. Controlling audience flow becomes the major factor with this new phenomenon.

Ten years ago, every broadsheet newspaper would have just one art critic. The critic was usually male and seemed to know automatically what he was going to write about every week. There was an obvious pecking order: important historical shows in major institutions; something at the Hayward Gallery perhaps; and that was it. Newspaper arts editors thought they knew what was best and, especially, what people could or couldn't understand. Contemporary art was considered difficult and to a certain extent it was. Now, at the end of a massive shift, contemporary art is everywhere – supposedly replacing pop music as the hottest, most fashionable medium. A limited list of artists have very high-profile personalities and their stardom is a far greater factor than the work they make. The introduction of a secondary, 'sidekick' critic on some newspapers started to mean shorter roundups and more risky coverage of lesser shows around the capital. The now infamous 'Freeze' exhibition, held in Docklands in 1989 and seen with hasty hindsight as the start of the Brit art thing, was covered by such a sidekick for only one national newspaper. But nobody was famous then, so the short article dealt with the work in the show, not the behaviour of the personalities involved. The relationship between London and the rest of the country remains even more awkward. Critics seldom venture out of the capital but coverage is all-encompassing. Even people who consider a particular critic stupid are nonetheless thrilled if he or she writes something good about their work. [...]

Tate Modern could not exist without substantial donations from America. Despite talk of Cool Britannia, very few people collect art here on a grand scale, and the government's professed thrill at all this is not accompanied by a shift away from the Tories' self-help attitude. Despite a solid chunk of Lottery money, the State would never assume responsiblity for such a project, as in Europe. In fact, Tate Modern continually has to raise massive amounts of funding to keep the machine going, in turn affecting all the country's other art centres. [...]

The Tate gallery's insistence on hosting the Turner Prize for the whole of the 1990s brought in thousands of punters and gave the impression that the institution was heavily involved with contemporary art. A shortlist of just four nominations a year simplifies it all for the press and allows greater concentration on personality. [...]

From the start, at art school, students find themselves involved in a justification process. The confusion between proper, critical practice and literal, often personal, narrative is established early on. The relationship between the need to justify and the guilt in pursuing the unreal does not seem to bother them in quite the same way as it once did. It culminates in a binge of popularism, concentration on attendance figures, and the strange contradiction of celebrating the lifestyle of a few. How does embedded moralistic guilt culminate in the celebration of the individual artist with romantic individualistic behaviour? Actually, quite easily, because the work itself becomes useful in a different manner. For this myth to work, one group of good artists must remain small and familiar to the public, while predatory curators hunt for the others – the unknown. The cacophony of build-up and self-congratulation has been exceptional. Newspapers are constantly writing about the new Tate: about the work, the architecture and the launch parties. The manufacturing industry's decline is turned on its head, apparently, by the conversion of an obsolete power station into a cathedral for modern art, and there is much jingoism and talk of doing better than the Americans. [...]

The word 'Modern' is in use again, but not in the strict, art-historical sense. Breaking with chronological display means that the contemporary can now be modern and, especially, the other way round. Art history, along with any history, is dead. Memories are short. And so drawings by Marlene Dumas are hung in a small gallery opposite Matisse's *Backs*. Fronts and backs, it might be thought, but the reason for making this work is not the front or back of anything. The chronological line-up of art, determining how museums used to be hung, has given way to displays in categories based roughly on old-fashioned painting genre. The labelling is too strong and limiting: 'Landscape, Matter, Environment' or 'Still Life, Object, Real Life', create a numbing, literal approach. Such divisions were done away with by modernism, yet Tate Modern's brief is to show work produced in the last hundred years. Ambiguity, in its true sense, is denied. Relationships are suggested between works of art, and such attention means an overbearing emphasis on the notion of comprehension, on subject matter as such. And so we come back full circle. For years, the media have been asking, 'What does it mean?' and worse, 'Is it art?' Attention always sought the strange and different, focusing on justification. A valiant attempt to circumvent that traditional limitation has unwittingly ended up with a defensive hang. Work is made for a number of reasons, in very different historical situations. The nuance of real conceptual difference must not be reduced to simple similarity, or similar appearance. It should be made clear to the public that selection is fallible, not totally authoritative; therefore, at a sophisticated level, everyone is part of the subject.

Mark Wallinger

Fool Britannia: Not New, Not Clever, Not Funny

Reprinted from *Who's Afraid of Red, White and Blue?*, David Burrows (ed.), ARTicle Press, University of Central England (Birmingham), 1998.

He who does not know history is destined to remain a child. Cicero

'Two bald men fighting over a comb' was how Borges described Great Britain's war with Argentina over the Falkland Islands. Sometimes the quarrel seems as distant and obscure as Jenkin's Ear. During the Miner's Strike (1984–85), people were incarcerated using any law on the statute-book, some dating back to the seventeenth century. A whole industry was dismantled to break union power in Britain. Hundreds of thousands of people marched against the trident missile and camped outside American airforce bases. Ronald Reagan's idea of a humorous aside was, 'let's bomb Russia'. These were the 1980s as I recall them.

During this time, I worked in a bookshop. It had a big Russian and Soviet department. The directors were Communist Party members, frequently at odds with the staff, who were predominantly Trotskyist, although Arthur in the storeroom was definitely a Tankie.

In retrospect, the factional disputes on the Left and changes in shop policy were an effective microcosm of the crisis of the Left in the world at large. Socialist Worker Party members were removed and replaced by Communist Party placemen. They turned out to be not very successful booksellers, so specialist booksellers and out-of-work actors began to take over as the business became more Thatcherite. In a

bizarre presage of history, the shop started selling t-shirts and badges with Bolshevik slogans and pictures of Lenin. Retro-Russian-Revolutionary chic became a fashion sensation; so much so that it eventually constituted over half the takings of the shop. I left in 1988. The following year was to see momentous upheaval. Fourteen staff who walked out in protest at the manner in which a colleague was dismissed were themselves fired. The shop was firebombed for stocking *The Satanic Verses*, and then closed altogether when the Soviet Union (which had payrolled it all along) collapsed.

Anyway, back in 1986 the National Front paid a visit and I got my head kicked in. Real things happened and sometimes I made works about them. *Tattoo* was made as a result of this attack. For all their violence, they struck me as a bunch of mother's boys scared of anything different, or 'other'. *Tattoo* was my attempt to come to terms with the passion of bigotry. Ironically, in the years to come, my work has been criticised for being too English. Middle-class squeamishness regarding self-analysis only allows 'Englishness' as a term denoting parochialism and nostalgia. Remember how the National Front successfully annexed the Union Jack as a symbol of white supremacy? Those wistful for an older order might do well to imagine what it is to be too Irish, too Serbian. In 1986, Englishness in extremis was imprinting itself firmly upon my mind. For those somewhat younger or

with narrower hindsight, the 1980s conjure something different. An age of opportunity, advantageous property deals, distressed jeans and Wham! The age of the entrepreneur, asset-stripping, privatisation, business built on hot air and recreational drugs. Advertising became hip. The exhibition 'Freeze' was paradigmatic of the 1980s and for many artists caught in that moment they have never ended. They are the first generation of artists to demand a lifestyle. Lofty ideas are for, well, ideal loft spaces in Clerkenwell. Man the barricades, I demand to be a restaurateur!

Charles Saatchi's gallery was the model for 'Freeze' and the warehouse and vacant-building shows that followed. These ex-industrial spaces were much too big for the exhibitions, and artworks became stunts – a small explosion here, a revolving bow-tie there. The spirit of PT Barnum infected the exhibitions, a sensibility that would persist into the 1990s. Empty buildings – or, strictly speaking, emptied buildings – were sought for a proliferation of artist-run shows. Buildings emptied of history and, by dint of the artworks, were removed from the context of urban blight and redevelopment. But never mind. 'Freeze' was received in terms of its own hype – as an event that was bigger than its actual content, which has never been properly evaluated. Even so, spurious claims have been made about the new relationship of art to galleries and collectors. The most bogus claim was that of

accessibility to a new audience. These were the most elitist of shows – a direct appeal to money, ladies who lunch, collectors and bigshots who were air-lifted into East London (*ich bin ein Londoner*).

Although much of the work was to leave locals as well as initiates nonplussed, contenders new to the field soon learnt the mantra, 'Great Space' and 'Who's curating that show?' In a uniquely tautological arrangement, to be invited to one of these shows was to be included in the in-crowd, a trend that reached its nadir in what might be called Scottish Mailing List Art. Specific art-world figures were targeted and asked for their contributions to an exhibition. Staggeringly, this obvious ruse sufficiently flattered the recipients, who were only too happy to oblige. What could be finer? They make the work for you and 'hey presto!', it has an instant Zeitgeist quality as well.

At this point, one begins to sense that something was missing. What was missing was the audience. In hot-wiring straight to the moneyed and the influential, the need for a discerning public was successfully avoided. In many ways, this resembled the radical overhaul effected by Direct Line Car Insurance – except the latter appealed over the heads of brokers direct to the public, rather than the other way around. Similarly, the effacement of a building as a productive space made of that loss a paradoxical kind of value. Art objects were invigorated by their capacity to empty out history; a no-space in no-time where nothing can fail to signify.

The search for vacant space with maximum headroom was shared with the nascent rave scene. Despite the claims made for a shared youth culture, Young British Art, as promoted by Saatchi, displayed little of the rave sensibility, preferring instead the *coup de theatre* so beloved of stadium rock (Harvey Goldsmiths College perhaps). Youth culture, which is as omnipresent and significant as acne, should not be confused with popular culture. It is just a phase art is going through because artists stay younger longer. Popular culture is the same team supported by generations of the same family. It is the kerbstones painted in Belfast. It is essential to people's identity.

Whilst popular culture hadn't much to answer for in new British art, it certainly influenced the way in which art was received at a critical level. For a number of reasons, art had given up the ghost under the weight of theory. The breakdown of distinctions between high and popular culture led to all manner of cultural produce and effluent being sifted and read as text. We were top-heavy with theorists (not to mention curators), who needed scant visual stimulus to write the work into the flat ergo of post-modernist irony: in short, what we had was nominalism. Artworks merely had to ring the appropriate bell to set the Pavlovian critics slav-

ering for interpretation.

If the artist has been reduced simply to repeating, appropriating, quoting or pointing a camera at a world awash with meaning and interpretation, the only meaningful position is to be a curator. Artists are too narrowly concerned to achieve an adequate overview of contemporary culture. Only the curator can bring any kind of authoritative commentary. Unafflicted by complacency, nepotism, sycophancy or careerism, they alone can provide artists with those links with collectors, or more often than not, taxpayers' money, in the quango-led non-meritocracy that constitutes the London art world.

Curators have the important advantage in that they need not take any responsibility for their actions. Any spin through the career of our most esteemed curators reveals how nimbly they can move from Conceptualism to Neo-Expressionism, Minimalism to mannequin abuse, without being court-martialled for dereliction of duty. Artists, however, are required to perfect their *schtick* and stick to it. It's tough enough for a curator, what with coming up with a title for a show, ringing up your mates, rummaging through art magazines. What would they do if the artist stopped painting, say, and took to the stage? In this brave new superstore it is unacceptable that the same people that make baked beans start manufacturing lawn-mowers. These modern-day Sophists have worked in concert

with a greedy market to ensure that artistic development is restricted to product placement and to niche marketing.

The artists themselves are curiously mute about their practice, perhaps because there is little to say about works that specialise in stating the obvious. Art is a commodity in the marketplace, women have had a raw deal, children's sexuality is spooky, we are all going to die, etc. The more feral artists have gone even further and forged a career by loudly proclaiming that they have nothing to say. However, they have learned one important lesson: context is all. What is lamentable on Jerry Springer is presentable in the gallery. The authority of the gallery creates a magical hiatus where pandering to the audience's appetite for sensation and vulgarity is seen in the guise of importance. However, nothing worthwhile can live long within inverted commas. The lazily adopted tag, 'Duchampian', that attaches to much current work is misleading. Far from being subversive, much of this work is subservient to the institution's validating power. But this 'radical' charade is of mutual benefit to the artists and galleries and the first step to success is to get yourself curated. ('They think it's funny, turning rebellion into money'.)

Artistic practice is the most critical practice. Art works should engage, articulate, problematise, open new ways of seeing, place the viewer in

jeopardy of their received opinions, move the artists to the limits of what they know or believe, excite, incite, entertain, annoy, get under the skin and when you've done with them, nag at your mind to go take another look.

Instead, today we have nominal triggers for regurgitating arguments better rehearsed elsewhere, which are neither illuminated nor in any sense present within the work. This is work that is essentially literary; work that repels the senses and takes us off to the library. The press release is the pitch, is the interpretation, is the whole work, ready to be phoned around the world; art that, in deconstructive logic, is a footnote to the text that justifies its existence. Young men and women emerging from the Courtauld and Sotheby's are guided by more pushy types towards young artists, anxious for their oeuvre to be bookended with scholarly appraisal. Once the artist is afflicted by this desire to be curated, or his work is deemed curatable, he or she is gradually but inexorably freed from accountability – hereafter the work need retain only a semblance of authenticity.

Paradoxically, the growth in numbers of curators has been accomplished at the expense of art history, which could be a thing of the past. At many art colleges, art history has been replaced as a mandatory part of fine-art courses by critical theory. An academy, an orthodoxy, a training scheme for artists has been created and, as in Mannerist paintings, gestures have lost their connectedness with meaning in the same way that sentiment comes apart from emotion. Within this academy, the student is best advised to choose between two basic strategies:

1 Be a swot and drop the right references in work that positively aches with its desire for approval.
2 Become a slag, an unholy innocent conduit of society's maladies and peccadilloes.

The first strategy gains Brownie points and is popular with curators who need the ballast of the dull and worthy to set against the raucous clamour of the second category.

Whichever the student chooses, they had better get on with it. I recently received a letter from a German museum:

It is really unfortunate that we could not consider your works for our project Urban Legends, London *– however, one of the main criteria of choosing the participants was not to exceed the age limit of thirty-five. This is of course a very bad reason to have, but strangely enough, it is an important one.*

Apparently, an artist's creative lifespan is similar to that of a footballer's – once the knees start playing up, the whole cerebral cortex shuts down. Myself, I've always preferred Piero to Ucello; he was so much younger.

Postmodernism, with its refutation of meta-narratives and ideology, has unfortunately served as a handy argument in favour of ignorance as an end-of-history stance. Andy Warhol, having already squeegeed history flat, left his successors nowhere to go, other than A to B (Anal to Banal). This, nevertheless, was the path chosen by the students of the 'Freeze' generation. 'Freeze' was the show in which student work broke through. Its greatest quality was its removal of expectations of depth and meaning, to be replaced by the society of the dilettante. In a world that begins and ends at one's fingertips, with an ineffectual past and a baseless future, all things are ever present and equivalent. Within this Fool's Paradise, if you look like an artist, live like an artist and behave like an artist, then you are indeed an artist.

NB. Some advice on deconstructing current critical terminology: simply replace 'not' for 'post', so that post-modern, post-conceptual and post-ironic become not-new, not-clever and not-funny.

Mark Wallinger, *Oxymoron*, 1996
flag, dimensions variable
© The Artist, courtesy of Anthony Reynolds Gallery, London

William Furlong

Conversation Piece

A constructed 'conversation' between Marcel Duchamp, Joseph Beuys, Andy Warhol and John Cage, 1998.

This artwork (which is available from Audio Arts), draws together four artists across time and space. All have 'appeared' individually on Audio Arts magazine and, apart from Duchamp, I have personally conducted the interviews.

Each of the artists' practice has made a significant intervention into contemporary culture, which has 'rippled out' from the centres of art to the wider spheres of social consciousness and discourse.

There can be no art-making by committee or consensus. The power and dynamic of art stems from its originality and independence. Art is not divisible by notions of audience and 'widening participation' and then realised. This isn't to say that strategies shouldn't be put in place to stimulate engagement (where it doesn't already happen) between the artist and audience. However, at the centre of any such engagement there has to be the dynamic experience of the artwork by the audience. Audiences are not anonymous constituencies easily reduced into categorised groups, but comprise individuals who participate in constructing the meanings and function of art: they should not be underestimated!

from left to right Andy Warhol on the occasion of his interview with William Furlong at Anthony d'Offay Gallery, London 1986, photo: Brian Westbury © Audio Arts; John Cage in his New York apartment on the occasion of his interview with William Furlong, 1983, photo: William Furlong; Marcel Duchamp photos by A. Rosenberg; Joseph Beuys and William Furlong at the Victoria and Albert Museum, London, 1983

Marcel Duchamp I have a very definite theory – call it 'theory', so that I can be wrong – that a work of art exists only when the spectator has looked at it. Until then, it is only something that has been done, that might disappear and nobody would know about it; but the spectator consecrates it by saying this is God, we will keep it, and the spectator in that case becomes posterity, and posterity keeps museums full of paintings today. My impression is that these museums – call it the Prado, call it the National Gallery, call it the Louvre – are only receptacles of things that have survived, probably mediocrity. Because they happen to have survived, there is no reason to make them so important and big and beautiful, and there is no justification for that label of 'beautiful'. It is because they have survived by the law of chance. We probably got many, many other artists of those same periods who are as beautiful or even more beautiful.

Joseph Beuys That is another problem. The artist now existing is a special type developed from the past. He runs the traditional line of the so-called culture without the ability to reach the body of the society. Therefore, he stands in an insulated field of action and cannot reach the point where everybody is involved with his life, is fully divided from the interests of the majority. Therefore from the point of view of the majority of the people with their sorrows and their problems, art looks like a special luxury – a luxury for the rich people, for privileged people, for people with more

advantage in class and those things, and therefore this is a division from art and society.

Andy Warhol I just do whatever I do, you know, just to get by.

John Cage Well, one could have those ideas, but what I was doing primarily was ignoring the difference between noises and musical tones to make a larger group that could be called 'sounds' and that would include both of those. Just as the word 'humanity' includes the rich and the poor, so my notion of sound is all of them, not just noises and not just musical tones but all of them.

MD All right, that is one way of looking at it. I do not consider myself any different from the others, and I think that my real feeling is that a work of art is only a work of art for a very short period. There is a life in a work of art that is very short, even shorter than a man's lifetime. I call it twenty years. After twenty years, an Impressionist painting has ceased to be an Impressionist painting, because the material, the colour, the paint has darkened so much that it is no more what the man did when he painted it.

JB Yes, you could also take this time of the necessity to change the understanding of art from the modern art – the ideology of moderns. You could shift it ten years later or ten years earlier, but in Germany that was the time when this modern art disappeared and a kind of revival took place, and some

very interesting painters appeared even after the Second World War. What I was missing with them was the theory of the thing. So in looking for the importance of modern art, which for me is very, very important, completely independent of whether it is German modernism or Dutch modernism or French or Italian modernism or Russian modernism – Mondrian for instance, or Malevich, Tatlin had Futuristic ideas, Cubist ideas, Surrealistic ideas. They are of the significance because they are the signalisation for future time where everything is done in person.

AW I guess so.

JC This is also for me the effect of modern painting on my eyes, so when I go around the city, I look, I look at the walls. And I look at the pavement and so forth as though I'm in a museum or gallery.

MD So I applied this role to all artworks, and they, after twenty years, are finished. Their life is over. They survive all right, because they are part of art history, and art history is not art. I don't believe in preserving. I think as I said that a work of art dies. It's a thing of contemporary life. In other words, in your life you might see things because it's contemporary with your life, it's being made at the same time as you are alive, and it has all the requisites of a work of art, which is to make, and your contemporaries are making works of art. They are works of art at the time you live, but once you are dead they die too.

JB It is especially interesting that Marcel Duchamp, who tried to destroy the whole kind of tradition, was hinting towards the common work with his *pissoir* piece, because he said 'this is an artwork only if it's shown in a special other context'. But he missed the point completely to find out the logic in saying that if this is a work of art that was done by some Mr Mutt or an anonymous worker in the factory, then the creator is really the worker. So he didn't enlarge all the work and all the labour to the new understanding of art as a necessity to study everything in humankind's labour from this point of view.

AW Uhmm

JC I think it must be because, you see, musicians at the beginning would not accept my work as music. They told me quite frankly in the 1930s that what I was doing was wrong. Whereas dancers accepted what I was doing. So I was accepted almost immediately into the world of theatre and the world of theatre includes the visual arts, includes poetry, includes singing. Theatre is what we're really living in.

MD Correct, yes, it's very important for me not to be engaged with any group. I want to be free, I want to free myself almost.

JB The idea of art is the principal means for other things in that the people do it by their own creativity: it is a very simple thing. I find it the rule that everybody is in a special way an artist in different fields. Surely, not all people are painters – this is a reduced understanding of art.

AW It's so exciting – it's just incredible.

JC I have a very good and close friend, William Anastasi, whose work I enjoy, and we play chess a great deal together, but we haven't collaborated on any actual work, though we might.

MD Yes, but this welding of two different sources of inspiration gave me a satisfactory answer to my research for something that has not been previously attempted. Being the young man who wants to do something by himself and copy the others, not use too much of the traditions. My research was in that direction, to find some way of expressing myself without being a painter, without being a writer, without taking one of these labels and yet producing something that would be an inner product of myself. The two things, mixing up the ideas and their visual representation attracted me as a technique after all. This hybrid form explains why I didn't have anyone to agree with me more or less, or to follow my ways of looking at it.

JB What would have been of very high importance because one could then have two kinds of discussions with existing ideology on society, the capitalistic systems and communistic systems. There is a germ in the right direction set down and practised by Marcel Duchamp,

but then he stays away from any other reflections, so he didn't understand his own work completely. So to be very modest, I could say that my interest was to make another interpretation of Marcel Duchamp, and I try at least to feel its most important depth, which was missing in this work. So, with such statements the silence of Marcel Duchamp is overrated.

AW Yes.

JC That it has to do also with the visual arts?

MD It is much more. It's been the non-conformist spirit which has existed in every century, every period, since man is man.

JB This whole project is my artwork, you know. This catalogue says exactly that the period of my drawings ended in principle in 1960. After 1960 the character of the drawings is going more in this direction, but there is not so much drawing, because I was interested more in action. Therefore the beginning of my activities is drawing. It is a time when I made sculptures, and I made objects.

AW I paint a lot, hand painting. I paint the background.

MD I thought it was a reaction against the retinal conception of painting, and I think it still is, because of the introduction of the conceptual, not entirely literary, because this is literary painting – it's been done before, of course, but

much deeper literary. It's using words, but everything that uses words is not necessarily literary, as you know.

JC You see, I found a way to collaborate with Merce Cunningham so that we really don't have to collaborate, we simply do our work separately after the most common-sense agreement, say twenty-five minutes, whether it's a humorous piece or whether it's going to be a serious piece. Then we simply work separately and we put it together in the theatre.

MD Very soon I felt impatience, so to speak, with Cubism – at least impatience in the way that I couldn't see any future for me in it. In fact I touched Cubism naturally, but the addition of movement in it, which seems to be Futuristic, is Futuristic only because the Futurists had spoken of movement, were speaking of movement at the time. That doesn't make it a new idea of theirs: movement was in the air. There was something more important than the Futurists for me in that case, which was the publication of photos of fencing or horses galloping and so on.

AW You did? Oh great.

JC After hearing a group of sounds, we say the name of the composer, like Beethoven. I would rather remember the sounds. This stems from a Buddhist idea that all beings, whether sentient, like human beings, or non-sentient, like sounds or stones, are the Buddha, so that we are living in an interpretation of

centres rather than moving towards one centre. Sometimes people get the idea, or get the experience, and it changes their way of living, and sometimes they don't.

MD Yes, it is ironical.

JB You could say it is a kind of 'sophia' – like philosophia – it is a sophia of humankind. This is the whole aspect of science. Then you find the special functions of science, the necessity to have materialistic science, because it is surely necessary.

AW Yes.

ANDY WARHOL

I JUST DO WHATEVER I DO, YOU KNOW, JUST TO GET BY

I GUESS SO

UHMM

IT'S SO EXCITING – IT'S JUST INCREDIBLE

YES

I PAINT A LOT, HAND PAINTING. I PAINT THE BACKGROUND

YOU DID? OH GREAT

1945

1997

SELECTED TEXTS

Lord Keynes

The Arts Council: Its Policy and Hopes

Reprinted from *The Listener* (London), 12 July 1945

In the early days of the war, when all sources of comfort to our spirits were at a low ebb, there came into existence, with the aid of the Pilgrim Trust, a body officially styled the Council for the Encouragement of Music and the Arts, but commonly known from its initial letters as CEMA. It was the task of CEMA to carry music, drama and pictures to places that otherwise would be cut off from all contact with the masterpieces of happier days and times: to air-raid shelters, to war-time hostels, to factories, to mining villages. ENSA was charged with the entertainment of the Services; the British Council kept contact with other countries overseas; the duty of CEMA was to maintain the opportunities of artistic performance for hard-pressed and often exiled civilians.

With experience, our ambitions and our scope increased. I should explain that whilst CEMA was started by private aid, the time soon came when it was sponsored by the Board of Education and entirely supported by a Treasury grant. We were never given much money, but by care and good housekeeping we made it go a long way. At the start, our aim was to replace what war had taken away; but we soon found that we were providing what had never existed even in peace time. That is why one of the last acts of the Coalition Government was to decide that CEMA, with a new name and wider opportunities, should be continued into time of peace. Henceforward, we are to be a permanent body, independent in constitution, free from red tape, but financed by the Treasury and ultimately responsible to Parliament, which will have to be satisfied with what we are doing when from time to time it votes us money. If we behave foolishly, any Member of Parliament will be able to question the Chancellor of the Exchequer and ask why. Our name is to be the Arts Council of Great Britain. I hope you will call us the Arts Council for short, and not try to turn our initials into a false, invented word. We have carefully selected initials that we hope are unpronounceable.

I do not believe it is yet realised what an important thing has happened. Strange patronage of the arts has crept in. It has happened in a very English, informal, unostentatious way – halfbaked if you like. A semi-independent body is provided with modest funds to stimulate, comfort and support any societies or bodies brought together on private or local initiative that are striving with serious purpose and a reasonable prospect of success to present for public enjoyment the arts of drama, music and painting.

At last the public exchequer has recognised the support and encouragement of the civilising arts of life as a part of their duty. But we do not intend to socialise this side of social endeavour. Whatever views may be held by the lately warring parties, whom you have been hearing every evening at this hour, about socialising industry, everyone, I fancy, recognises that the work of the artist in all its aspects is, of its nature, individual and free, undisciplined, unregimented, uncontrolled. The artist walks where the breath of the spirit blows him. He cannot be told his direction; he does not know it himself. But he leads the rest of us into fresh pastures and teaches us to love and to enjoy what we often begin by rejecting, enlarging our sensibility and purifying our instincts. The task of an official body is not to teach or to censor, but to give courage, confidence and opportunity. Artists depend on the world they live in and the spirit of the age. There is no reason to suppose that less native genius is born into the world in the ages empty of achievement than in those brief periods when nearly all we most value has been brought to birth. New work will spring up more abundantly in unexpected quarters and in unforeseen shapes when there is a universal opportunity for contact with traditional and contemporary arts in their noblest forms.

The Part Played by the BBC

But do not think of the Arts Council as a schoolmaster. Your enjoyment will be our first aim. We have but little money to spill, and it will be you yourselves who will by your patronage decide in the long run what you get. In so far as we instruct, it is a new game we are teaching you to play – and to watch. Our war-time experience has led us already to one clear discovery: the unsatisfied demand and the enormous public for serious and fine entertainment. This certainly did not exist a few years ago. I do not believe that it is a merely war-time phenomenon. I fancy that the BBC has played a big part, the predominant part, in creating this public demand, by bringing to everybody in the country the possibility of learning these new games, which only the few used to play, and by forming new tastes and habits and thus enlarging the desires of the listener and his capacity for enjoyment. I am told that today, when a good symphony concert is broadcast, as many as five million people may listen to it. Their ears become trained. With what anticipation many of them look forward, if a chance comes their way, to hearing a living orchestra and to experiencing the enhanced excitement and concentration of attention and emotion that flows from being one of a great audience all moved together by the surge and glory of an orchestra in being, beating in on the sensibilities of every organ of the body and of the apprehension. The result is that half the world is being taught to approach with a livelier appetite the living performer and the work of the artist as it comes from his own hand and body, with the added subtlety of actual flesh and blood.

I believe that the work of the BBC and the Arts Council can react backwards and forwards on one another to the great advantage of both. It is the purpose of the Arts Council to feed these newly aroused and widely diffused desires. But for success we shall have to solve what will be our biggest problem, the shortage – in most parts of Britain, the complete absence – of adequate and suitable buildings. There were never many theatres in this country or any concert halls or galleries worth counting. Of the few we once had, first the cinema took a heavy toll and then the blitz; and anyway, the really suitable building for a largish audience that the modern engineer can construct had never been there. The greater number even of large towns, let alone the smaller centres, are absolutely bare of the necessary bricks and mortar. And our national situation today is very unfavourable for a quick solution. Houses for householders have to come first.

Rebuilding of Our Common Life

And so they should. Yet I plead for a certain moderation from our controller and a few crumbs of mortar. The rebuilding of the community and of our common life must proceed in due proportion between one thing and another. We must not limit our provision too exclusively to shelter and comfort to cover us when we are asleep and allow us no convenient place of congregation and enjoyment when we are awake. I hope that a reasonable allotment of resources will be set aside each year for the repair and erection of the buildings we shall need. I hear that in Russia, theatres and concert halls are given a very high priority for building.

And let such buildings be widely spread throughout the country. We of the Arts Council are greatly concerned to decentralise and disperse the dramatic and musical and artistic life of the country, to build up provincial centres and to promote corporate life in these matters in every town and county. It is not our intention to act on our own where we can avoid it. We want to collaborate with local authorities and to encourage local institutions and societies and local enterprise to take the lead. We already have regional offices in Birmingham, Cambridge, Manchester, Nottingham, Bristol, Leeds, Newcastle-upon-Tyne, Cardiff and Edinburgh. For Scotland and for Wales, special committees have been established. In Glasgow, in particular, the work of the Citizens' Theatre is a perfect model of what we should like to see established everywhere, with their own playwrights, their own company and an ever-growing and more appreciative local public. We have great hopes of our new Welsh Committee and of the stimulus it will give to the special genius of the Welsh people. Certainly, in every blitzed town in this country one hopes that the local authority will make provision for a central group of buildings for drama and music and art. There could be no better memorial of a war to save the freedom of the spirit of the individual. We look forward to the time when the theatre and the concert-hall and the gallery will be a living element in everyone's upbringing, and regular attendance at the theatre and at concerts a part of organised education. The return of the BBC to regional programmes may play a great part in reawakening local life and interest in all these matters. How satisfactory it would be if different parts of this country would again walk their several ways as they once did and learn to develop something different from their neighbours and characteristic of themselves. Nothing can be more damaging than the excessive prestige of metropolitan standards and fashions. Let every part of Merry England be merry in its own way. Death to Hollywood.

Plans for London

But it is also our business to make London a great artistic metropolis, a place to visit and to wonder at. For this purpose, London today is half a ruin. With the loss of the Queen's Hall there is no proper place for concerts. The Royal Opera House at Covent Garden has been diverted to other purposes throughout the war. The Crystal Palace has been burnt to the ground. We hope that Covent Garden will be re-opened early next year as the home of opera and ballet. The London County Council has already allotted a site for a National Theatre. The Arts Council has joined with the Trustees of the Crystal Palace in the preparation of plans to make that once again a great People's Palace.

No one can yet say where the tides of the times will carry our new-found ship. The purpose of the Arts Council of Great Britain is to create an environment to breed a spirit, to cultivate an opinion, to offer a stimulus to such purpose that the artist and the public can each sustain and live on the other in that union that has occasionally existed in the past at the great ages of a communal civilised life.

Wyndham Lewis

Bread and Ballyhoo

Extract from *Wyndham Lewis on Art, Collected Writings 1913-1956*, Walter Michel & CJ Fox (eds.), Thames and Hudson (London), 1969, originally published in *The Listener*, 8 September 1949

[...] Those imposing institutions, the Arts Council or the British Council, by their mere existence serve to conceal from the public the neglect of contemporary art. It would be far better, from the artist's standpoint, if they were not there. Things could scarcely be worse: and without these make-believes it might become plain to the public how desperate things are.

Can we Afford a Renaissance?

When and why the building of this cultural facade began, we know. Lord Lloyd, actually, was the pioneer. That initiative 'to assuage the conscience of the age' – to show how art blooms in the midst of bloodshed – was sooner or later taken up on all hands. The action of the Pilgrim Trust developed into what is now the English equivalent of a Ministère des Beaux Artes, namely the Arts Council (the Chairman of the Arts Panel presumably the *de facto Ministre*). The great national collections, boroughs, even counties (Leicestershire for example) joined in. Now the Festival of Britain looms in the distance.

By 1945, such a facade had been run up, suggestive of a 'cultural awakening' – like a Renaissance façade in a Hollywood set – that, echoing the slogans of official propaganda, the public must have said to itself 'there has never been such an interest in the arts!' But there is of course no renaissance or rebirth. You cannot have a renaissance of the living arts without patrons, or patronage. Artists unfortunately cannot live on hot air. But the State has killed the geese that laid the golden eggs (or is in the process of discouraging them financially with such efficiency that most, as patrons, are already dead), but it has not itself become a giant goose, occupying the economic vacuum. If it believes it has done that, with its Councils, it is deceived, or has been deceived.

From the official attitude, the natural deduction would be that visual art in England today, though of course its existence had to be recognised, is not deserving of much attention. This estimate is violently unfair. Actually, England is so well-endowed with artists of first-rate quality at the moment that, given the opportunity (i.e. the official economic support) it could in fact be what it is merely advertised to be. The ballyhoo would be transformed into reality. There is an unusual wealth of young talent, at last up-to-datedly equipped, not harking back to French Impressionism, or to pre-Impressionist romanticism. But there can only be promise, in the absence of substantial support. All that Nash, myself and others – to put it that way – worked to create in England is here. From my standpoint, the country is bursting with good painters. I feel, and for the first time, at home. But the capital needed to exploit this creative outburst is spent in other ways.

What is the total outlay, annually, of HM Treasury for the purchase of work by living English artists? It is in fact so small that it would not do much more than keep a half-dozen artists, were they the sole beneficiaries. Three grants are involved, namely that to the Tate and those to the Arts Council and the British Council. The sum that the latter institutions elect to spend is modest but not very clearly defined. £2,000 may be spent by the Arts Council, but only if there are 'enough interesting pictures' available. The British Council would not agree it spent anything like that yearly: but both are fairly regular purchasers in picture exhibitions. I would guess that between them they spend £2,000 or £3,000 yearly. The Tate's £2,000 grant has to cover foreign and British works for over a century.

The State is not necessarily mean, but, one supposes, ignorant. The responsibility lies elsewhere. A phoney list could very easily be drawn up purporting to show that an extremely large sum is spent every year for the purchase of contemporary works of art – by the provincial cities, societies, the Chantry Bequest, the Transport Board, and indomitable collectors. Such an inventory would be highly misleading. Our society is being socialised at top speed, and the main buyer of good pictures has always been the middle class, most deeply affected.

The subject is so intricate – there are so many official alibis to be dealt with, the multiplicity of conflicting values where pictures are concerned is such a source of confusion – that all that can be done in an article is to stimulate attention. We have, however, one piece of first-rate evidence, of the utmost concreteness. I refer to the 'Income and Expenditure' pages in the *Third Annual Report of the Arts Council* (1946-7). They are not very explicit, but the following facts stand out. The sum finally at the disposal of the Council that year was roughly £450,000. As I have said, of this, a maximum of £2,000 is ear-marked for the work of living artists. But Covent Garden pulled down over £90,000. Music, all told, received £212,000 – theatrical companies £56,000 odd. But the essential – the stupefying – figures are 450 and 2.

The Council's Arts Department has much less money to spend than the Drama, but it spends it practically all on exhibitions, lectures and salaries. There are no lectures listed in the above report on 'How to act' or 'How to play the oboe'. Drama is treated as creative art, Opera and Ballet the same. The visual arts, however, are treated as a branch of education. The artist, the producer, is sacrificed to some idea of consumption; he is smothered beneath a mountain of 'cultural' advertisement. The cultural publicity man, the educationalist and the 'amateur' have supplanted the artist: the painter is being talked and explained. Art is being boosted, off the face of the earth.

The Arts Council of Great Britain

Basic Policy of the Arts Council

Extract from Chapter III of *The First Ten Years*, The Arts Council of Great Britain (London), 1956

1 The Pursuit of Quality

What are the main policies that the Arts Council has been developing during its first ten years? The primary responsibility imposed by its Royal Charter is to preserve and improve standards of performance in the various arts. The Arts Council interprets this injunction, in relation to its income, as implying the support of a limited number of institutions where exemplary standards may be developed. [...]

Covent Garden, Sadler's Wells and the Old Vic, then, as three national institutions endeavouring to provide exemplary performances in the metropolis, are a primary responsibility of the Arts Council. From time to time the Arts Council is criticised for showing a bias in favour of London and, especially, for spending a large portion of its budget upon these three establishments. To this criticism, the first answer is that a capital city is also the metropolis of the nation's art: the home, for example, of its National Gallery and British Museum. It is both proper and inevitable that its National Opera House should be located there as well. Secondly, it was not the Arts Council that decided to establish these three institutions. The Arts Council did not decide to give half its money to London; it decided to act as patron to certain institutions already established, and of these, the most meritorious and representative were situated in London. If any provincial city had assumed the responsibility for creating and maintaining, say Sadler's Wells, the Arts Council would gladly have become its patron. It is highly improbable, in fact, that any large city in the provinces could provide a continuous home for opera and ballet; they have insufficient catchment areas (or visitors) to supply the large audiences and income an operation of such magnitude requires. No provincial city at present seems able to sustain more than four weeks a year of the major tours.

There are other exemplary institutions, some of them in London but most of them in the provinces, which, without being national or traditional monuments of the arts in the sense that the Old Vic is, or Sadler's Wells, are nevertheless engaged in maintaining the highest standards of performance. Some of them, like the Stratford Memorial Theatre, are happily in no need of subsidy. Glyndebourne, that brilliant demonstration of private patronage and bastion of impeccable standards, has received one grant of £25,000 from the Arts Council. The Scottish committee of the Arts Council took part in the inauguration of the Edinburgh Festival and continues to vote an annual subsidy to this most distinguished and successful institution.

2 Making the Arts Accessible

The Arts Council believes, then, that the first claim upon its attention and assistance is that of maintaining in London and the larger cities effective power-houses of opera, music and drama; for unless these quality institutions can be maintained, the arts are bound to decline into mediocrity. The maintenance of standards, in static centres, must come first. Yet the Council is also aware of its obligations to make the arts increasingly accessible to populations outside these few centres. Its achievement of this object has been considerable. For example, it finances the tours of the popular Carl Rosa, the Sadler's Wells Theatre Ballet, the Ballet Rambert and the seasons of the Welsh National Opera Company, apart from assisting the expensive and complicated operation of sending out for several weeks Covent Garden and Sadler's Wells productions that are not designed for the purposes of touring. A substantial part of its subsidies to the symphony orchestras is intended to encourage them to visit smaller towns that are not economic propositions; and it makes grants to several smaller orchestras, such as the Boyd Neel, which, with this assistance, can afford to develop its own specialised repertory and to play in the less populous centres. On another front, the Arts Council finances several local festivals of the arts that provide an annual assembly of music and art in places that could not normally enjoy such offerings. Its diffusion of the visual arts is similarly determined by the principle of maintaining standards. On this basis, it arranges exhibitions of major importance in London and selected provincial cities; its biggest venture of this kind in 1956 was the exhibition of Van Gogh shown in Liverpool, Manchester and Newcastle – and not in London. [...]

3 Other Limits to Diffusion

Even if the Arts Council had more money to spend, it would need to ponder several other questions before deciding upon extended diffusion. There are many towns that have consistently failed to reveal an interest in 'live' plays or concerts, and which have allowed their local repertory theatre to collapse. Is public money to be used in the long and expensive business of coaxing the cultural appetites of such places? Are seats to be subsidised whether they are full or empty? The Arts Council lacks the means to pursue diffusion on a massive scale and, since there exist methods more apt for diffusion than those it can command or afford, it seems wiser that the Arts Council should now concentrate its limited resources primarily, but not exclusively, on the maintenance and enhancement of standards. Standards can best be raised in permanent centres: music and drama must have fixed abodes where resident companies can develop their skill and esprit and sense of purpose. There is no reason to conclude that the Arts Council will diminish its present scale of diffusion, but, faced with a problem of choice, and a limited budget, the Arts Council must seek to consolidate rather than enlarge its own particular responsibilities to the arts in Britain. It can do so, moreover, in the solid confidence that municipal patronage is taking a large and increasing share of the cost of providing the arts to those communities that express an articulate desire to enjoy them. If Local Authorities will continue at the present rate to carry some of the load of diffusion, there will still be an inevitable dearth of the 'living' arts, but there will be no famine. But unless high standards can be maintained in selected strongholds, diffusion will be a fruitless and improvident effort.

Jennie Lee, MP

A Policy for the Arts: The First Steps

Extract from *Introduction to A Policy for the Arts: The First Steps*, Her Majesty's Stationery Office (London), 1965

1   The relationship between artist and State in a modern democratic community is not easily defined. No-one would wish State patronage to dictate taste or in any way restrict the liberty of even the most unorthodox and experimental of artists.

2   But if a high level of artistic achievement is to be sustained and the best in the arts made more widely available, more generous and discriminating help is urgently needed, locally, regionally and nationally.

3   In some parts of the country, professional companies are non-existent. Even amateurs find it hard to keep going. And lack of suitable buildings makes it impossible to bring any of the leading national companies, orchestral, operatic, ballet or theatre, into those areas.

4   Fortunately, this state of affairs is coming increasingly under fire. So too are those of our museums, art galleries and concert halls that have failed to move with the times, retaining a cheerless, unwelcoming air that alienates all but the specialist and the dedicated.

5   No greater disservice can be done to the serious artist than to present his work in an atmosphere of old-fashioned gloom and undue solemnity.

6   If we are concerned to win a wider and more appreciative public for the arts, all this must be changed. A new social as well as artistic climate is essential.

7   There is no easy or quick way of bringing this about, the more so as too many working people have been conditioned by their education and environment to consider the best in music, painting, sculpture and literature outside their reach. A younger generation, however, more self-confident than their elders, and beginning to be given some feeling for drama, music and the visual arts in their school years, are more hopeful material. They will want gaiety and colour, informality and experimentation. But there is no reason why attractive presentation should be left to those whose primary concern is with quantity and profitability.

8   Some of our new civic centres and art centres already demonstrate that an agreeable environment and a jealous regard for the maintenance of high standards are not incompatible. Centres that succeed in providing a friendly meeting ground where both light entertainment and cultural projects can be enjoyed help also to break down the isolation from which both artist and potential audience have suffered in the past.

9   Another encouraging trend is the growing recognition of the importance of strengthening contacts between regional and civic art associations in different parts of the country.

10   But we have a long way to go before effective associations of this kind become common form everywhere. If a sane balance of population between North and South, East and West, is to be achieved, this kind of development is just as essential as any movement of industry or provision of public utility service. If the eager and gifted, to whom we must look for leadership in every field, are to feel as much at home in the North and West as in and near London, each region will require high points of artistic excellence. Of course, no provincial centre can hope to rival the full wealth and diversity of London's art treasures, but each can have something of its own that is supreme in some particular field. This too must be the aim of the new towns, if they are to win and to hold the kind of residents they most need.

11   From the combined efforts of the Government and of regional associations that include representatives of industry, the trade unions and private donors as well as local authorities, the money must be found to provide the buildings needed to house the arts.

12   If we are prepared to accept this challenge, we must also be prepared within the limits of the resources that can be made available to give expenditure for these projects a higher priority than in the past.

13   The financial difficulties that so many of today's artists have to contend with must also be realistically examined.

14   In any civilised community, the arts and associated amenities, serious or comic, light or demanding, must occupy a central place. Their enjoyment should not be regarded as something remote from everyday life. The promotion and appreciation of high standards in architecture, in industrial design, in town planning and the preservation of the beauty of the countryside, are all part of it. Beginning in the schools, and reaching out into every corner of the nation's life, in city and village, at home, at work, at play, there is an immense amount that could be done to improve the quality of contemporary life.

15   There is no short-term solution for what by its very nature is a long-term problem. This is a field in which, even in the most favourable circumstances, it will never be possible to do as much as we want to do as quickly as we want to do it. But this is no excuse for not doing as much as we can and more than has hitherto been attempted. [...]

Rt. Hon. Viscount Eccles

Politics and the Quality of Life

Extract from *Politics and the Quality of Life*, a pamphlet based on the address delivered by Lord Eccles to the Conservative Political Centre (London), 1970

[...] A policy to raise the quality of life is not a new social service. This distinction would be vital if we had to plan the machinery to carry out what I am proposing to you this evening. The Social Services – not including Education among them – are the means by which the Community helps those in some particular trouble. It may be the weak – children and old people – or it may be the unfortunate – the poor, the unemployed and the sick. Action is taken to enable identifiable persons to reach the standard that the Community regards as the tolerable minimum. This is a rescue operation firmly anchored by material criteria. A policy to raise the quality of life is a constructive operation in another dimension, that of the spirit. It has therefore to proceed from the opposite direction to that taken by the Social Services. It begins by identifying the best, supporting it with government resources, and then spreading it across the population. In the field of the arts, it is the job of the Arts Council to select and fortify the highest standards in drama and music and of the British Film Institute to do the same for the cinema. But the procedure holds good for improving the environment, for industrial conditions and for teaching moral and aesthetic values. The criterion for choosing what is best differs sharply from the statistical methods of the Social Services. The quality of life demands that we should support that which enhances the individual's understanding of himself and his society, and which arouses in him the desire and the capacity to use his own powers to the full. We know that in favourable circumstances art can do this, but judging by the way the British people are reacting to life today, we shall not get very far unless the other two partners, industry and education, are working on the same plans as those who are responsible for the arts. As I said earlier, life today does not make enough sense either at work or in leisure, nor are the values well enough taught by which we can discriminate between good and bad conduct and good and bad taste. To give you one example, I doubt whether a real improvement in the environment will be achieved until architecture has become a regular subject in school and on television. Local people will resist disturbing, expensive changes in their surroundings until they have some grasp of the principles on which their living-space must be organised if human relations are not to be sacrificed to economics. In the meantime, it costs less to put electric cables on poles than underground, and more to dispose of waste on the premises than to tip it somewhere else.

You may challenge the proposition that the arts should be part and parcel of a policy that embraces industrial conditions and education. Why should the arts be in such company? I will end my remarks by trying to give you a satisfactory answer.

To set out deliberately to improve the quality of anything implies a desire to understand more about it, to discover its true character, and by what means to get the best out of it. So in putting forward a policy to improve the quality of life, we are aiming to increase the understanding of life and to help men and women to develop themselves in harmony with this better understanding. If it is true, as the great thinkers have said, that you cannot find life's meaning in bread alone, where do you find it? Let me ask a specific question: 'Today, what are the British people living for beyond money?' You might well give me the answer 'We do not exactly know, but at any rate they are not much interested in religion and art'. Suppose I press for a more positive reply, you might then add that the British people live for sport, gambling, sex, motor-cars and so on. But however long your list, all the items would share one interesting characteristic. As distinct from religion and art, none of them helps us to discover the meaning of the whole of life. I take religion and art to be very close relations, for both go below the surface of things to penetrate the inner reality of human existence. In times gone by, States heaped favours on religion because it afforded an explanation of life that held society together. What holds us together now? We seem to think ourselves rich enough and well enough educated in the sciences to make the experiment of living in a vacuum without any explanation of life, and it is becoming very uncomfortable. What shall we do to fill this vacuum? We cannot go back up the stream of history. Now that technology has revolutionised the apparatus of life, the old expositions of the truth of the human condition are not relevant. To find new expositions becomes extremely urgent. For the first time, the mass of people are asking for a share in life of a quality that satisfies the expectations aroused by better education and the defeat of poverty. They are determined to know themselves as individual men and women, not submerged in crowds manipulated from some distant headquarters. Surely, to come to their aid in this predicament is right in line with Tory doctrine that the character of the people counts above everything?

To advance towards a society in which the quality of life is as important as economic growth calls for a new social strategy. So politics must change, and Governments go beyond the satisfaction of material needs and show an increasing concern for the imagination and spirit of all the members of the community. Look around you with compassion and hope at how the young are behaving and you will descry the outline of the new dimension in politics. From the United States to Soviet Russia, from France to Cuba, from India to Nigeria, intelligent groups like the CPC are searching for the political philosophy to succeed Capitalism, Marxism and Socialism. Essentially, this means healing the split between work and leisure as incomes rise. I like to think that the Conservative Party, under Mr Heath's leadership, will pioneer this adventure and set the world a fresh example of British skill in political evolution.

The Arts Council of Great Britain

Community Arts

Extract from *The Report of the Community Arts Working Party*. Arts Council of Great Britain (London), 1974

[. . .] CLAUSE 3 (B) OF THE CHARTER READS: 'TO INCREASE THE ACCESSIBILITY OF THE ARTS TO THE PUBLIC THROUGHOUT GREAT BRITAIN'. MOST COMMUNITY ARTISTS ARE NOT CONCERNED WITH INCREASING THE ACCESSIBILITY OF THE ARTS IN THE TRADITIONAL SENSE, E.G. BY PERFORMANCES OF SHAKESPEARE OR VISITS TO ART GALLERIES, BUT THE AIM OF INVOLVING WIDER SECTIONS OF THE PUBLIC IN ARTISTIC ACTIVITY DOES SEEM TO COME WITHIN THE SPIRIT OF THIS CLAUSE; INDEED THEY WOULD CLAIM THAT THEY ARE DOING SOMETHING TO PROMOTE THIS OBJECT OF THE COUNCIL IN AREAS AND AMONG STRATA OF SOCIETY WHERE OTHERWISE IT COULD HAVE NO HOPE OF FULFILMENT, AND THAT THEREBY THEY ARE HELPING TO MAKE THE PHRASE 'THROUGHOUT GREAT BRITAIN' MORE OF A REALITY THAN IT IS AT PRESENT. IF THEIR SUCCESS IN CARRYING OUT THIS AIM IS OFTEN MOST MARKED AMONG YOUNG PEOPLE, THEY ARGUE THAT WORK WITH THIS AGE GROUP IS OF THE GREATEST IMPORTANCE FOR THE FUTURE. THE WORKING PARTY, WHILE AWARE THAT THE RESULTS THEY ACHIEVE ARE VARIABLE, BELIEVES THAT THEY ARE MAKING A CONTRIBUTION THAT THE COUNCIL, UNDER CLAUSE 3 (B), HAS GOOD REASON TO SUPPORT. [. . .]

Labour Party

The Arts and the People

Extract from Introduction to *Policy Towards the Arts*, Labour Party (London), 1977

The arts[1] are politically important. Their funding and administration are as dependent on political decisions as housing, education, defence or any other function of government.

For too long, governments of both parties have considered the arts as outside politics and of secondary importance – worthy of a junior ministry; worthy of a tiny proportion of local government rates; worthy of afterthought paragraphs in manifestos and of infrequent debate at conference: worthy of scant consideration because worth few votes. Successive governments have financed the Arts with small, if growing, subsidies. But money spent in the absence of a coherent policy will inevitably reinforce existing tendencies. In the case of the arts, those tendencies have been towards the metropolitan and the institutional – in both attitude and architecture. Thus, the enormously high quality of artistic achievement that we have in this country in almost every medium has been presented for a small – if slowly growing – proportion of the population.

This report sets out to formulate a socialist policy for the arts with the following main objectives:

1 to make the arts available and relevant to all people in this country;
2 to increase the quality and diversity of the arts with greater emphasis on those based in communities;
3 to increase public finance for the arts;
4 to ensure that the context of the arts is not controlled by government and that artists are free to produce their works without external constraints;
5 to restructure the administration and finance of the arts by making them both democratic and decentralised;
6 to improve the wages, conditions of employment and security of all people professionally engaged in the arts.

To achieve these objectives we recommend that:

a A new separate Ministry for Arts, Entertainment and Communications be created.
b The Arts Council be radically reformed.

The implementation of such policies will demand two actions by the Government – a considerable increase in expenditure over the next decade; and, more important still, a new and urgent commitment to the arts, which can only stem from a recognition of their vital role in the life of the country. [...]

By placing the arts in the political forum, such changes will no doubt result in pleas to 'keep politics out of art', but we maintain that politics are inextricably sewn into the fabric of the arts. At present, we have an arts policy through which the most heavily subsidised arts are catering for a predominately middle-class audience. It is a policy through which a high, if decreasing, percentage of those subsidies go to London and the metropolitan areas. The effect of such a policy is political – to favour one area or one type of artistic preference against another. Further, in so far as most works of art are concerned with man as subject matter – his ideals, beliefs, fears, joys – they are inevitably political in content. It is difficult, not to say impossible, to tell a story that does not take an attitude – either questioning or reassuring. Such an attitude may be implicit or explicit but it will be there, and the cumulation of such attitudes is political. In the same way, where you present a work of art, how much you charge for it, what forms receive subsidy, will have an inevitable political effect. There will be those who point out the dangers of political manipulation and censorship of the arts, with numerous illustration from totalitarian countries – both left and right. We deplore without reservation such practices since freedom of the arts is an essential part of socialist policy. But we believe that the most effective way of safeguarding the fundamental right to express any lawful view through any art medium will be to ensure that the arts are under the same democratic scrutiny as the rest of our social policies. [...]

All such reforms, however, presuppose that the arts are a vital part of this country's life – a valuation that is not universally held and which thus requires justification. We maintain that the arts are not a rarefied world – approachable only with a university degree, or relevant only to a small, highbrow elite. Rather, the greatest works of art in any medium appeal equally to the emotions and the mind of any person prepared to open himself to them. In essence, such works of art are the means of telling a story or conveying ideas and impressions. As such, they are special only because of their quality and intensity. At their most successful, they are capable of placing each one of us in contact with the best and finest possibilities of man. At their most effective, they challenge us to question our morality and our beliefs.

For these reasons, we are convinced that the arts are important. They are not a social luxury worthy of our consideration and finance only when other aspects of life have been satisfied. If we neglect or ignore them, we jeopardise the very quality of our national life.

This document urges policies that we believe will bring the arts firmly into the centre of our society. Such policies are unashamedly socialist since by placing the arts in a democratic and decentralised structure they will give people of all political and cultural views the opportunity to create, participate in, benefit from, and, above all, enjoy, our great artistic heritage and our artistic future.

1 In this statement we use the term 'arts' to include all cultural activities – including those often termed as 'entertainment'.

Kingsley Amis

An Arts Policy?

Reprinted from *An Arts Policy?*, a lecture given by Kingsley Amis under the auspices of the Centre for Policy Studies at the Wintergardens, Brighton, during the Conservative Party Conference, October 1979, published by Centre for Policy Studies (London), 1979

As you'll see soon enough, what I have to say carries no special authority. I've been selling my work for nearly thirty years and living off it for over fifteen. I have some experience of other arts as what's now called a 'consumer'. I'm a member of the Writers' Guild, but not a very active one, I'm afraid, and I've never sat on any panel or board or committee concerned with administering the arts. So at any rate, I have no vested interest in the matter. I've a vested interest in surviving, like everybody else, and also like everybody else, another one in not being told what to do. More of that in a minute.

You may not think so, but I chose my title with some care. *An* arts policy? Only one single policy for all those different arts? An *arts* policy? What a horrible bureaucrat's phrase, with 'arts' used as an adjective. An arts *policy*? As Mr St John-Stevas asked, 'Why should a political party have an arts policy at all?'[1] and I think any Conservative approaches the subject not with the eagerness of the planner, but with the feelings of someone reluctantly settling down to a not-very-exciting duty. I hope so, anyway. The question-mark in my title is meant to show that reluctance. It also shows indecision: I'm not sure what policy is best. And that's rare; my friends will tell you that for Amis not to be absolutely certain what he thinks on any topic from Aberystwyth to Zoroastrianism is almost unknown. The question-mark stands for another kind of uncertainty too: I had to give the organisers the title before I wrote the talk, and as usual, didn't know a lot about what I was going to say until I was down to the job.

One thing I'm absolutely sure about is that any kind of socialist policy for the arts must be sternly resisted at every point. When the State takes a really passionate interest in the work and other activities of its artists, creative and executive alike, the artists had better start running. Many a writer in the Soviet Union, for example, must feel he could well have done without the kind of official recognition he's attained. It would be foolish to pretend that there are not plenty of people in the Labour Party and elsewhere who would like to see a British government concern itself with culture to the same sort of degree. Any kind of totalitarian hates all artists, not only writers, because he can never own, or direct, their talent– that which makes them artists.

What is the official arts policy of the Labour Party? I strongly recommend *The Arts and the People*;[2] notice it's not *The Artists* or *Artists and the People*; it's *The Arts*, the commodity, and *the People*, the consumers. I thought I was going to be bored, but I wasn't; I was fascinated, and horrified. If I spend a few minutes on it, that's not only because it pays to know your enemy, though it does. Preliminary thanks are offered to the people who made their experience and expertise available to Labour's NEC: Government ministers, MPs, trade unionists and individual party members – I suppose that some of them might have been artists. First sentence of text: 'The arts are politically important'. Footnote: 'In this statement we use the term "arts" to include all cultural activities – including those often termed as "entertainment"'. Next page: 'Politics are inextricably sewn into the fabric of the arts'; quite a vivid image. There, of course, the authors are telling us something about their brand of politics, not about the arts. You won't find much political content in a given string quartet. I suppose they might tell you that that content is in string quartets as a whole, something to do with a leisured, affluent class, perhaps. That would be a pity, because what is interesting about any string quartet is how it differs from all the others written up to that time. After studying Shakespeare politically, which I did once, you can be pretty sure he wasn't a Republican and he wasn't anti-English, and that's about it. Enough; we know where we are there.

What the authors call in so many words a socialist policy for the arts, has six clauses. (a) goes: 'To make the arts available and relevant to all people in this country'. To call something 'relevant' like that, as a synonym for 'meaningful' or 'interesting', is a very unpopular use in some quarters. I'm all for it; it's a useful or even infallible sign that the writer is a victim of appalling herd-instinct, getting his ideas from some fashionable source and passing them on without taking them in or thinking for himself. Also, you can't do that: make the arts relevant to all people, who are not interested in them. Before sitting down to frame arts policy, it's essential to understand that.

It's a traditional Lefty view, the belief that anybody can enjoy art, real art, in the same way that everybody is creative. In the words of that old idiot and very bad artist Eric Gill, 'The artist is not a special kind of man; every man is a special kind of artist'.[3] That's only possible if making mud pies counts as art, which admittedly is beginning to happen. Can you imagine a novel, say, that was relevant to everybody in the United Kingdom, including the ones with an IQ of 80? But I think that's what these chaps are getting at. You notice they say 'available' as well as 'relevant'. Obviously, a novel is physically available if it's in print; they must mean 'accessible', another fashionable use, 'understandable' by an 80 IQ. So the novelist is to write down to his readers and thereby cease to produce art. The trouble with bringing art to the people is that it tends to get fatally damaged in transit.

I may have come a bit too far too fast. Anyway, clause (b) of the socialist arts policy goes: 'To increase the quality and diversity of the arts with greater emphasis on those based in communities'. So my duty is clear. I must write better, which had never occurred to me before, and I must write more sorts of things, epic poems and introductions to catalogues of exhibitions of experimental paintings and gags for TV shows – remember they're art too, even though they are often termed as entertainment. Actually, more than this is required. 'A socialist policy', they say further, 'requires more books, and a wider range and higher quality of books to be published, written by authors of every sort of social background'. Naturally. But why aren't people writing these high-quality books already? Our friends seem to think quality is a sort of optional ingredient or extra like HP sauce on sausages: 'Don't forget the quality, Mum!' Years ago, when the universities were beginning to expand their intake, I wrote of university students, 'You cannot decide to have more good ones. All you can decide to have is more. And more will mean worse'.[4] So with books, so with paintings, so with everything. An artist is a special kind of man, or woman; there are never many around at one time and there's no way of making new ones, even by spending money. Authors are certainly going to have some money spent on them, though, because literature is, 'an underfinanced artistic area'. Would you let someone who talked about 'underfinanced literature areas' recommend you a book?

What about those arts based in communities? What are they? There's community singing, of course, but I'm sure they don't mean that: much too spontaneous and uninstructive. It's hard to make out what they do mean. Community arts are a 'process of art activity' rather than a product. They include drama, but it's community drama; music and dance, also community; silk-screen painting, video, murals and neighbourhood newspapers – 'all aimed at involving the community', they tell us, and – they don't tell us, but I know – all left-wing. Community theatre would be very, very poor man's Brecht, Arnold Wesker, etc. There's a good give-away passage about encouraging 'fringe experimental and community theatre that most regional and national theatres have neglected from lack of finance and lack of interest'. In other words, we'll supply the finance and you'd better supply the interest; a very clear example of the Socialists' habit of giving the public not what it wants but what they think it ought to want. And it's the Tories who get called paternalistic! Happily, the public won't take what it doesn't want. It goes somewhere else. It changes the channel.

The last point I want to make about this vile document, which manages to disgrace the Labour Party, concerns its answer to the question, 'Who will run the arts?' Well, a policy-making National Conference for the Arts and Entertainment will be set up, comprising of' – this is really elegant stuff – 'elected representatives from local authorities, Regional Arts Associations, arts and entertainment trade unions, individual artists, subsidised management, and other relevant bodies' – got it right for once – 'such as those directly representing the consumers of the arts'. So this lot decides what the public ought to want and a reformed Arts Council doles out the cash. It, the reformed Arts Council, will comprise of, one-third, Ministerial appointees suggested by what they call 'interest groups in the arts' – hold on a minute – and two-thirds 'representatives of most of those interest groups represented at the National Conference', and a list follows. Since it's only 'most of', who's missing? Local authorities? No, they'll be there. Trade unionists? No. It's individual artists. We're not having any of them on our new Arts Council; who do they think they are?

So under a Labour government we'd have the TUC controlling the arts in this country. And it's well enough known that he who pays the piper calls the tune, except that these days it wouldn't be a tune but a succession of meaningless noises that nobody asked for. The principle doesn't change when a Conservative government comes to power, though I obviously wouldn't be here if I didn't think that such a government would exert its influence more wisely and far more gently than the contenders on the other side. And yet ... The whole question of paying for the arts is a very difficult one, not only at the doling-out end but also at the receiving end, the end that isn't so often considered from this point of view. The truth is that the way an artist is paid profoundly affects his product, whether he's an opera producer, what used be called a lyric poet, or anything in between. Most artists are subject to two quite different pressures, one to do with their material, the other to do with their public. In the twentieth century, a lot of artists have got heavily involved with their material at the expense of their public. In other words, they tend to produce something very technical, complex, unfamiliar, in some way unexpected, and the public doesn't understand it, is bored, baffled or outraged. And the public – I belong to it myself most of the time – is usually right. This was happening long before there was any government support for the arts, but that support encourages the tendency. In

explaining his resignation from the Arts Council in 1977, the distinguished poet and novelist Roy Fuller wrote: 'The bestowal of money for the arts inevitably attracts the idle, the dotty, the minimally talented, the self promoters'.[5] He might have added that their typical product is plays without plots, a canvas entirely covered with black paint offered as a picture, poems that are meaningless patterns of letters – I needn't go on. If you're paid in advance or have your losses underwritten, the temptation to self-indulgence is extreme. If you have to please to live, you'll do your best to please.

The standard answer to that, of course, is that I'm suggesting that artists should pander to the public's whim and that new work, innovatory work, should not be encouraged. The public's whim is better than the critics' whim, or the experts' whim, or the bureaucrats' whim, and what we should encourage is good work, not new work. Actually the public's whim can be pretty constant – a whim of iron. Take one field, music. A new work, called say *Distortions*, is commissioned. It's to be played at a concert. You have to put in other works as well, by Beethoven, Schubert, Brahms and other composers who pandered to the public's whim. When you work out the order of performance, *Distortions* has to be played second. If you put it first, nobody comes until it's over, except the composer's party and the critics. If you put it third, before the interval, everybody goes out before it starts. If it's after the interval, they all have a drink and go home. And it's been like that for fifty years – some whim. A cynical friend of mine, a very able keyboard player and conductor, said that the really rare event in musical life is the second performance of a modern work; no subsidy for that. Well, I could go on about this for hours, as you may well imagine, so I'll round off this bit just by stating flatly that if you really are interested in quality, one way of allowing it to improve would be to withdraw public money from the arts.

As well as being tempted to be self-indulgent, the State-supported artist is more likely to be wasteful. We all spend other people's money more

IT'S A TRADITIONAL LEFTY VIEW
THE BELIEF THAT ANYBODY CAN ENJOY ART, REAL ART
IN THE SAME WAY THAT EVERYBODY IS
CREATIVE
IN THE WORDS OF THAT OLD IDIOT
AND VERY BAD ARTIST
ERIC GILL
'THE ARTIST IS NOT A SPECIAL KIND OF MAN
EVERY MAN IS A SPECIAL KIND OF ARTIST'*

THAT'S ONLY POSSIBLE IF
MAKING
MUD PIES
COUNTS AS ART
WHICH ADMITTEDLY
IS BEGINNING TO HAPPEN

SOMEWHERE IN THE WORKS OF ERIC GILL. I'M NOT GOING TO READ THROUGH THEM TO FIND OUT WHERE freely than our own, with less regard for value. It doesn't really matter if a chap overspends an individual grant, which is likely to be pretty small anyway. It matters rather more if he's in charge of a new production of *Carmen*. Let's call him Entwistle. He'll be very lavish on the production itself, because that's what gets talked and written about. It's Entwistle's *Carmen* you go to see, and when you've finished discussing that you go on to the singers' *Carmen*, and after that you might get on to the conductor's *Carmen*, and possibly you might have a word or two to say about Bizet's *Carmen* if there's time, or room. I was told on excellent authority a terrifying story about a recent production of *Rosenkavalier*. There's a drunken-brawl scene in which, at every performance, half a dozen glasses were smashed on the stage. One of the singers noticed that they seemed posh affairs, and asked how much they'd cost. 'Seven or eight pounds', he was told. 'What!' he said. 'Why aren't you using tooth-glasses?' 'Oh, the audience would see, and it would seem wrong to have rich characters drinking out of cheap glasses'. I'm glad I'm not playing the Bleeding Sergeant in that fellow's *Macbeth*; presumably he'd stab me every evening before I made my entrance so the audience wouldn't be put off by seeing artificial blood. I don't think he'd be spending fifty quid a week on glasses if the money came out of the takings, do you? As a footnote, I similarly doubt whether you'd give £2,865 you'd earned and paid tax on to something called Harry's Big Balloonz, with a z. Well, the Arts Council gave that sum to a body so named in 1975-6. Actually, it's a performance art group, whatever that is, but I wouldn't give a cent of your money to anything called that, even if it were a charitable home for distressed old ladies. That strikes me as quite a good wheeze for go-ahead charitable homes. I offer it free.

So taxpayers' money paid to the arts encourages waste and irresponsibility in those who do the spending as well as self-indulgence in the artist. On the second point, I might have said further about *Distortions* that as well as not writing for the public, the composer is writing for the critics, which means he'll inevitably strive after orig-

inality. It's annoying, but originality will come of its own accord or not at all, and striving for it must have a harmful effect. Anyway, am I arguing for the abolition of subsidies? For the moment I am. A third argument on this side concerns the supposed experts who sit on the central panels, the awful Regional Arts Associations and so on. A full study of the rise of the expert in this century, especially its second half, would make enthralling and very depressing reading. It's all part of the great loss of confidence that has shaken our society, beginning at the time of the First World War. In the past, you didn't know anything about art, but you knew what you liked. Of course you did, and what was even more important, you weren't afraid to say what you liked, and didn't like. You were a Victorian businessman and you came down to London from Birmingham and you bought a Pre-Raphaelite picture because you liked it, not because some interfering git called Ruskin said you should. Now you ask an expert because you don't trust your own judgement. It's comically appropriate that one of the most totally committed expert-worshippers of our time should be Sir Roy Shaw, the amiable head of the Arts Council, or its Secretary-General as he's forbiddingly known. Roy Fuller, in his why-I-resigned article in Encounter magazine,[6] gave as one minor reason what he called 'the hideous contemporary paintings' bought by the Council and hung in its Piccadilly offices. In his reply the following month, Sir Roy Shaw said that Roy Fuller was an excellent poet, but, 'he is not an authority on contemporary painting and neither am I; the paintings were bought on the advice of people who are.'[7] We learn from that that Sir Roy must himself be an authority (up-market term for an expert) on contemporary poetry, or he'd have had to ask one to find out whether Roy Fuller was an excellent poet or not. Imagine telling Lorenzo the Magnificent that the painting he thought he liked had been pronounced bad by an expert.[8] Imagine telling our Victorian businessman. Their descendants are afraid of being thought unprogressive.

The present system exalts the expert and institutionalises him. The panels and study-groups

and regional boards he sits on officialise and bureaucratise and politicise art. They might have been designed for the needs of the Left and probably were: new and expanding bodies with ill-defined powers and fields of operation and endless public money, money the public won't pay. For the moment, I'm objecting not to Leftist politics, as such, but to the consequences of those politics on the various bits of art that get publicly promoted or financed. It's strange that some of the members or supporters of what rather sadly likes to think of itself as a mass party should have such elitist tastes, that left-wing views should go with an apparent liking for avant-garde, experimental, nonsensical and certainly minority art. The explanation must be that the Lefty's settled hostility to tradition, to things as they are, overrides his feelings or class solidarity, perhaps not very strong in the first place.

So do we phase out the Arts Council and all the other bodies, withdraw in the end every shilling of public support? It's tempting. Think of a Minister for the Arts with no functions at all, his title a pure honorific like Warden of the Cinque Ports, a symbolic figure to be seen only at first nights or private views. Certainly some parts of the system could be closed down: grants to individual writers and other artists whose materials aren't expensive could well go, and there seems an unanswerable case for closing down the National Film Finance Corporation and the other bodies it has spawned, what with their classic demonstration that investment in failure ends in failure. But things like that wouldn't save very much, any more than closing down arts centres, however desirable that would be on every ground you can think of. The really big spenders are the national opera and theatre companies. What the question boils down to is whether we seriously think the day will come when Covent Garden or the National Theatre can get along without any taxpayers' money and also without lowering the quality of their productions, though putting a 50p ceiling on any glasses they may break. If we do think that, then the argument is over.[9]

Where's the money to come from? David Alexander, of the Selsdon Group,[10] thinks it could come from where it most certainly should come from: the individual as consumer, not as taxpayer. Enough private money would be set free by radical cuts in taxes on capital and on incomes to cover the gap left by the withdrawal of subsidies. Dismissing as a red herring the idea of business patronage, David Alexander sees what he calls 'mass patronage' as the answer. Colin Brough, of the Bow Group,[11] sees things differently. He doesn't think the arts can ever be free of State support, but a large injection from business could be gained by changes in the laws affecting capital gains, covenants on such matters. I don't know what I think. I am very conscious of the idea that any transition involving a large increase in the price at the box office would have to be managed with almost superhuman care, and I hate the thought of any of these important institutions being endangered. If they had to shut for a month or two, they'd probably shut for ever. But what I do think is both important and practicable is the lifting of VAT on the arts, if not on all of them, then on theatre, opera and concert seats. Even the authors of the Labour Party pamphlet agree with me here. To take this action would be to give a huge invisible subsidy of the best kind, one that doesn't benefit individuals or individual groups. I urge the government to consider this seriously and soon.

I've said nothing so far about the Conservative document about arts policy,[12] because it's very disappointing, to put it as mildly as possible. The subtitle, 'The Way Forward', bodes ill. The first sentence goes, 'Any Government, whatever its political hue, should take some active steps to encourage the arts'. No. The arts aren't like housing or public health; they have their own momentum and rate of development, and must be allowed to pursue it unmolested by encouragement as much as by censorship. The extra reason why I said so much earlier about the Labour pamphlet is that long stretches of the Tory one read just like it, though they're rather better written. 'The arts are menaced by public indifference.' No: public interference. 'The bur-

eaucrats who dole out the money lean towards the conventional and established.' No: they lean towards experimentalism and non-art, because they're afraid of being thought unprogressive. 'Fringe activities should be encouraged.' No, no, no. I won't go on. Apart from suggestions that VAT should be reduced, State subsidies limited to 50% of revenue, and business support actively encouraged, the authors have nothing useful to say and a good deal that's pernicious. Their statement is a sad example of Tory me-tooism.

I'd like to say thank you to the Government for establishing the principle of the Public Lending Right for authors, and to explain to the doubtful that payments under the PLR would not be grants to individuals but returns for services already rendered to borrowers of library books, the money coming not out of those borrowers' pockets but out of taxation. Perhaps I might also point out that so far no money has even started to come. Action, please.

You'll understand if my final point is also about books. One of the simplest ways, not of bringing art to the people, but of letting the people get at art, is by way of bookshops. In this country there are about 500 chartered bookshops, that is, shops where you can't buy toilet requisites or pop records, just books. In West Germany there are 6,000. There are large provincial towns in Great Britain with no decent bookshop at all. Somebody willing to start one could be supported in one or more of several ways: with a grant or loan for fitting out the premises, buying the initial stock, meeting some of the overheads, etc. To bring such a shop into being would be a real community service, and those many who live out of reach of one will probably agree with me that it's as important as establishing any sort of theatre, and much cheaper. The arrangement would also benefit authors, which is no bad thing. Some of the expense could be offset by stopping the subsidies to little magazines that mainly or largely publish poetry. The provision of unearned cash, cash that comes in whatever and whoever you print, almost inevitably results in a magazine of that kind becoming the preserve of a clique, a

disability to which poetry is peculiarly liable, and that is a bad thing, and not a trivial one either. As so often, public funds turn out to be harming to the very people they were intended to help. It's odd that Conservatives of all people should seem not to have noticed that after thirty years.

1   *The Arts: the way forward*, Conservative Political Centre (London), September 1978

2   *The Arts and the People*, Labour Party (London), October 1977

3   Somewhere in the works of Eric Gill. I'm not going to read through them to find out where.

4   *What Became of Jane Austen? and Other Questions*, Cape (London), 1970, p. 163

5   *Encounter*, October 1977

6   Ibid.

7   *Encounter*, November 1977

8   I have no quarrel with the expert as such, who can be very useful in his proper role of supplying me with specialist information and helping me to form my taste. If, instead of making up my own mind, I let him tell me what's good and what's bad, I'm abdicating my responsibility, encouraging in him an inflated view of his own importance and increasing his already excessive power. Art is for the public, not for experts.

9   Some part in that argument would be taken by the example of the Glyndebourne opera, which is privately supported. It is, however, a comparatively small scale venture, and was founded at a time when conditions were more propitious.

10 *A Policy for the Arts: Just Cut Taxes*, The Selsdon Group (London), July 1978.

11 *As You Like it: Private Support for the Arts*, Bow Publications Ltd (London), n.d.

12 *The Arts: the way forward*, op. cit.

Raymond Williams

The Arts Council

Extract from *Political Quarterly*. vol. 50, no. 2. April/May/June 1979

[...] 'Intermediate' or 'Arm's Length'

In the broad perspective of a theory of institutions, the Arts Council is an important and relatively original attempt to create a kind of intermediate body that distributes public money without being under the direct control of a governmental organisation. The whole question of such intermediate bodies is now being widely discussed. In the case of the arts, and within anything at all like the present social order, the principle can be strongly supported on the grounds, first, that it is impossible for the arts to be adequately supported by the ordinary operations of the market or by occasional private patronage (as the banks and industrial companies would soon discover and indeed know already; their prestige advertising support is only practicable at all on the basis of substantial long-term public funding); and secondly, that while public finance, from the general revenue, is essential, it is undesirable that any governmental body, subject to changes of political emphasis, should have direct control over artistic policies and practices. We have only to compare the intermediate principle with either of its probable alternatives – a consortium of commercial sponsors, or a government arts department – to see how desirable it is that it should be realistically attempted. A commercial consortium would necessarily subordinate its policies to its own interests, however generally conceived, sustaining certain metropolitan institutions, certain activities in its commercially relevant areas, and certain amenities. It could not undertake the comprehensive regional provision, the deliberate extension of access, and the broad mix of established and experimental arts that the public interest requires. On the other hand, a government department, from such comparative evidence as we have, would be likely, even if it stopped short of direct political interference, to be radically insensitive to the highly varied, often untidy and at times unpredictable practice of so many kinds of art. An intermediate body, responsibly and accountably disposing of public money and including in itself people with direct current knowledge of the arts and their administration, is a much more attractive proposition. [...]

Definition of 'The Arts'

A further characteristic of an adequate intermediate body is that it should have a clearly defined and effective area of responsibility. This is not now the case with the Arts Council. In its first formulation, under the 1946 charter, it came directly under the Treasury and was concerned with 'the fine arts exclusively'. This notoriously difficult category was taken in practice to include theatre, opera, ballet, concert music, painting and sculpture. Under the 1967 Charter the category became the generalised 'the arts', and, in certain ways, literature, film, photography, 'performance art' and 'community arts' were taken on board; the Council was also moved (in 1964) to come under the Department of Education and Science.

The later definition is more in line with real needs, but the former, for all its evidently residual character, in a way just because of it, had more consistency. Socially, the original arts were the cultural interests of an older upper-middle and middle class: a limited government initiative – a financial rather than a cultural or educational intervention – would help to sustain them and make them more widely accessible. But the cultural situation was already rapidly changing. Radio was already the primary distributor of concert music and of drama; television, if unevenly, was to become the major distributive channel of all arts, in terms of numbers. Moreover, once the shift to a cultural and educational rather than financial policy had been made, quite different social relations were in question; not just increased access to a relatively enclosed and continuing culture, but a complex and interacting set of new and old arts, new and old media and institutions, new and older audiences. Throughout, meanwhile, there had been the relative exclusion of literature: not because it was clearly outside the 'fine arts' – there had been no period since 1620 when it could be even plausibly argued that the theatre contained more serious art than printed books – but because public provision, at the level of access, was already provided at the level of free libraries. However, once it had happened that the greater part of the Council's money went to sustaining primary producers, and only after that to sustaining and developing means of distribution, this exclusion became in principle untenable, though in terms of relative sums allotted, it has continued to this day.

The whole complex of changing social and cultural relations has produced major problems for any kind of Arts Council. The development of socially as well as formally experimental art (the fringe drama companies presenting plays in more public places than theatres; public performance art and the area of locally based community arts) led to problems in assessment which the talisman of 'standards' (itself difficult enough in a restricted 'fine arts' category) could not resolve. Yet strict assessment of the quality of these uses of public money was still obviously necessary. The Council found itself caught between residual notions of quality (the continuing professional 'fine arts'), new notions of quality (movement beyond academic and establishment art) and new social and cultural notions of the inevitable relation between quality and situation: the specific relations of works of art to their audiences, which were relevant not only to problems in non-theatre drama companies and community arts but, by a crucial twist, to the educational aims embodied in the new Charter and the new responsibility to an educational rather than a financial government department. And if these problems of assessment were not already difficult enough, the Council found itself given responsibility for 'the arts' in a period in which the broadcasting organisations and a significant number of publishers (especially in paperback) were becoming major providers.

It is not the Arts Council that has failed to resolve this developing complexity and the consequent muddle, though its consensual tone has led to repeated attempts to accept the muddle, to take it as something that has to be lived with. The central failing is at a more public level and specifically at the level of Government organisation. Institutions and problems relating to the arts, though of course often relating inextricably to other matters also, are distributed across the responsibilities of government departments in what looks like the work of a sorcerer's apprentice. No consistent cultural policy, even at the simplest level of the provision of public money, is, for example, possible without some minimal correlation of the work of the Arts Council and of the broadcasting organisations. Yet broadcasting, from its original context of security in the early 1920s, comes under the Home Office. The Press and publishing come under the Department of Industry. [...]

The British State and Its Ruling Class
It would be naive to discuss the principles and problems of intermediate bodies without paying some attention to the character of the British State and its ruling class. Indeed, it can be argued that intermediate bodies of the kind we have known were made possible by this character. The British State has been able to delegate some of its official functions to a whole complex of semi-official or nominally independent bodies because it has been able to rely on an unusually compact and organic ruling class. Thus it can give Lord X or Lady Y both public money and apparent freedom of decision in some confidence, subject to normal procedures of report and accounting, that they will act as if they were indeed State officials. The British State gets a surprisingly large amount of its public work, from the House of Lords to the Governors of the BBC, from Royal Commissions to Consumers' Councils and from Committees of Inquiry to the Arts Council, done by these processes of out-work and administered co-option. [...]

But we have now to face the fact that the principle of an intermediate body, sometimes described as if it were a British democratic innovation, is administered by this essentially different principle of a relatively informal but reliable and consensual ruling class. We have to test the mix in each specific case. The University Grants Committee, distributing public money between universities, is drawn on the representative principle from people in universities – and thus looks like an authentic intermediate body – but the representatives are in fact chosen by the Department of Education and Science, in the familiar practice of administratively controlled intermediacy. The Arts Council is not even a mixed case. It is politically and administratively appointed, and its members are not drawn from arts practice and administration but from that vaguer category of 'persons of experience and goodwill', which is the State's euphemism for its informal ruling class.[...]

Cultural Policies
The social relations of British culture have been changing so fast, together with changes in media and in forms of art, that neither the residual model of government patronage of the fine arts, nor the succeeding model of funded extension of the received arts, is now adequate. It is then, of course, true that there will be intense controversy about new models of cultural policy to replace them. This is already clear from the public arguments of the last twenty years. At the special conference, Richard Hoggart, who does not share all my views about the Arts Council and about ways of reorganising it, correctly identified one area of choice: between a Council constituted to represent the existing (second) model, with any necessary improvements in that direction; and a Council in which the now essentially alternative conceptions of the cultural policy could be theoretically and practically argued out and developed. The first type of Council would be consensual; the second essentially disputative. He did not go on to declare his own preference:

there are obviously practical arguments both ways. But if I am right about the nature of the current problems, and about their origins in real changes of circumstance and demand, the case for the second type of Council makes itself. There must be some specific and continuing national body in which the merits of alternative general policies, and at the same time the practicalities of the detailed and complex choices that flow from them, can be properly argued through and decided. Such a Council would necessarily be open to public attendance and report, and to parliamentary questioning, preferably by a specific Select Committee. Until we get such a Council, some form of National Standing Conference, open to all the organisations concerned, is urgently required. [...]

Sir William Rees Mogg

The Glory of the Garden

Extract from the Preface to *The Glory of the Garden: The Development of the Arts in England – A Strategy for a Decade*. The Arts Council of Great Britain (London). 1984

[...] Whatever may be the controversies in economics, I remain an avowed Keynesian in the arts. When one reads his remarkably far-sighted talk [see page 142], it is clear that the Arts Council has in nearly forty years kept faith with his ideal of giving sup-port and opportunity rather than trying to teach or censor the artist.

We might indeed follow Jefferson's example in framing the Declaration of Independence and apply John Locke's celebrated principles of liberty to the arts:

> As the highest perfection of intellectual nature lies in a careful and constant pursuit of true and solid happiness, so the care of ourselves, that we mistake not imaginary for real happiness, is the necessary foundation of our liberty ... The variety of pursuits shows that everyone does not place his happiness in the same thing, or choose the same way to it. Men may choose different things and yet all choose right.

Care for real excellence, encouragement of variety for the audience, support of freedom for the artist, are the foundation of liberty for the arts. The counterpart of liberty is responsibility. An Arts Council that stands back to respect liberty, puts the responsibility for art on the artists, and the responsibility for practical success on the managers of companies.

It is clear also that Keynes' second aim of making London 'a great artistic metropolis' has been achieved, to a degree even beyond what he envisaged. With the four national companies, the London orchestras, the post-war development of galleries and exhibitions, London is probably the greatest artistic metropolis of the modern world, challenged only by New York and more than bearing comparison with any continental European city. Considering the part Arts Council funding has played in this development, and the fact that London was indeed 'half a ruin' when it began, this is an achievement that alone would justify the comparatively modest public expenditure on the work of the Arts Council in the period.

It is, however, also clear that his first aim, 'to decentralise and disperse the dramatic and musical and artistic life of this country', has not been adequately realised. Despite the excellent work that has been done in Scotland, Wales and the English regions, the Arts Council has fallen short in its first priority, just as it has surpassed expectations in its second. The quality of London itself as an artistic metropolis shows up the deficiencies of the arts provision in the rest of the country. For this, the Arts Council must accept its share of the blame. The decision in 1956 to abolish the regional offices that Keynes had created was an almost unbelievably retrogressive step. Fortunately, they were replaced by the Regional Arts Associations, and fortunately also the Regional Arts Associations were a partnership between the Arts Council and the local authorities just as Keynes envisaged. But time was lost and the Regional Arts Associations were funded only on a modest scale.

The same underfunding occurs throughout regional provision. Neither in drama, music, art nor opera is the regional provision other than badly funded by comparison either with London or with what is demonstrably needed. One comparison will show how wide the gap is. No theatre company based entirely in the regions enjoys an Arts Council subsidy equal to one-tenth of that given to either of the two national theatre companies, the National Theatre or the Royal Shakespeare Company. Most receive less than a fiftieth. That does not mean that these two theatre companies receive too much. Indeed, the Priestley Report found to the contrary. But it is a clear indication that some provincial theatres receive too little. There are many good drama companies, orchestras, exhibitions and opera and dance companies throughout Great Britain that would not exist without the Arts Council. But we live as two artistic nations – London and everyone else.

No fair examination would therefore conclude that Keynes' first priority had been adequately achieved. It would be a great mistake to try to strengthen the regions by destroying the metropolis, to achieve Keynes' first priority by losing the achievement of the second. London is 'a place to visit and to wonder at' and that achievement – one of the most important of the post-war achievements of British culture – must not be put at risk.

On the whole, I prefer to argue the case for funding the Arts Council on the contribution of the arts to British civilisation. But it is obvious that the attraction of London as an artistic metropolis is essential to Great Britain's appeal to tourists. The loss of London's arts would cost the balance of trade as much as the loss of a major industry. The economic argument is quite clear-cut and it applies most strongly to London, though it also applies to the regional arts.

Nevertheless, after forty years, it is time to get to grips with Keynes' first priority, to decentralise and disperse the dramatic and musical and artistic life of this country. The measures required to do so include the institutional, the administrative and the financial.

Geoff Mulgan and Ken Worpole

Saturday Night or Sunday Morning?

Extracts from Chapters 1 and 8 of *Saturday Night or Sunday Morning? From Arts to Industry – New Forms of Cultural Policy*, Comedia (London), 1989

Chapter 1

New Definitions for Old

Who is doing most to shape British culture in the late 1980s? Next, Virgin, WH Smith, News International, Benetton, Channel 4, Saatchi and Saatchi, the Notting Hill Carnival and Virago, or the Wigmore Hall, Arts Council, National Theatre, Tate Gallery and Royal Opera House? Most people know the answer, and live it every day in the clothes they wear, the newspapers they read, the music they listen to and the television they watch. The emergence (and disappearance) of new pursuits, technologies, techniques and styles – whether windsurfing, jogging, aerobics, Zen, compact discs, angling, wine-making, CB radio, rambling, hip hop, home computing, photography, or keeping diaries – represent changes that bear little relation to traditional notions of art and culture and the subsidised institutions that embody them.

With the special exception of broadcasting, State policies have for too long been directed at only one small corner of the world – the world of theatres, concert halls and galleries. It is as if every energy has been directed to placing a preservation order on a Tudor cottage, while all around, the developers were building new motorways, skyscrapers and airports. In this, Labour has always been complicit. It has failed to make the links between the old arts and the new, electronic forms. It has failed to break out of the false divisions between high and low culture, and has never challenged the power of the tiny, metropolitan elite that views the world of the arts as its own private playground. Nor do traditional socialist solutions have much to offer. The prospect of nationalising newspapers, record companies and advertising agencies is rightly viewed with enormous suspicion. The idea that 'art' can simply be mobilised in the service of socialism has little resonance in an age when the most radical liberation struggles around gender, race, sexuality, disability and imperialism have only a partial relationship to a socialist hegemony.

Yet, after years of electoral decline, there is a dawning awareness that socialism without a cultural programme is a barren project. Unable to muster visions and fictions, the economic programmes for change lose their resonance and become just so many more new – and possibly unreal – figures and false promises. Throughout its history, reflecting its base in workplace organisation, the Labour Party has been lukewarm about culture. The rich and varied heritage of the Chartists, William Morris and the Socialist League, the Clarion Clubs, the ILP choirs, the workers' theatre movement, was never incorporated into the kind of all-embracing party culture of the other great European socialist parties like the Swedish or German SDPs and the Italian PCI. When in power, Labour has mostly promulgated bi-partisan, 'non-political' arts policies. Its key interventions have been in support of Covent Garden rather than working-class culture. Its radicalism has taken the form of calls for more spending on the arts, though in practice this has involved an even greater transfer of resources from working-class taxpayers to subsidise the pleasure of the metropolitan elite.

The price paid for the absence of a coherent socialist perspective has been marginalisation. While the Arts Council funded a few more theatres and the occasional touring opera company, the real popular pleasures have been provided and defined within the marketplace. The cultural industries that produce the words, sounds, images and meanings that surround and bombard us have been immensely dynamic in recent years. The Marxist superstructure, the realm of ideas and ideologies, has become a primary motor for the economic base. Converging around the television set, a host of new, information-based industries is growing up, linking computing, telecommunications and the diffusion of culture. In this context, the marginalisation of State intervention and the artificial governmental division between art (The Office of Arts and Libraries), the economy (Treasury and Department of Trade and

Industry), broadcasting (Home Office) and education (Department of Education) have left the commercial marketplace with all the best tunes. While the State concentrates on a fairly limited opera repertoire and a Shakespearean heritage for the tourists, the corporate planners and strategy executives of the multinationals are only too keen to write the real cultural policies for themselves.

The worst result would be a two-tier culture: on the one hand a world of subsidised or sponsored arts and public service broadcasting for the elite, and on the other, commercial, mass-produced, largely imported culture for the rest. In this book, we argue for an alternative based on supporting the rich diversities of activity in Britain within all forms of culture, popular and traditional. We argue for a shift away from the traditional, patronage-based models of funding towards new forms of investment and regulation more suited to the realities of culture as a modern industry, and geared to the independence of those who make culture. These policies are not blind to the fundamental politics of culture so vehemently denied by the arts elite. The traditional bipartisan approaches have allowed dominant ideologies and institutions to dominate. They have failed to recognise the massive social power of culture for those on the receiving end of material and ideological oppressions, and the ways in which struggle takes place within commercial forms and the market as much as in the corridors of the State. [...]

Chapter 8

Conclusions

What Would Happen if Labour Came to Power?

This book has been written with a sense of urgency. For the first time for many years, there is now a strong possibility that the Labour Party might regain power at a national level within the next two years. Yet Labour is still a long way from being able to project a radical and attractive policy for the arts and culture. It remains constrained by the dead weight of the past in the form of lingering attachments to the traditional arts and a deep, puritan suspicion of the modern forms of popular culture. Despite advances in recent years, it still lacks a coherent media policy capable of encompassing both community newspapers and satellite broadcasting. Meanwhile, the important new movements around community arts and the arts of the 'new communities' developing out of distinctive women's, ethnic, gay and lesbian cultures, do not in themselves address directly what we see as some of the most crucial cultural battlegrounds of the late 1980s.

These battlegrounds lie largely outside the scope of traditional arts policies. We believe that it is no longer enough for a socialist policy to call, for example, for more community artists to be sent to the estates, for gallery charges to be scrapped, for the Arts Council to be reformed, or for a small network of community recording studios to be set up; unless it can also begin to tackle the problems of how key monopoly distributors such as WH Smith and John Menzies can be taken into social ownership, of how the Murdoch empire can be broken up, and of how support can be given to an independent, self-sustaining cultural economy, it will be condemned to marginality. Successful intervention in the macro-dynamics of the cultural sector is, for us, one of the key long-term tasks of a radical cultural policy. Without such an intervention, the cultural movements of the 'new communities' will continue to run the risk of being marginalised, co-opted and eventually destroyed.

This sort of intervention is also vital if the economic strength of the British cultural economy is to be exploited in the historic task of bringing Britain back to some form of full employment. Youth culture, alongside its offshoots in style, fashion, music and design has been one of the few areas of the economy successfully to make the transition to the late 1980s, creating jobs and finding new international markets. Arts policies

have almost totally ignored it, while economic development programmes have preferred the more orthodox problems of manufacturing and services like tourism and catering. Meanwhile, media policy has largely been seen as the personal prerogative of the Prime Minister, used primarily to service short-term party political needs.

The costs of not having a coherent strategy for the arts and communications are more than economic. Allowing the new media to develop along the lines of Fleet Street, mortgaged to international capital through wilful neglect, would be unforgivable. To the extent that such a lack of policy allows other, more powerful, international forces to determine the nature of change, it admits defeat from the start.

Alongside work done as part of the GLC's London Industrial Strategy, at GLEB and other local authorities and enterprise boards, we hope that this book will be part of a shift towards a more forward-looking and relevant cultural policy. Our shopping list outlines the kind of fundamental institutional reforms that would be needed before such as shift could become a reality at the national level. The key existing cultural institutions such as the BBC and the Arts Council are tired and out of step with their times. They belong to a time when the British elite could unproblematically universalise its own beliefs and prejudices.

Happily, that time is past. (A recent survey of young people showed that their favourite television channel was, perhaps surprisingly, Channel 4, a choice that we believe is significant and deserves serious attention.) The new institutions will have to be both more clearly accountable, and more clearly open to the demands of audiences. They will have to be able to support experiment, risk and innovation without the contempt for the popular that linked the traditional elites to the avant gardes. And

they will need to recognise their wider social and economic responsibility: art has never been sovereign and accountable only to itself. When resources are scarce, the arts have no inherent rights over the demands of health, education or any other area of public spending.

In this section, we outline some of the basic institutional elements of the policy. In the first place, the existing division of responsibilities between the Office of Arts and Libraries, the Department of the Environment, the Department of Trade and Industry and the Home Office needs to be urgently rationalised by the creation of an integrated Ministry of Arts and Communications. On its own, such a reform would do little. But without it there is no prospect of a coherent national approach to the range of policy issues that will undoubtedly face governments in the last years of this century.

Such a Ministry would be responsible for overseeing the development of the sector as a whole, establishing a National Media and Cultural Industries Enterprise Board to invest in strategic areas in the press, music and publishing, a Film Finance Board for funding film and video productions, providing funding towards regional boards (which would also be funded through local taxation), directly funding national arts institutions, museums and galleries, overseeing broadcasting regulation, establishing training bodies, establishing a framework for levies and redistribution of the proceeds, developing copyright law, and ensuring the divestment of multinational press and other holdings.

Alongside such a Ministry, some form of elected broadcasting authority will be needed to supersede the current role of the IBA and BBC board of governors. As technologies of transmission proliferate, regulation will inevitably become more complex. An elected body, including co-opted members from voluntary organisations, national and local government, would establish sub-committees to regulate different parts of the system – ITV channels, licence-fee-funded channels, cable channels. It would be responsible for the allocation of the licence fee between different services, the allocation of national franchises, and issues such as rights of reply. Alongside the Ministry it would be responsible for determining policy with respect to new areas of broadcasting. This national Broadcasting authority would operate under statute with a responsibility to ensure that broadcasting reflects the full range of cultures and perspectives in British society. Having an elected base, it would gain a legitimacy and independence from government impossible in the present, patronage-based system.

Alongside a National Media and Cultural Industries Enterprise Board, elected regional development boards need to be set up responsible for investment, grant aid and regulation of some of the local media. These boards would combine directly elected and co-opted members. They would provide the base of democratic accountability that has been so lacking in the past. Some argue that democracy would sound the death knell of experiment and excellence, diverting state support to a bland, populist mush, and that only the cognoscenti can be trusted to understand the vanguards of national change. Though we have our doubts as to the cultural literacy of many local politicians, there can be little doubt that many local authorities have shown themselves far more receptive to the real vanguards of cultural change than the Arts Council, which recently identified the growth of early music societies as the key musical development of the early 1980s.

Local boards would be funded both from local taxation (following an updating of local government arts and general economic powers) and through central government. Just as at a national level an enterprise board would probably work best with relatively autonomous units within it

(responsible perhaps for investment in women's publishing, or black music, or new printing technologies) so at a regional level, groups of officers should be able to make investments independently rather than passing all decisions through a single, probably over-cautious, committee.

Alongside new institutions, new criteria are needed for appraising funding choices, which encompass the creation of work, and the needs of audiences, as well as a wider set of aesthetic considerations that break free from redundant divisions between high and low art. The capitalist world has made enormous strides in understanding the ways in which people use and enjoy its products. Unless the public sector can develop its own categories and techniques for understanding how leisure services, community radio stations or arts centres are used and perceived it will deserve to be ignored.

Blueprints have a habit of remaining blueprints. The more detailed and structured they are, the less chance there is of them ever turning into reality. The details of the programme advanced in this book and of how the local, national and indeed transnational state can begin to influence transnational corporations, will of course have to emerge from practice and experience.

More important, perhaps, than the detailed policies are the principles that underlie them. In the long run we are calling for a major conceptual shift that may prove difficult for those for whom art is still exclusively about theatre rather than television, easel paintings rather than design, live opera rather than recorded music. It will require a shift towards understanding how the modern popular arts as commodities are produced, marketed and distributed by industries dependent on skills, investment and training, and a development away from older pre-industrial ideologies of art that emphasised personal development and the sacrosanct value of individual self-expression (but for only a few).

The Arts Council of Great Britain

Towards a National Arts and Media Strategy

Extracts from Introduction and Chapter 4 of *Towards a National Arts and Media Strategy*, Arts Council of Great Britain (London), 1992

This strategy is about the central place of the arts in society. It is also about helping to create the conditions in which arts of all sorts, from all cultures, can flourish; in which opportunities to practice the arts are open to all; and in which active reading, looking, listening, making and discussing the arts take place throughout society. It is produced by the Arts Council of Great Britain, the British Film Institute, the Crafts Council and the Regional Arts Boards. That is the 'we' to be found throughout this document, since we were the bodies charged by Richard Luce, then Minister for the Arts, with producing this strategy. In addition, it has benefited from a partnership between the organisations commissioned by the Minister, the local authorities and the museums funding bodies. More generally, we received advice by means of the largest consultative process on the arts that has ever taken place in Great Britain. [...]

These are a few of the key themes that underlie what follows.

I. The Arts and Culture at the Core of Citizenship

The arts are both individual and communal; spiritual and earthy; celebratory and subversive; special and everyday. The increasing public and political prominence of the arts has led to a growing expectation that they justify themselves in terms of local or national image and economic development. Certainly, they often can. But this must not drive out the inherent, and unquantifiable, value of the arts, in terms of the creative spark and spiritual enrichment. It is hard to discover an aesthetic language that carries the same weight as the 'hard facts' of attendance figures and invisible export earnings. But a new balance must be established between them, and this strategy is, in part, an attempt to do just that.

II. The Arts and Culture as an Integrated Whole

The arts that receive support from public funds are part of the broader picture of our cultural life. They have no special status because they are funded. Distinctions between 'high' and 'low' culture, between 'commercial' and 'non-commercial' arts, between professional and amateur, do not reflect the way in which most people experience the arts: high quality and cultural significance are what matter, and they can be achieved in a whole range of forms from opera to television drama, from sculpture to folk song.

III. Culture and 'Cultural Provision'

The phrase 'cultural provision' suggests that there is a clear set of cultural goods to be delivered to people. This is too passive a model for now and the future, if it ever was appropriate. At the start of their book *Saturday Night or Sunday Morning*, Geoff Mulgan and Ken Worpole pose this question:

> Who is doing most to shape British culture in the late 1980s? Next, Virgin, WH Smith, News International, Benetton, Channel 4, Saatchi & Saatchi, the Notting Hill Carnival and Virago, or the Wigmore Hall, Arts Council, National Theatre, Tate Gallery and Royal Opera House? Most people know the answer, and live it every day in the clothes they wear, the newspapers they read, the music they listen to and the television they watch. The emergence (and disappearance) of new pursuits, technologies, techniques and styles ... represent changes that bear little relation to traditional notions of arts and culture and the subsidised institutions that embody them.

One need not accept the implication that for many years public money has been backing the wrong horse; after all, almost every interest is a 'minority interest'. But there is a truth here as well. To use a high-flown metaphor: the arts, cultural industries, recreation and entertainment are a sea, and the Arts Council and its partners are swimmers in it. The more that we can learn about the tides and currents, the better. That too, is what this strategy is about. [...]

Variety and Quality in the Arts
A Hierarchy of the Arts?

This chapter discusses two areas crucial to the arts – variety and quality – which in practice are more closely related than in theory. They meet over the issue of the hierarchy, or supposed hierarchy, of art forms – which can be summarised in the misleading question: is a Keats poem better than a Bob Dylan song lyric?

The question is misleading because those who pose it are not actually talking about the work of those particular artists, but are using the question as a surrogate for the issue of relative or absolute values in the arts.

To over-simplify, on the one side are those who argue that all opinions on quality in the arts and culture are subjective and thus that none has greater validity than any other; at the extreme, that Shakespeare's work is neither better nor worse than, but merely different from, the contents of a telephone directory. In practice, they would argue, the accepted canon of great art has been determined by issues of history and power – it is a question of who was in a position to make the judgements, rather than of inherent quality. On the other side, the argument tends to be not that a particular Keats poem is better or worse than a particular Dylan lyric (after all, so what?) but that there is something inherently superior in the form in which one of these artists worked. The subtext to this point of view is that there is a real gulf between 'high' and 'popular' art; that art as a whole has degenerated over the past 180 years; and that it is the duty of those who care about the arts to make and be seen to make judgements of quality.

Despite the gulf separating these positions, what they have in common is a refusal to make such judgements – since the latter group is judging on the basis of labels or categories rather than individual works of art. However one defines artistic quality, it is rather restrictive to suggest that it is found only in particular forms of art. There is also the point that any supposed hierarchy is likely to be culturally determined. How are those schooled only in Western visual arts traditions to place, for instance, Russian Orthodox icon painting or Islamic weaving?

One of our key responsibilities is to make judgements about the allocation of scarce resources. The concept of quality is central to the making of such judgements (as to its complexity, see below), and we believe that it should be central to all those who work in the arts. But the concept is not associated solely with particular art forms, and we entirely repudiate the idea that some forms are of themselves superior or inferior to others.

Variety and the Role of the Funding System

Variety was an issue that arose implicitly rather than explicitly during the strategy consultation process. It is when one puts together the range of art forms, ideologies and ways of delivering and participating in the arts that were raised during the process that variety becomes an overwhelmingly strong theme. We shall seek to encourage variety of arts provision and activity by every means we can.

One implication of this is that the family of art forms in which we should take an interest goes well beyond what in the past we have been able to support. Architecture is as good an example as any.

The last twenty years have seen a phenomenal growth in general public awareness and interest in environmental issues. As part of this, architecture is now rightly and widely seen to have a major influence on the quality of life, rather than being a technical matter of little concern to the general public. Hence the establishment of the Arts Council Architecture Unit, which is intended particularly to stimulate public debate in this vital area, but which has also been widely welcomed within the architecture profession. The

cultural dimension of architecture and its links with the rest of the visual arts have for too long been undervalued, and the funding system is well placed to reverse the trend in the 1990s.

Similarly with the whole issue of design, which, as Helen Rees argued in her strategy discussion paper, is a central but neglected cultural issue.

Then there are forms that have been more widely accepted as coming under the banner of the arts, but which have been marginalised by the funding system: for instance, folk and traditional art, new circus, carnival, puppetry – and, many would argue, photography and literature.

There are several reasons why these attitudes must change. First, it is simply myopic to focus in the future only on what has been supported in the past. Second, these issues and forms are significant to the artistic and cultural life of a large part of the population to which we are accountable. Third, as we argued in Chapter 3, development in the arts is crucially hampered if support structures are based around rigid existing divisions. Design and architecture influence and are influenced by the visual arts generally. Developments in new circus affect physical theatre. The freedom of carnival, its lack of distinction between spectator and participant, has wider implications for theatre. Thus, even if it were not necessary to take an interest in these issues and forms for their own sake – which it is – it would be worth doing so for their impact on those arts that we have traditionally supported. (It is, of course, also worth mentioning the need for each of the funding bodies to keep in touch with developments in areas in which the others work: visual arts and crafts practices act and react on one another; emerging practices in film, video and television influence many other arts; and so on.)

What sort of intervention by the funding system is appropriate in such areas? There is no single answer to this. For major issues such as design

and architecture, where our financial stake will be very small, our responsibility must be largely to foster debate and raise awareness among the public as well as the experts, as for instance the BFI did in its series of publications in 1990 about issues in broadcasting, and as will be the main task of the Arts Council Architecture Unit.

The situation is different in relation to such specific but influential forms as puppetry, illustration, mime and carnival. In such cases, the best help that the funding system can provide is threefold: first, funding opportunities that are flexible and not tied down to rigid artform divisions; second, explicit acknowledgement that they are indeed art forms; and third, organisational and financial help for meetings of practitioners including, if appropriate, assistance with setting up national or regional membership organisations.

Acknowledging the value of variety in the arts and repudiating the idea of a hierarchy of art forms does not mean that all forms should attract subsidy. It does mean that we must not rule out subsidy for any form simply because of its name. Innovation, quality, need and competing priorities are relevant factors; the art-form label is not.

Quality

The issue of quality is so complex that the main contribution of this strategy may be no more than to state its complexity and to call for wider debate. Nonetheless, some attempt will be made to define the main areas of discussion.

We have argued above that quality is an inescapable concept in the arts, and in support of the arts. This conclusion may stand even if one has sympathy for Rupert Murdoch's view in relation to 'quality television' (though it applies as much to the other arts) that:

> *Much of what is claimed to be quality television here is no more than the parading of the prejudices and interests [of broadcasters] and has*

had debilitating effects on British society, by producing a TV output that is so often obsessed with class, dominated by anti-commercial attitudes and with a tendency to hark back to the past.

It may well be an unwilling agreement with this view – in effect, guilt at traditional 'top down' notions of quality – that has prompted some to retreat from the issue. Nonetheless, such critiques should lead one to improve and refine the concept, not to abandon it: that would be an abdication of responsibility. As Geoff Mulgan has argued, again in the context of television:

Criticism and judgement are part of the very pro-cess of making television. If critics and audiences do not repeatedly criticise pro-grammes, developing a more sophisticated armoury with which to judge, then it is all too likely that standards will slip, that bad tele-vision will displace good.

If one accepts that judgements can and must be made, then the minimum consensus arising from consultation is that there is more than one scale, and indeed more than one type, of critical judgement. A few different types of quality may be listed here:

(i) Creator or producer quality
This is quality in terms of the creator's gut feelings, or by reference to such standards as 'production values'. Alongside quality as defined by expert advisers or critics, it is probably the most generally understood use of the term in the arts. It is intimately bound up with issues of artistic freedom, and is essentially subjective.

(ii) Expert assessor/critic quality
This is similar to (i) but the assessment is now carried out by someone – however expert or well informed – who is outside the work in question; again subjective.

(iii) Consumer quality
At its crudest, this is purely a numbers game: an exhibition receiving 5,000 visitors each day is better than one receiving 3,000; quality is a full theatre. This sort of measure can be used, as Rupert Murdoch used it in the quotation above, as a stick with which to beat a presumed elite. But our starting point for this document was that the arts are not a numbers game. So if 'consumer quality' is to be a useful concept, it must be at least as much about the nature of the artistic experience as it is about the numbers involved.

(iv) Quality in community
As our public-attitudes research demonstrated, the arts can be powerful agents for bringing people together in communities defined by geography, ethnicity, gender, religion, or simply shared interest. To the extent that they succeed in conveying a shared vision – giving voice to what had previously been silent – the arts may be considered to be of high quality.

(v) Quality in variety
This is the other side of the coin of (iv): it is a concept of quality based on the overall avail-ability of the arts rather than on individual works of art. The argument runs that in a society of many different interests, views, cultures and experiences, one of the essential tests of artistic quality is that the arts reflect that diversity.

(vi) Quality in longevity
Is it reasonable to suggest that works that have 'passed the test of time', which still appear alive to us, after centuries, say, are for that reason of high quality?

(vii) Quality as 'fitness as purpose'
The essence of this approach to quality is that it is not an abstract issue but one that arises from its context: in certain places, at certain times, opera is more appropriate than rock; at others, vice versa. As to what constitutes great opera or great rock music, one of the tests will have to apply!

Assessing Quality – the Role of the Funding System
We believe that funding decisions should be int-imately bound up with issues of quality, and it is this that makes the above discussion of more than academic importance. If the resources available to us were vastly larger than they are, judgements of quality would be less necessary, because there would be enough money to go around. The less money there is, the more necessary and the more difficult it is to make judgements based on quality. Thinking must be developed not by the funding system alone, but in partnership with others who work in and care about the arts. A few general points can be made.

First, one can draw up a list, though not a comprehensive one, of factors relevant to the assessment of quality. Such a list would include aesthetic ambition, artistic and social innovation and significance and likely durability; each of which terms, of course, requires further analysis.

Second, it is important to focus as much on the artistic process as on the artistic product. Factors more appropriate for objective analysis arise at that stage.

Third, we accept the strong view of artists and arts organisations during the consultation pro-cess that self-assessment should become an important part of assessing quality. This should be as rigorous as any other form of assessment – it is far more than an organisation saying 'We think we did well (or badly)'. Its starting point must be an artistic mission statement – a state-ment in advance of overall aims and objectives, against which performance can be assessed. But if an artist or organisation wishes to receive fund-ing then this is clearly not enough: criteria and assessment must be a matter for negotiation between the organisation and the funder.

Fourth, in order to discharge our responsibility to assess quality, we need to broaden the range of experience available to us from both our advisers and our staff. The role of advisers needs to become more coherent. The wider the range of the arts we support, the more diverse are the scales of judgement and notions of quality that we must apply, and the greater is the range of arts experience and knowledge necessary to help develop and assess the work.

Fifth, and related to this, assessment is one of a funding body's most difficult and most vital tasks. We argue in Chapter 7 that if we wish to have the best assessment of the widest range of work, we may need to pay our assessors. Perhaps they should be paid as a matter of principle also: the creation of a contractual relationship with assessors could have beneficial consequences in terms of responsibility and accountability.

Finally, we must use measures and indicators of performance for no more than they are worth. They are substitutes for performance, not the thing itself. They cannot be 100% reliable and thus 100% reliance on them is inevitably a mistake. Those being assessed may work to score well on the assessment scales, rather than actually to focus on quality. (This is related to the sad phenomenon of arts organisations attempting to construct projects to meet inflexible funding criteria, rather than fulfil their own aims.) Measures of performance are no more than 'material', to be used critically as any other in judging how well an arts organisation is doing.

Conclusion

If we have an obligation to recognise and support new and evolving art forms, we have an equal obligation to act when art forms or ways of delivering the arts are losing their relevance. It is difficult to recognise such processes, but given lack of resources it is painful but necessary to respond to them. Flexibility of funding was one of the major themes of consultation and one of the areas seen as most in need of improvement. This is easy to accept in principle but tougher in

practice; reducing or ending the support of institutions or whole areas of activity is inevitably painful. If such tough decisions are to 'stick', there are two prerequisites that have been widely identified: an increase in the respect enjoyed by the funding system and in the range of advice available to it, an issue that recurs repeatedly in the strategy; and a more contractual relationship between public funders (including local authorities) and those they fund, which is considered in the next chapter.

We must be prepared to act as advocates in the arts even when we are not major financial players. This is not as arrogant as it may sound; our activity in these areas should only be by invitation, and it is surprising how often such activity is welcome. Thus, those working in the public libraries, major publishers and bookstore chains are entitled to look to the funding system for support in the 'cause' of literature. We should be prepared to argue for the recognition of movies as an art form as much as part of an industry. Arts broadcasters are entitled to whatever support and lobbying power, regional and national, the funding system has at its disposal.

Chapter 3 and 4 have argued for our developing imaginative ways of encouraging innovation, variety and ever higher quality, and acknowledging that there is no single scale of judgement or method of achievement for any of these. We must work with existing and potential clients, producers, promoters and others. This is a positive and exciting prospect.

The Arts

Mr Cormack (Staffordshire South): [...] We are dealing with one of the most important subjects that Parliament can debate, because, in a few years' time, amid the furore of a Tuesday and Thursday, the particular issues that might have excited passions today on many other fronts will be forgotten. If our civilisation is to survive, it is important that the buildings that encapsulate it and the works of art that speak of our heritage and history are preserved. It is now the responsibility of the National Heritage Department to do that. I am sure that there is not a single hon. Member in the House who would not wish my right hon. and hon. Friends success in the tremendous task, but we need to give higher priority to the subjects that we are debating today, in financial terms as well as parliamentary time.

Mr Terry Dicks (Hayes and Harlington): After the last few words of my hon. Friend the Member for Staffordshire, South (Mr Cormack) I feel almost like breaking out and singing 'Rule Britannia' or perhaps even the national anthem, so deeply do I feel about such matters. This is a club: it is the 'we all love the arts' club – the luvvies' club – and I am not a member. I am on the outside – a Philistine. Indeed, if you, Madam Deputy Speaker, will excuse the ethnic expression, if it were down to the unanimity of many hon. Members, I would be blackballed. I am delighted about that, because it is not the sort of club that I want to belong to.

I have heard a couple of things that interest me. The hon. Member for Caithness and Sutherland (Mr Maclennan) talked about bringing the arts to prison. The mind boggles. Imagine the Krays dressed up in tights and prancing around – that sounds rather good – or Ronnie Knight singing like an opera singer instead of like a bird? Perhaps we should bring in the Trojan horse for those on the other side – they might be able to use it for other purposes.

In the Whips Office, there is a Conservative research department brief on the arts. Under the heading 'The Government's Approach' it says: 'The central aim of Conservative arts policy has always been to encourage wider access to, and higher standards in, the arts. This aim applies at every level of artistic activity, from amateur dramatics to Grand Opera'. That is very good, very narrow, very exclusive and very elitist, is it not? There is no mention of anything but amateur dramatics in the arts. Why not darts? That is a game played in most working men's clubs throughout the world and in this country, particularly in the Northeast and Northwest, but there is no mention of improving the standard of darts playing. Ten-pin bowling is one of the most enjoyed leisure pursuits. Those who play have to pay the full cost of using the bowling lanes, but there is no mention of the Government becoming involved in improving standards there. The same is true of tiddlywinks. Table tennis is probably played by more people in this country than any other sport, but there is no mention of that. What always angers me about arts debates is that they are too damned elitist and closed shop.

There is no reference to the sports that I mentioned because they are not Establishment sports or pursuits – although given the decimation of the arts world in America and here due to a particular kind of illness, one wonders what the arts world gets up to in respect of some leisure pursuits. Our heritage is what the Establishment says it is. Time and again, I have asked for somebody to tell me in simple words – because I am a simple chap – what is so special about the arts and what is so ordinary about working-class pastimes.

I refer, for example, to the sport of my hon. Friend the Member for Falmouth and Camborne (Mr Coe). Watching him dashing for the tape in the Olympics, either just behind or just ahead of Steve Ovett – the sheer form of that man running for his country – was to witness an artistic form. It was something special and really nice. Compare that with the comments of my hon. Friend the Member for Staffordshire, South about looking at churches, which would bore me to tears. Once, I visited Athens. It seemed like a Wimpey building site and I was absolutely bored. However, that is my view. If somebody else thinks that old broken brick is marvellous, that is up to them – but do not expect me to accept your view of what is special. In the same way, I do not expect you to accept my view of my hon. Friend the Member for Falmouth and Camborne.

Madam Deputy Speaker (Dame Janet Fookes): Order. The hon. Gentleman should not bring me into it. He probably did not intend to.

Mr Dicks: I beg your pardon, Madam Deputy Speaker. We must be more generous and take a more general view of leisure pursuits. Take Pavarotti. Nowadays, he has to be helped onto the stage and leans against a backdrop. He has to be supported by other singers in case he falls over. He holds a handkerchief that is soaking wet, and he weighs 25 stone. His voice is going now. How on earth can he be seen to be singing a love song to a supposedly young lady but in reality to a woman of the same age and nearly the same weight who rocks and rolls every time she stands up? If others want to say that watching such a performance is their pastime and heritage, let them do so, but they should pay the full cost and not expect me, my constituents or anyone else to put our hands in our pockets to the tune of nearly £40 a seat to support them. If they are daft enough to follow that pursuit, let them be daft enough to pay for it.

For my sins, I have supported Bristol Rovers for fifty years. They are now struggling in the second division of the Endsleigh league. They are not doing well and are almost broke. When I attend their matches, and if I am not invited to the Chairman's box, which is just a little wooden structure – nothing like the luxury box in which the hon. Member for Newham, North-West (Mr Banks) sits when he goes to Chelsea …

Mr Tony Banks: The hon. Gentleman amuses me, but he is not getting away with that calumny. I am a Chelsea season-ticket holder and I have been a regular supporter for forty years. I queue for my ticket, sit in the stands, and pay for my seat – which is more than I can say for some Members of Parliament.

Mr Dicks: I will take a guess that the hon. Gentleman has a cup final ticket, which many Chelsea supporters do not and I bet that he did not have to queue for it. However, I am sure that the hon. Gentleman agrees that those of us who support soccer and appreciate its beauty – and the artistry of Manchester United, Newcastle and Blackburn Rovers in particular – pay the full economic cost of entering the grounds. Nobody says, 'The cost of a stand seat is £60, but we will give you £40 towards it because it is important in the wider context of the heritage of our country'. I suppose I should go down on one knee when I say that.

Football is our heritage. It was founded in this country, but nobody seems to care whether Hartlepool United goes out of existence, because the luvvies do not watch Hartlepool United but go in their droves to watch opera and ballet, kiss each other on both cheeks and say, 'Darling, how nice to see you'. That is why poor Hartlepool United and, to a lesser extent, Bristol Rovers have to struggle to make ends meet, week in and week out. I get fed up with it. I am sick and tired of it, and I hope that one day some common sense will be shown by members of my Front Bench and that something will be done.

The Conservative Research Department brief also states that the West End theatre is a success and that '11.5 million people attended shows at West End theatres in 1993-94'. However, it does not reveal that the most successful shows are those where supply and demand come together – as in the case of Sir Andrew Lloyd Webber's musicals – and make a price. The public are prepared to pay the full cost to see a damned good show. They are prepared to queue for tickets, or even to wait three or four months for them. In the arty-farty world, where it is a case of an obscure opera staged in the back of beyond, it is said, 'It will go out of business unless we give it money'. Of course it will go out of business if it is a load of rubbish and nobody wants to see it unless someone else pays for the ticket. That is the problem with the arts: so much rubbish is put on that nobody wants to see unless someone else makes a contribution.

I mentioned Manchester United and Arsenal. People pay the full cost to see them. The hon. Member for Hemsworth (Mr Enright) mentioned the wonderful game that Wigan played against Leeds last Saturday. Everyone involved paid their own way. There was no subsidy of the kind given to transporting musical instruments. Players

and fans paid the cost of their own journeys. They went to Wembley, where it cost them a fortune not only to watch the game but to pay for the barrels of beer afterwards – and good luck to them. There is no subsidy for those working-class lads up North who – unlike a load of middle-class twits swanning around in their bow ties and long frocks – support their team and pay their own way out of their hard-earned wages. They paid the full cost, and quite right. We are all very proud of them. The Conservative research document also makes reference to an access initiative, 'aimed at encouraging a wider range of people to participate in the arts, and at' – this is the best bit – 'improving (or deepening) the quality of their experience of the arts'.

Will my right hon. Friend the Secretary of State share with me – to use the 'in' phrase – what is meant by 'deepening the quality of experience of the arts'? That is politically correct tripe of the worst kind. Nobody wants to improve or deepen the quality of my experience of Bristol Rovers, but now we are to have a chap with a little hat and a badge saying, 'I can deepen your understanding of the arts – let me talk to you and help you to understand the arts'. I have never read so much tripe. If that is the sort of rubbish coming out of Central Office, God help us.

The briefing also states that 'Conservatives have provided record resources for the Arts Council. Between 1979 and 1993, the Arts Council's grant increased by 45% – over and above inflation'. What a boast! What a record! Some of my constituents have a job to survive, yet we boast of giving the Arts Council increases 'over and above inflation'. What sort of society does that? Value Added Tax has been imposed on domestic fuel because of the need to overcome the Government's debts or the country's debts, yet we can fire off money to arty-farty people and the luvvies. The poor, the sick and the elderly would be offended if they ever bothered to read that. They would ask, 'Why do we have to struggle?' Am I to tell them, 'If you cannot heat your flat tonight, I will put you in a car and take you to the Royal Opera House, and the Government will give you £40 to get in – and that will keep you warm as well'. That is the logic of this nonsense. How can we talk of making savings to get Government finances right when that sort of money is sent down the plughole? It is a disgrace and a shame and I hope that common sense will take hold one day and that some of us will have a chance to put things right.

The briefing adds that although the Arts Council grant will fall in 1994-95, it will still stand at £186 million, which will still be '£800,000 more than was originally planned in the 1992 autumn statement'. The luvvies will not like that. They will say that it is not enough. On the other hand, an extra £1.6 million will be provided in 1995-96 – again, more money wasted.

I did not vote for the National Lottery because 20% of the funds raised will go to the same gang of vested interests who seem able to bend the ear, neck and both legs of my right hon. Friend the Secretary of State. It is estimated that that 20% will be worth £75 million. I say to my right hon. Friend the Secretary of State: give me that £75 million and I will make the life of some of my constituents a lot better. I could ensure that life was a bit easier for the many old-age pensioners who have to live in those dreadful flats in Lambeth and who have to bar themselves in at night because they are unsafe. I would arrange a holiday for them – a cruise – instead of giving money to the plonkers in the arts world. Words fail me.

I have a new definition of the arm's-length principle. The arts world in general, and the luvvies in particular, should be at arm's length from taxpayers' pockets. Their grubby hands should be kept as far away as possible from taxpayers' pockets.

If the European Parliament can have Eurosceptic members, why cannot the Arts Council have 'arts-sceptic' members? I am available when my right hon. Friend the Secretary of State wants someone on the Council to pull it apart and close it down or to close down his Department, which is costing the taxpayer £1 million.

Mr Tony Banks (Newham, North-West): I am still trying to absorb the fusillade of the hon. Member for Hayes and Harlington (Mr Dicks). I did not expect him to finish so quickly, but I am glad that he did.

I offer my apologies. Like other hon. Members, I have tried to keep in touch with the debate, but I have treated it somewhat like a buffet – dipping in and out while electioneering elsewhere. I register my support for the right hon. Member for Old Bexley and Sidcup (Sir E. Heath), who, like others, complained that this important debate on the arts is being held today. We all know why that is so. If elections are going on in which we have a great interest – why should we not have an interest as politicians of sorts? – the House should rise for a day. We should get away from this nonsense. The last arts debate took place four years ago on the day of the European elections. No doubt the Government's business managers will be thinking of some other subject for 9 June.

Mr Cormack: We are not here on 9 June.

Mr Banks: Good. In that case, the Government will not have to think of a subject.

I am not criticising the Secretary of State – no doubt he takes the opportunity that he is given – but such arrangements convince me that the Government use arts debates such as this as a throwaway, a chuckaway and a sort of filling. The hon. Member for Hayes and Harlington made a number of points that are worth dealing with, and it would be worth doing so at a time when the House could consider them properly, without its mind being fixed somewhere else or hon. Members hoping to get away as quickly as possible to do a bit of last-minute fanatical canvassing – not that we need to do so in the London Borough of Newham, but I understand why Conservative Members might be panicking tonight.

I always know that the hon. Member for Hayes and Harlington will attend the arts debate, as he knows that I will. He certainly could not be described as a 'luvvy'. There is nothing luvvy about him. He is a sort of artistic anti-Christ who comes into our Chamber. He made a number of arguments, however, that we need to deal

with. One thinks of Andy Warhol's dictum that everyone is famous for fifteen minutes. It seems a pity that the hon. Member for Hayes and Harlington always chooses his quarter of an hour in an arts debate. One has the image at times that he would probably be happiest if he were out vandalising a Van Gogh, burning a book, or bombing a ballet, but the question that he asked – 'what is art?' – is an important one. Even the ramblings of a lunatic – I am not suggesting that the hon. Gentleman is a lunatic – contain the odd gem.

We addressed that question when the Labour Party controlled the Greater London Council. I was fortunate to be Chairman of the Arts Committee and I looked at which organisations were receiving the money. I found that the money was going to the great institutions: the National Theatre, English National Opera, London Festival Ballet and London orchestral concerts. I did not argue with that, but I wondered where the rest of the money was going. Why was it not going to regional organisations, community arts, ethnic arts or working-class activities, a description that the hon. Member for Hayes and Harlington might prefer? Middle-class people, particularly white middle-class people, were determining what was art. They decided that art was what they liked most. The hon. Gentleman is right to touch on that subject. Often, one found that those people went to opera not because they appreciated the music but because it was a good place to be seen. It makes me want to throw up a bit when I go to an artistic event and see people posing because it is a good place to be seen. I have some sympathy with the hon. Gentleman because some of the people who attend such events could easily pay a much higher price for their tickets. Why should people in the London Borough of Newham subsidise the arts for them?

I want to make opera, ballet and wonderful concert music available to the people of Newham. Subsidies are not targeted, as they should be, to expand audiences for those great art forms; they are targeted at a narrow group of people who have the fortune and economic ability to enjoy those art forms. One must consider other factors when considering arts funding. In the GLC days, we said that we should not dismiss transport. If there is no public transport or scant public transport by the time concerts, opera and theatre performances finish, ordinary people who do not have cars will not be able to get home. That is another in-built disadvantage that they face and another in-built advantage that those with a higher economic mobility have in enjoying the arts. We must consider the arts in their totality.

The hon. Member for Hayes and Harlington is right to point out that one needs to consider carefully who is defining what art is, because when that has been defined, public money and investment can be directed to it. I am not arguing against such investment being made – this is where I part company with the hon. Gentleman – but we should ensure that those who could benefit most from investment in the arts do so and that those who could afford to pay somewhat more do so too. I listened to the hon. Gentleman's speech, but it would be almost beyond anyone to deepen the appreciation of Bristol City …

Mr Dicks: Rovers.

IT IS ESTIMATED THAT

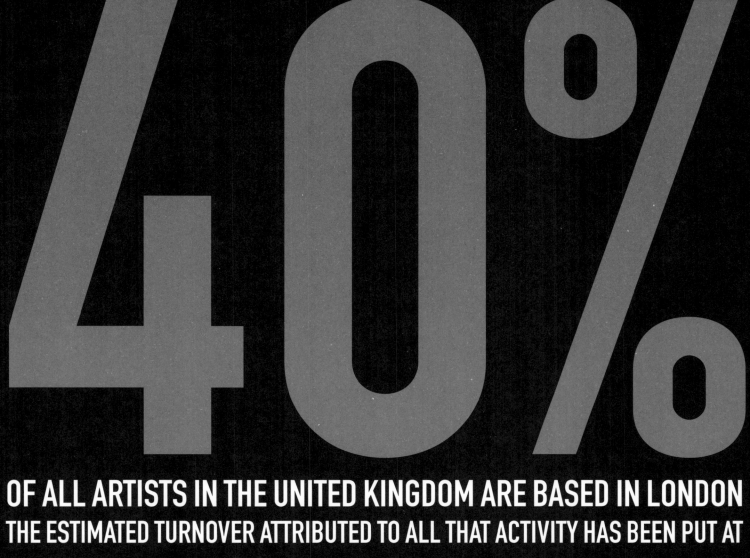

40%

OF ALL ARTISTS IN THE UNITED KINGDOM ARE BASED IN LONDON
THE ESTIMATED TURNOVER ATTRIBUTED TO ALL THAT ACTIVITY HAS BEEN PUT AT

£7,465 MILLION
THAT IS ALMOST 6%

OF OUR GROSS DOMESTIC PRODUCT
PUBLIC SUBSIDY AMOUNTED TO NO MORE THAN £500 MILLION OF THAT

Mr Banks: Or, indeed, Bristol Rovers. That would probably be even more challenging than deepening an appreciation of Bristol City. The hon. Member for Twickenham (Mr Jessel) spoke of the economic advantages of the arts. He has left the Chamber. I will forgive him doing that, but I could forgive him almost anything having sat at a concert in Smith Square and having heard him play Mozart. It is fantastic to have such ability and talent, which I did not associate with the hon. Member for Twickenham. Given the way in which he jerks around all over the place, I thought it would be impossible for him to play Mozart, but he did so – and to concert-performance standards. I found that it was a wonderful experience and I am deeply grateful to him for it. I could forgive him anything because of that ability to enrich my life and the lives of others through that beautiful music. He is a talented guy in artistic, if not political, terms. One should consider some of the arguments that the hon. Member for Twickenham advanced on the economic contribution of the arts. I should have thought that this was something that monetarists could grasp. Although we go over the statistics from time to time, they do not seem to sink in with the Government in the way that they should. London is the region about which I am most concerned. Some 11,700 organisations in the capital are involved in arts, culture and entertainment. They employ more than 200,000 people, which is equal to London's construction industry during the boom and to 6% of total employment. The hon. Member for Hayes and Harlington should think about those facts. A number of people from Hayes and Harlington may be employed in the arts industry – not just those who perform, but those who provide the background services, carpenters, scene painters and those who move the sets around. Thousands of people are associated with the arts. They do skilled and unskilled work. There are those who provide the food and so on.

So the hon. Member for Hayes and Harlington must think a little beyond the 'arty-farty' group, as he describes it, and realise that involved in and supporting the arts are many thousands of Londoners who work hard, not necessarily for large amounts of money, and contribute greatly to the economy of the capital city.

It is estimated that 40% of all artists in the United Kingdom are based in London. The estimated turnover attributed to all that activity has been put at £7,465 million. That is almost 6% of our gross domestic product. Public subsidy amounted to no more than £500 million of that. I assume that that is taking central government and local government investment together. That is a wonderful return. I say that to the hon. Member for Hayes and Harlington because he is the main, or indeed the only, sceptic here. Such arguments are worth bearing in mind, but he never touches on them during his fifteen-minute rants in our rare arts debates. Overseas earnings from the arts were estimated at £3,800 million, against imports of £2,500 million, giving a net balance of £1,300 million to the economy of the capital and the nation. That is a significant economic contribution. The hon. Member for Hayes and Harlington dismissed the people involved in the arts as 'luvvies'. I have some sympathy with him about some of the people involved in the arts. However, when one examines the people who enjoy the arts, one realises how significant the figures are. It has been estimated that in 1990 there were 94 million attendances at cultural events, 27 million at the cinema, 21 million at museums and galleries, 17.5 million at clubs and smaller music venues, 12 million at theatre, opera and dance, 11.6 million at historic houses and 4 million at concerts.

I am an avid soccer supporter, so I can perhaps say this to the hon. Gentleman more easily than anyone. Those figures are a hell of a lot higher than the figures for those who go to support football, although I take what he said about the fact that football and football supporters often get a rum deal.

Mr Dicks: I do not disagree with anything that the hon. Gentleman says. All that I am asking is why people want to attend arts events only if part of the cost is paid by someone else. If the hon. Gentleman went to Arsenal, he would have to pay the full cost. I cannot understand why one aspect of life receives a subsidy. I accept the figures that the hon. Gentleman has given, but I do not understand why the arts should expect to be subsidised by the rest of us.

Mr Banks: I am a Chelsea supporter. I would rather die than go to Arsenal.

The reason why the arts expect to be subsidised is that there is a good return on the investment. We invest in education and we invest in the arts. The hon. Gentleman seems to have picked out one area of public investment. I do not like the word 'subsidy' for the arts. I think that we subsidise defence, but we invest in the arts and in education. We invest in people's creativity – their manual and their mental creativity. That is a perfectly reasonable thing to do. The hon. Member for Hayes and Harlington should come to the Theatre Royal in my constituency in the London Borough of Newham. It is heavily subsidised by the Arts Council, the London arts board and the local authority. It is difficult for us to do that. We have kept seat prices as low as possible because the theatre is in an area of economic deprivation. The hon. Gentleman should come to the theatre and see the pensioners and unemployed people who come and enjoy performances. He tends to confine his criticisms – as I do at times – to something like the Royal Opera House. If he came to the Theatre Royal at Stratford, he might see the type of people whom he would be happy with in Newham or Hayes and Harlington, enjoying theatre and receiving the benefit of a seat subsidy. The subsidy costs us dear in the London Borough of Newham because we are a hard-stretched Local Authority.

I should like to deal with Local Authority support for the arts. The Secretary of State praised Local Authorities and said what an excellent job they were doing. I wonder how much he appreciates how difficult it is for those Local Authorities to maintain that level of funding for the arts. During National Heritage questions I often ask – not recently, because I seem to be unlucky in getting into the frame and being called – how many times the Secretary of State has talked not to the Treasury but to the Department of the Environment about the arts provision that local authorities make.

Arts provision is one of the discretionary areas of local government expenditure. If hard-pressed, locally elected councils face cuts in statutory areas of expenditure, it is not surprising that they chop away at the discretionary areas. I feel deeply annoyed that Newham and Waltham Forest – two Labour authorities – but mostly Newham, work hard to keep the Theatre Royal open while just down the road in Liberal Democrat Tower Hamlets the council has closed down the Half Moon theatre. It is easy for local authorities to talk about how they show up in terms of overall expenditure. If they shut out discretionary areas of expenditure, they can save money for people in their area, but those people simply move into areas such as Newham. They can use the facilities that the Newham charge payers have to keep going. That is parasitic. That is what is happening in London local authorities.

Newham tries to keep open its recreational facilities such as swimming pools and leisure centres. Other Tory and Liberal authorities close them down. People who live in Tory or Liberal areas cannot be prevented from coming to Newham. It is grotesquely unfair. It is made even worse if Ministers start slagging off my authority for being a high spender. We subsidise people around us in the arts, leisure and recreational facilities and we deeply resent it.

Mr Brooke: I take the point that the hon. Gentleman raises. It is one that we have discussed with some of the great city auth-orities in the context of their regional hinterland. Does the hon. Gentleman acknowledge that it is possible for the process that he describes to work in the opposite direction – that Camden Coun-cil tax payers can use Westminster facilities and that Westminster maintains a music library on behalf of the whole country?

Mr Banks: Of course I acknowledge that. I was talking about the East End of London. In the spirit of friendship, on this rare occasion, I will concede that point to the right hon. Gentleman. But I suggest that he examines the problem. We are talking about discretionary areas of local authority expenditure. Clearly, something has to be done. There must be some acknowledge-ment that when the Department of the Environment makes its standard spending assessments it looks at what services are provided, not what services are needed in discretionary areas. That is a matter that he could usefully discuss with his colleagues in other Departments.

It is true that in the past two years, cultural provision has been seriously affected by the reduction in Local Authority exp-enditure on the arts in London. The further reduction of standard spending assessment allowances for London for 1994-95 will exacerbate the position. SSA settlements have seriously affected some of London's poorest boroughs, including my own of New-ham, neighbouring Hackney, Haringey, Islington and so on. All those boroughs are associated with strong support for the arts.

I acknowledge that the City of London has increased its expenditure on the arts. That is good; but the City is in the unique position of being far and away the wealthiest local authority in the country. It worries me that there is still so much uncertainty about arts expenditure. The cuts that the Department of National Heritage has announced for the next four years are worrying. We reached a good position when we had a rolling programme and some predictability about arts funding – not about cuts but about an increase. One must pay tribute to the right hon. and learned Member for Putney (Mr Mellor) for achieving that. Many people said that, for a Tory, he would have made a good Arts Minister. That was until he took the hands-on artistic policy rather too literally. That greater certainty about money for the arts was what was most needed.

I understand that a decision is due any day about the Lottery. I am an agnostic on lotteries. I would also like to be seriously rich, so I shall undoubtedly buy some tickets when they come my way. If I win, you will not see my bottom for dust, Mr Deputy Speaker.

I agree with what the hon. Member for Staffordshire, South (Mr Cormack) and others have said – the money generated by the Lottery must be new money for the arts or whatever. Perhaps I am a cynic or suspicious, but I do not think that that will happen, because, when Treasury Ministers make their assessments, they will take into account the global amount of money available.

The Secretary of State, or whichever Conservative – or Labour – Member has the job, will find it difficult to argue that the Treasury should simply dismiss that money and not take it into account when deciding the arts settlement. It is all right to give an undertaking in the House and to set out with good intentions, but I can well imagine the sort of pressures a Secretary of State will be under when faced with that spending round. The Treasury will say, 'But hell, you're getting an awful lot of money from the National Lottery'.

I should like a guarantee from the Secretary of State that Mr Branson will not get responsibility for running the Lottery. My suspicions about Mr Branson are very deep. I feel that he injected £5 million into the County Hall Leisure Complex recently to bail out the Japanese group Shiryama, which was due to hit the wall. I remain firmly convinced of that. His involvement might have saved the group's bacon and in doing so he has also saved the face of Ministers. If County Hall – immediately opposite the Pal-ace of Westminster – had ended up the sort of shell that Battersea power station is, imagine Ministers' embarrassment. Am I being basely and groundlessly suspicious or could Mr Branson have been given a nod and a wink that if he stepped in to bail out the County Hall project he would get the Lottery? I hope that that is not the case, but I shall be watching closely who gets the Lottery and I hope that it is not Mr Branson, or all my suspicions will be proved correct. [...]

Chris Smith

A Vision for the Arts

Adapted from a speech to the Annual Dinner of the Royal Academy, London, on 22 May 1997. Published in *Creative Britain*, Faber & Faber, (London) 1998.

One of the defining differences between the parties at the recent general election was this Labour Government's fundamental belief that the individual citizen achieves his or her true potential within the context of a strong community. For years the absurd assertion that 'there is no such thing as society' held sway. The philosophy brought about a palpable decline in the quality of communal and personal life in Britain; and our first aim must be to rebuild – piece by piece – the nation's sense of community. Our cultural life – embracing artistic and sporting endeavour, the quality of our media and the sense of our heritage – has a key role to play in this. It is culture in its widest meaning that gives us our sense of identity. It draws us together. It enables us to understand and to articulate our experiences, our values and traditions. It opens up our minds. It helps to make life worth living.

For too long governments have considered the arts as something of a sideshow, an add-on to the main business in hand. I strongly dissent from this view. Enhancing the cultural life of the nation will be at the heart of New Labour's approach. The arts are not optional extras for government; they are at the very centre of our mission.

It is surely sad that governments for many years have failed to understand this simple truth. We have many inspirational artists in Britain; our theatres draw audiences from around the globe; our film-makers and television programme-makers are world leaders; our designers and architects are in universal demand; our music industry goes from strength to strength. Yet recent governments have shied away from giving arts and cultural activity either the importance or the support they need.

Other administrations have, by contrast, recognised the importance of cultural life to their people. In France, the transformation of Paris over twenty years has given an enormous sense of civic pride to its citizens. In Australia, Paul Keating deliberately set out to forge a new sense of Australian identity from cultural endeavour. And here in Britain, when Jennie

Lee was appointed as our first ever Arts Minister by a Labour government, we saw the flourishing of cultural life in a way undreamt of by earlier generations.

It is my passionate belief, therefore, that there is a duty on any civilised government to nurture and support artistic and creative activity, and to put in place the conditions in which the arts can thrive. In doing so, I want to set out four cardinal principles against which that commitment is given.

The first – and perhaps the most important – is that the arts are for everyone. Things of quality must be available to the many, not just the few. Cultural activity is not some élitist exercise that takes place in reverential temples aimed at the predilections of the cognoscenti. The opportunity to create and to enjoy must be fostered for all. Enjoyment of the arts – be it of Jarvis Cocker or of Jessye Norman, or of Antony Gormely or Anthony Hopkins – crosses all social and geographical boundaries. The arts fire the imagination and inspire the intelligence; there can be no artificial barriers erected to prevent or discourage access to those experiences.

Take an obvious and current example: the availability of world-class opera at the Royal Opera House in Covent Garden. I believe strongly that London needs a first-rank, globally recognized venue for opera. I think it is right for us to ensure that public support is available to it. But I want to see better access for the ordinary people of Britain in return for that support. That is why the commitments already given, for some cheaper seats and for more television broadcasting, are welcome. Let us see how we can build on those.

And let no one try to tell me that the appetite is not there. Look at the barnstorming success of Classic FM. Look at the crowds waiting in the rain for Pavarotti in Hyde Park. Look at the great surge of public interest when the GLC so marvellously opened up the foyers of the Festival Hall to the public. Look at the sheer pressure of visitor numbers that has led to the Tate Gallery having to close it doors from time to time at weekends because there are too many

people inside. And listen to my own constituent, chair of her tenants' association for the last ten years, who told me – after hearing an opera singer who had come to sing some arias for a local Christmas concert – that she had loved opera for years, she had a stack of tapes at home, but she had never seen an opera singer performing live, ever before. Let us aim to make that exclusivity a thing of the past.

I have been impressed, too, by the way in which some of the Lottery awards have recently been moving in this direction. The Arts for Everyone programme has now begun to put small-scale grants in place at community and neighbourhood level, fostering local artistic activity in a way that has a real impact on people's lives. I welcome this enormously, and wish to give every encouragement to the Arts Council – and to the other distributing bodies – to continue their emphasis on grass-roots projects and local schemes. The Lottery, after all, is the people's money. More of it should go to where the people are.

This brings me to my second major theme. It is a related and important point. I spoke earlier about ensuring that the arts were not simply associated with activity in special – sometimes intimidating – temples. Of course there is a bit of magic to be preserved, but not to the exclusion of the enjoyment of creative flair in the most accessible settings. In short, I want to see the arts becoming much more a part of our everyday lives. You should not need always to make the conscious decision to step across a special threshold in order to experience cultural activity. Art, and good-quality design, and architecture that arrests and pleases, and cultural enrichment should be part and parcel of everything we do and everywhere we go. I want to encourage cultural activity to come to the people, rather than always expecting the people to go to the activity.

Think, for example, of the way in which Northern Arts – in its hugely successful Visual Arts 96 programme – turned a number of carriages on the Gateshead Metro into travelling art galleries. You would not know when it was going to happen, but from time to time, on your journey to work or to the shops, you would step into a carriage that had been transformed. Think also of the wonderful work that Hospital Arts in Manchester has for years been doing, bringing artistic pleasure to patients in local hospitals. The changed face of Birmingham's city centre by the imaginative use of public open space and bold sculpture has been dramatic, too.

Let us try, over the coming years, to put more energy and thought into how we can transform our public spaces, our street architecture, and our creative activity. Let us consider public-art projects – not ones that dump unwanted sculpture in the middle of a much-loved high street, but ones that involve local communities in creating fine spaces. And let us consider bringing live art and contemporary painting and sculpture to some of those places we have to be in or at – the office block, the shopping mall, the airport waiting lounge. Would it not be good if we could turn off the Muzak and have some live music for a change?

My third theme is the enormous economic importance of the creative sectors. As I have said elsewhere, the arts, sport, media and cultural industries together amount to some £50 billion of economic activity each year. Some 500,000 people are employed in the arts sector alone. The arts represent a massive boost to local economies: when the new Tate Gallery opened in St Ives, the levels of economic activity in the town rose by 25 per cent almost overnight. Cultural activity, therefore, has an important contribution to make in working towards our goal of high and sustainable levels of employ-ment. This is why I am particularly anxious for the cultural sector to play a full part in our Welfare to Work programme, helping young people in particular to come off benefit and into work or high-quality training.

The fourth and final theme I would put in place is simply this: we need to ensure that the arts and creativity are made an integral part of our education

service, above all for young people, but throughout the whole of life as well. Our education needs to teach us to reason and to question and to analyse, but it needs to teach us to wonder too. And the arts are central to this.

For any of you who have never done so, I recommend a trip to the Micro Gallery computers in the Sainsbury Wing of the National Gallery. There you will see young people – and those young at heart too – sitting in fascination, gripped by what they are seeing on the screen in front of them. Here is the most important thing of all. Having chased the digital image round the screen for a while, they then want to go and see the real thing. And their experience of it has been enormously enriched by what they have just learned.

That I believe, is art in education at its best. It is why I want to see a digital archive emerging in this country, taking the best of all the great national collections we have, putting it into on-screen form, and then making it available free to every school and every public library in the country. The idea is that any pupil, anywhere in the land, can walk into their classroom, sit down at a computer, and conjure up in seconds the glories of the Science Museum or the Tate Gallery. And the glories too, I hope, of the Royal Academy.

I have tried to set out tonight some of the vision I have of how public policy on the arts can develop in the years ahead. The arts are for everyone; part of everyday life; economically vital for the nations; and part and parcel of our education system. These are bold objectives. But let us never forget that the primary joy of art is the value it has, of and for itself.

William Hazlitt, two centuries ago, put it better than I possibly could. He was perhaps a little hard on the Scots, but he made the point very movingly:

> Scotland is of all other countries in the world perhaps the one in which the question 'What is the use of that?' is asked oftenest. But where this is the case, the Fine Arts cannot flourish, or attain their high and balmy state ... for they are their

own sole end and use, and in themselves 'sum all delight'. It may be said of the Fine Arts that they 'toil not, neither do they spin', but are like the lilies of the valley, lovely in themselves, graceful and beautiful, and precious in the sight of all but the blind. They do not furnish us with food or raiment, it is true; but they do please the eye, they haunt the imagination, they solace the heart. If after that you ask the question, Cui bono? there is no answer to be returned.

Gilbert and George

Postal Sculpture 1969

sent to fellow participants in '18 Paris IV. 70' exhibition (courtesy Andrew Wilson)

'ART FOR ALL'   LONDON, 1969

" All my life I give you nothing
and still you ask for more."

from the sculptors

....   *and*   ....

Notes on the Authors and Artists

Kingsley Amis (1922–95) was one of Britain's most successful and influential twentieth century writers. His twenty-five novels include *Lucky Jim* (1954) and the Booker Prize-winning *The Old Devils* (1986). A poet, critic and prolific anthologiser, he was awarded a CBE in 1981 and a knighthood in 1990.

ART IN RUINS is the collaborative practice, formed in 1984, of Hannah Vowles and Glyn Banks. Their installations and writings have been exhibited and published internationally. In their own words, 'Art in Ruins, as a form of cultural activism, explores sites of voluntary and involuntary collaboration that challenge the (political) management of appearance in both art and life'.

Terry Atkinson (b. 1939) is an artist. He is a founding member of Art & Language and teaches in the Fine Art Department of the University of Leeds.

BANK is the collaborative name of artists Simon Bedwell (b. 1963) and Milly Thompson (b. 1964). Recent projects include cover artwork and book reviews for *Modern Painters* magazine, Summer 2000, and a downloadable screensaver and posters for BBC web page 'Artzone/takeaway'. Recent shows include 'Protest and Survive', Whitechapel Gallery, London (2000) and 'The Armchair Project', Cinch, London (2000). A book detailing the first ten years of BANK was published in December 2000.

Tony Banks (b. 1943) joined the Labour Party in 1964 and has been the Labour MP for West Ham since 1997. He was Parliamentary Under-Secretary of State for the DCMS from 1997–99 and has sat on two Select Committees and on the Council of Europe and the WEU. He has been a board member of the ENO, London Festival Ballet and the National Theatre. He is the author of *Out of Order* (1993).

David Bartholomew (b. 1964) is a Belgian-born writer who now lives in Sheffield. He is the author of the novel, *Socrates and the Pig Probably* and is currently working on a collection of short fictions. 'The Proposed Sculpture' is based on recent events in Sheffield.

David Batchelor (b. 1955) is an artist and writer based in London. Recent exhibitions include 'Electric Colour Tower' at Sadler's Wells Theatre, London (2000), 'Apocalypstick' at Anthony Wilkinson Gallery, London (2000) and 'The British Art Show 5', Edinburgh, Southampton, Cardiff and Birmingham (2000). He has recently published the book, *Chromophobia* (2000), on the fear of colour.

Big Sister Colum Leith (b. 1968) and Victoria Stevens (b. 1968), have described themselves as 'an artist/design group who, through the production of our work, hope to be truth against lies, good against evil, the moralist versus the scum of the earth. We are cheap and throwaway'.

Baroness Blackstone, Tessa (b. 1942) has been Minister of State for the Department for Education and Employment since 1997. She was Chairman of the Royal Opera House (1987–97) and a member of the Planning Board of the ACGB (1986–90). She is Vice President of VSO and Governor of the Royal Ballet. Her published work includes *Social Policy and Administration in Britain* (1975), *Prisons and Penal Reform* (1990) and *Race Relations in Britain* (1997).

Earl of Clancarty see Nick Trench

Martin Creed (b. 1968) is an artist who investigates the nature of everyday things and often invests them with a simple yet poetic resonance. He has participated in many group shows in Britain and abroad such as the Sydney Biennale (1998) and 'Intelligence: New British Art 2000', Tate Britain. Solo exhibitions include; Mark Foxx Gallery, Los Angeles; Cabinet, London (both 1999); Gavin Brown's enterprise, New York (2000) and 'Martin Creed Works' at Southampton City Art Gallery and travelling to Leeds City Art Gallery, Bluecoat Gallery, Liverpool and Camden Arts Centre, London (2000).

Lord Bragg, Melvyn (b. 1939) has been the presenter and Editor of the South Bank show since 1978, and Controller of Arts Programmes at LWT since 1990. He was a member of the ACGB and from 1977–80 chaired its Literature Panel. He has been President of the National Campaign for the Arts since 1986 and Governor of LSE since 1997. Recent publications include *On Giant's Shoulders* (1998), *A Time to Dance* (televised 1992) and *The Soldier's Return* (1999).

Ian Breakwell (b.1943) is an artist and a writer. He exhibits regularly at Anthony Reynolds Gallery, London. His work is in a number of private and public collections including the Tate. Since 1993, survey exhibitions of his work in all media including film and video have been held at Ffotogallery, Cardiff; Ferens Art Gallery, Hull; John Hansard Gallery, Southampton; the V&A Museum and the ICA, London.

Andrew Brighton (b.1944) is a critic and the Senior Curator of Public Programmes at Tate Modern. He was co-editor of *Towards Another Picture: An Anthology of Writings by Artists Working in Britain 1945–77* (1977). Other publications include, *The Economic Situation of the Visual Artist* (1984), *Ana-Maria Pacheco* (1993) and *Francis Bacon* (forthcoming). He has published in, amongst others, *Art in America, Art Monthly, London Review of Books, Studio International, Artscribe* and *The Guardian*. He is a Contributing Editor of *Critical Quarterly* and a Trustee of Peer.

Adam Chodzko (b. 1965) is an artist who has shown extensively both in the UK and abroad, at the Venice Biennale; De Appel, Amsterdam; and The Walker Art Center, Minneapolis. Forthcoming exhibitions include solo shows in Los Angeles, and Turin, and projects commissioned by London Film & Video Umbrella, BookWorks, London, the Arts Council Single Screen Film & Video and the UKS Biennial, Oslo.

Roger Cook (b. 1940) is a Lecturer in Fine Art and a Ph.D candidate in History of Art at the University of Reading. Along with colleagues on the MA course, 'The Body and Representation', at Reading, he is co-editor of a collection of essays entitled In/Determinate Bodies published in 2001.

Sacha Craddock (b. 1955) is an independent art critic and lecturer. She has written regularly for The Times, as well as many art magazines and catalogues. She is the Chair of New Contemporaries, and was a juror for the Turner Prize in 1999. She is currently setting up rgb monitor, a new project for critical writing, discussion and the commissioning of work.

Penelope Curtis (b. 1961) is a curator who has primarily been based in new galleries outside London. From 1988, she worked as Exhibitions Curator at Tate Liverpool, and since 1994 has been Curator at the Henry Moore Institute in Leeds. She has been committed to working with collections as well as on exhibitions, and with historic as well as contemporary art.

Jeremy Deller (b. 1966) is an artist working in London. He has exhibited widely in Europe and the UK, most recently in 'Intelligence: New British Art 2000' at Tate Britain. He has also curated a number of exhibitions including 'Unconvention' at Centre for Visual Arts, Cardiff (1999). An ongoing project is his collection of contemporary British folk art (see www.folkarchive.co.uk).

Terry Dicks (b. 1937) was the Conservative MP for Hayes and Harlington and a Member of the Council of Europe from 1983–97. He was the administrative officer to the GLC between 1971 and 1986.

Lord Eccles, David (b. 1904) was Conservative MP for Chippenham from 1943-62. He was Minister of Education (1951–54 and 1954–57), President of the Board of Trade (1957–59) and Paymaster General (1970–73). He has been Chairman of both the British Museum and the British Library and is a Senior Fellow of the Royal College of Art.

Jes Fernie (b. 1969) is a freelance art consultant and writer. She also works part time as Project Director of the RSA Art for Architecture scheme. She studied Art History at Manchester University and has worked at Cubitt Gallery, London, Art Projects Management and the Hayward Gallery, London.

Jean Fisher is a freelance writer on issues of contemporary art practice. She is the former editor of Third Text and currently teaches at Middlesex University and the Royal College of Art, London.

Lord Freyberg, Valerian (b. 1970) is an artist. From 1989–94, he studied at Camberwell College of Art. He has sat as a cross-bencher in the House of Lords since 1995 and was re-elected to the House in 1999 as part of the interim reform.

William Furlong (b. 1944) is an artist living in London. In 1973, he established Audio Arts Magazine, which he continues to edit and produce, as part of his practice. He is currently Director of Research at Wimbledon School of Art. Recent exhibitions include 'Intelligence: New British Art 2000', held at Tate Britain.

Ben Gibson (b. 1958) is Director of the London Film School and an independent producer. From 1989-98, he was Head of Production at the BFI, executive producing The Long Day Closes (1992), Wittgenstein (1993), London (1994), Gallivant (1996), Robinson in Space (1997), Under the Skin (1997), Beautiful People (1999) and Love is the Devil (1998). He has been a distributor, cinema proprietor/ programmer and film journalist.

Lord Gibson, Richard (b. 1916) was Chairman of the ACGB from 1972–77. He has also chaired the National Trust (1977–86), was Director of Financial Times Ltd (1957–58) and Honorary Treasurer to the Commonwealth Press Union (1957–67). He has sat on the board of the Royal Opera House and has been a Trustee of Glyndbourne Festival Opera.

Gilbert and George (b. 1942 and 1943) are an artist who lives and works in London. They have exhibited their pictures widely, including museum exhibitions recently in Paris, Moscow, Kraków, Zurich, Vienna, New York, Budapest, Beijing, Tokyo and Shanghai. They adopted the slogan 'Art for All' for their work in 1969.

René Gimpel (b. 1947) is an art dealer and Director of Gimpel Fils, London.

Antony Gormley (b. 1950) has created museum-based and major public sculpture since the early 1970s. His most ambitious work includes Field for the British Isles (1993), Angel of the North (1995–98) and Quantum Cloud (2000) on the Thames in Greenwich. He has created large-scale installations both in Britain and abroad, has participated in group shows such as the Venice Biennale and Documenta 8, and has held solo exhibitions at the Whitechapel Gallery, the Serpentine Gallery and White Cube, London. He was awarded an OBE in 1997, the Turner Prize in 1994 and the South Bank Prize for Visual Art in 1999. He is a member of the board of the ACE.

Helen Gould (b. 1965) began her career as a journalist and editor in the arts policy field but has more recently worked with the role of culture in sustainable development. She founded Creative Exchange in 1997, has served as Editor at the National Campaign for the Arts and Culture, and as Development Consultant at the British Council. She is a member of the culture committee of the UK UNESCO National Commission.

Richard Grayson (b. 1958) is an artist, writer and curator who divides his time between the UK and Australia. He was a founding member of The Basement Group, Newcastle upon Tyne (1979–84) and Director of the Experimental Art Foundation, Adelaide, Australia (1991–98). Recent exhibitions include 'Sporting Life', Museum of Contemporary Art, Sydney (2000); 'Negative Space', Yuill Crowley Gallery, Sydney (1999); '1000 Accidents', Institute of Modern Art, Brisbane (1999), and 'ahistoryofreading', Contemporary Art Centre of South Australia, Adelaide (1998).

David Heathcoat-Amory (b. 1949) is a Chartered Accountant and has been MP for Wells since 1983. In 1988 he joined the Government and served in a number of Departments before being appointed Minister for Europe in the Foreign Office in 1993, when he also became Paymaster General at the Treasury. Two years later, he resigned from the Government over the issue of Europe. He is now shadow Chief Secretary to the Treasury. He was made a Privy Councillor in 1996.

Graham Higgin (b. 1968) was born in Belfast and educated at Cambridge and Yale. He is a writer and curator working in London. Recent projects include *Porcupines: a Philosophical Anthology* (1999) and the exhibitions 'Porcupines/Arthinking', 298 Gallery, London (1999), and 'The Insanity Benefit', Vilma Gold gallery, London (2000).

Matthew Higgs (b. 1964) is an artist and curator. He is the publisher of Imprint 93, an ongoing series of artists' multiples and editions, and is currently Associate Director of Exhibitions at the ICA, London.

Stewart Home (b. 1962) is the author of a number of novels and works of cultural commentary including *Blow Job, Cunt* and *Confusion Incorporated*. He has also released several music and spoken word CDs, and occasionally shows work in galleries and makes videos. He lives in East London.

Joan Key (b. 1948) teaches at the Kent Institute of Art and Design and Goldsmiths College and works as a painter, writer and curator. The work in this book is the basis for a series of paintings that form a collaborative project with the cellist Christopher Mansell. Her work has recently been shown at the Richard Salmon Gallery, London, and has been included in the British Council exhibitions 'Pittura Britannica' and 'O Pas La' and the Arts Council touring exhibitions 'Sublime' and 'The British Art Show 5'.

Lord Keynes, John Maynard (1883–1946) is arguably the most influential figure in twentieth century economics. His book *The Economic Consequences of Peace* (1919) made him famous overnight, although he is best known for *A Treatise on Money* (1930) and *General Theory of Employment, Interest and Money* (1936). He was also a statesman, a journalist, a collector and patron of the arts, closely associated with the Bloomsbury Group. In 1942 he took his seat in the Liberal Benches of the House of Lords and became Chairman of the newly formed Committee for the Encouragement of Music and the Arts, which in 1945, was renamed the Arts Council of Great Britain.

Jennie Lee (1904–88) was Labour MP for North Lanark (1929–31) and for Cannock (1945–70). She was Minister of State for the Department of Education and Science between 1967 and 1970. In 1981 she was made an Honorary Fellow of the Royal Academy. Although she was a life peer, she remained in the Commons and never took up her seat in the Lords.

Wyndham Lewis (1882–1957) was a novelist, painter, essayist, poet, critic and polemicist. He was the founder of Vorticism, arguably the only original movement in twentieth century British painting. His books include *Tarr* (1918), *The Lion and the Fox* (1927), *Time and Western Man* (1927), *The Ages of God* (1930), *The Revenge for Love* (1937) and *Self-Condemned* (1954). He was also Editor of *BLAST* (1914) a 'Review of the Great English Vortex', a quarterly journal, which ran to only two issues as a result of the war.

Lord McIntosh, Andrew (b. 1933) has been Captain of the Yeoman of the Guard (Deputy Government Chief Whip) since 1997. He is a member of the House of Lords and was Deputy Leader of the Opposition from 1992–97. He is President of the North London Abbeyfield Housing Society, Vice-President of the National Association of Local Councils and a Trustee of the Working Men's College. He published Women and Work in 1981.

Michael Madden (b. 1954) is an artist who is both apprenticed and artschool trained. He has worked mainly on heritage buildings, most recently at the Natural History Museum, London, as a painter/muralist. He was active in trade unions until October 2000, when he moved to Cumbria to concentrate on his own work with a political and environmental emphasis.

Christopher Mansell (b. 1971) is a cellist with wide experience as a classical musician, now working with the Quartet Viotti and the D'Oyly Carte opera company, and teaching in London. For this publication, he has collaborated with Joan Key.

François Matarasso (b. 1958) spent fifteen years working in community arts before concentrating on research into cultural policy and practice. Since joining the independent consultancy group Comedia in 1994, he has undertaken work on the impact of culture, first published in 1997 as *Use or Ornament? The Social Impact of Participation in the Arts*, and on new approaches to evaluation. He has been commissioned by international and national agencies, local authorities and NGOs as well as cultural organisations and foundations in Europe and further afield. He is currently writing a book about the role of culture in democratic societies.

Roland Miller (b. 1938) is a performance artist and lecturer at the University of Huddersfield. He holds a doctorate in performance art and has been a member of several Arts Council and Regional Arts Board committees. For the last four years, he has been an Arts Council Lottery Grant assessor.

Geoff Mulgan (b. 1961) is Director of the Performance and Innovation Unit at the Cabinet Office. He was previously the Prime Minster's special adviser on social exclusion, welfare, family and urban policy. From 1993–97 he was Director of Demos, an independent think-tank, which he co-founded. His most recent books are *Connexity* (1998) and *Politics in an Antipolitical Age* (1994). He has been a presenter on radio and TV, a newspaper columnist and is a visiting professor at University College London.

Nicholas Murray (b. 1952) is the author of a collection of poems, a short critical biography of Bruce Chatwin, and literary biographies of Matthew Arnold, Andrew Marvell and his current subject, Aldous Huxley. His poems, essays, and reviews have appeared in a wide variety of newspapers and literary magazines and he has lectured at universities and literary festivals in the UK, Italy and the US. He lives in London and Wales.

Richard Noble (b. 1958) is a Canadian political philosopher who lives in London. He has written a book on Rousseau's conception of freedom, and articles on eighteenth century political thought, as well as a number of articles on contemporary art, politics and philosophy, including a catalogue on the Canadian artist Jana Sterbak. He is currently working on a book about tolerance.

Janette Parris (b. 1962) is an artist who lives and works in London.

John Pick (b. 1936) is Professor Emeritus of Arts Management, City University, London and is currently visiting professor of Arts Management, South Bank University, London. He has lectured internationally on the arts and arts policy-making and is the author of more than twenty books, including *Building Jerusalem: Art, Industry and the British Millennium* (1999) and the forthcoming *Managing Britannia*, a critique of New Labour's cultural managerialism.

Lord Rees-Mogg, William (b. 1928) was Chairman of the ACGB from 1982–89. He is currently Director of EFG Private Bank, Informa plc, Pickering and Chatto (Publishers) Ltd and Value Realisations Trust plc. Editor of the Times from 1967–81, he has written extensively for many other newspapers and journals. He is author of *The Great Reckoning* (1991) and *The Sovereign Individual* (1997).

Gerry Robinson (b. 1948) has been Chairman of the ACE since 1998. He was Managing Director of Coca-Cola between 1983–84 and has been Chairman of LWT (1994–96), ITN (1995–97) and BSkyB (1995–98). From 1991–96, he was Chief Executive of Granada Group plc, becoming Chairman in 1996.

Mark Ryan (b. 1960) is an events organiser and writer on contemporary culture. Creative Director of the Institute of Ideas, London, he is an editor of its forthcoming *Conversations in Print*.

Alex Sainsbury (b. 1968) is an art collector and a Trustee of Peer.

Stella Santacatterina (b. 1959) is a curator, lecturer and a writer on art theory and contemporary aesthetics. She is based in London.

Charles Saumarez Smith (b. 1954) is Director of the National Portrait Gallery, London. He was previously Head of Research at the V&A Museum, London, and was a contributor to *The New Museology*, edited by Peter Vergo in 1989.

Arthur Scargill (b. 1938) has been involved in union politics since he began working in the mid-1950s as a miner in South Yorkshire. He played a leading role in the unofficial miners' strike of 1969 and was elected President of the Yorkshire Miners' Union in 1973. Throughout the 1970s he was also active in the wider Labour movement and in peace and environmental campaigns. He was elected Chair of the British Anti-Nuclear Campaign (1977) and President of the NUM (1981), leading it through the year-long strike of 1984–85. In 1995, he helped establish and was elected General Secretary of the Socialist Labour Party. He is the author of several publications including *Miners in the Eighties* (1981) and *New Realism: the Politics of Fear* (1987).

Brian Sedgemore (b. 1937) has been Labour MP for Hackney South & Shoreditch since 1983 and has also worked as a civil servant, barrister and TV journalist. He has written three novels and a number of books including *The How and Why of Socialism* (1977) and *The Insiders Guide to Parliament* (1995). A passionate supporter of the arts, he gives occasional talks and lectures to art colleges and universities on cultural and political practice and theory.

Bob & Roberta Smith (b. 1963) is the assumed name of artist Patrick Brill. Recent solo exhibitions were held at Anthony Wilkinson Gallery, London; Arnolfini, Bristol; and Chisenhale, London (1998). Group shows include 'Intelligence: New British Art 2000' at Tate Britain.

Chris Smith (b. 1951) has been the Labour MP for Islington South and Finsbury since 1983 and Secretary of State for Culture, Media and Sport since 1997. He was principal opposition spokesman on environmental protection (1992–94), National Heritage (1994–95), social security (1995–96), and health (1996–97). He was on the Executive Committee of the National Trust (1995–97), Governor of Sadler's Wells Theatre, London (1987–97) and a Trustee of John Muir Trust (1991–97). His book, *Creative Britain*, was published in 1998.

Ingrid Swenson (b. 1960) has been the Curatorial Director of Peer since 1998. From 1988–94, she was Exhibitions Co-ordinator at the ICA, London, after which she worked on independent projects and as a freelance curator at a number of arts organisations in London including The Economist (for the Contemporary Art Society), Camden Art Centre and the Serpentine Gallery.

Nick Trench (Earl of Clancarty) (b. 1952) is an artist living in London. He sat as an Independent in the House of Lords from 1996 – 1999.

George Walden (b. 1939) worked for the British Foreign Office from 1962–83. From 1983–97 he was Conservative MP for Buckingham, and from 1985–97, Minister for Higher Education. His books include *Morality and Foreign Policy* (1990) and *We Should Know Better* (1996). His memoirs, *Lucky George* (1996), were published to great acclaim and controversy in 1999.

Mark Wallinger (b. 1958) is an artist who has exhibited internationally since the mid-1980s. Following his 1994 one-person exhibition at the Serpentine Gallery, London, he was shortlisted for the Turner Prize in 1995. Major one-person exhibitions have been presented in Basel, Brussels, Frankfurt (all 1999) and Tate, Liverpool (2000). His most recent project in London was 'Ecce Homo' (2000) for Trafalgar Square (2000). He will represent Britain at the Venice Biennale in 2001.

Baroness Warnock, Mary (b. 1924) is best known for her writings on Sartre and on imagination. A philosopher, who has taught at both Oxford and Cambridge, she has chaired various government committees of inquiry, most notably that on Human Fertility and Embryology (1982–84). She was made a life peer in 1985 and sits in the House of Lords as a cross-bencher. Her recent publications include *Women Philosophers* (ed.) (1996), the controversial *An Intelligent Person's Guide to Ethics* (1998), and the first part of her autobiography, *Mary Warnock, A Memoir* (2000).

Raymond Williams (b. 1921–90) was adult education tutor for Oxford University Delegacy for Extra-mural Studies until 1961, when he was elected Fellow of Jesus College, Cambridge, becoming Professor of Drama there between 1974 and 1983. He part-edited *Politics and Letters* (1947), to which George Orwell was a contributor. He has also published, among other books, *Keywords* (1976), *Marxism and Literature* (1977) and *Writing, Culture and Politics* (1980).

Ken Worpole (b. 1944) is a freelance writer and policy researcher. He has lived in Hackney for more than thirty years and has been active in local cultural issues. His most recent book is *Here Comes the Sun: Architecture and Public Space in the Twentieth Century European Culture* (2000).

Index

A

access 10, 11, 14, 15, 16, 21, 29, 32, 34, 40, 44, 66, 101, 114, 132, 145, 156
    Accessibility for All. Freedom for the Few (Noble) 76-7
    Culture and Accessibility (Murray) 58-63
    disabled 21
    ethnic minorities 21
    external 55
    to museums 55-6
Adler, Carine
    Under the Skin 42
advertising 29
Alexander, David 155
Anastasi, William 138
An Crann/The Tree 69
Angel of the North 15
architecture 15, 163
Aristotle 58
arm's-length principle 10, 24, 35, 156-7
Arnold, Matthew 24, 120
    Culture and Anarchy 58-9, 60, 62
    Numbers 61
Art & Language 126-8
Artangel 34
Art for Everyone 36
art history, study of 112-13, 134
Artist Placement Group (APG) 31
art market, British 122
Art in Ruins
    Untitled 33
art schools 28, 106-9, 110, 130
    access to 114
    art history, study of 112-13, 134
    cultural studies 112-13
    fees 106, 114
    overseas students 106
Arts Council 14, 15, 26, 34, 36, 129, 144, 147, 151, 160-1, 162
    access as policy cornerstone 78-9, 145, 156
    Agreement between the Department for Culture, Media and Sport and the Arts Council of England 20-1
    An Arts Council for the Future (Robinson) 18-19
    Architecture Unit 163
    arm's-length principle 156-7
    Arts Council of England Christmas Card (1999) 118-19
    The Arts Council (Williams, 1979) 156-7
    Basic Policy (1956) 145
    Cultural Diversity Action Plan 76-7
    Glory of the Garden (1984) 158
    hierarchy of arts funded by 156-7, 159-61, 162-3, 166-71
    Report of the Community Arts Working Party (1974) 148
    The Arts Council: Its Policy and Hopes (Keynes, 1945) 142-3, 158

Towards a National Arts and Media Strategy (1992) 39, 162-5
Arts and the People (1977) 149
Atkinson, Terry
    Eurostar Avant-Gardism Secured in Both Directions by Dumbing Down from London and Wising Up from Paris 126-8
attendance figures 90-1, 130, 162
avant-garde model 126-8

B

Bacon, Francis 49, 127
Baldwin, Michael 128
Bank
    Just imagine... 22-3
Banks, Tony 166-71
Barrett Browning, Elizabeth 58
Bartholemew, David
    The Proposed Sculpture 82-3
Batchelor, David 70-2
    Electric Colour Tower 73
    Unpopular Culture 70
Bautista, Jaime 54
Bayley, Stephen
    Labour Camp 25
Beethoven, Ludwig van 70
Bell, Clive
    Civilisation 70
Benjamin, Walter 32
Berkeley, Michael 59
Bernerd, Elliot 14
Beuys, Joseph 136-8
Bevan, Aneurin 16, 49
Bigger Picture, The 43
Big Sister
    Beware the Influence of Public Opinion 102-3
Birtwistle, Sir Harrison
    Panic 58-9
Bizet, Georges
    Carmen 58
Blackstone, Baroness 107, 109
Blair, Tony 16, 25, 36, 57, 111, 120
Blake, William 104
Bloom, Harold 67
Bloomsbury Group 26, 36
Blunkett, David 14
Bourdieu, Pierre
    The Rules of Art 104-5
Bournemouth Symphony Orchestra 14, 34
Bragg, Lord 34-5
Breakwell, Ian
    The Caller 78-9
Half the Work 30-1
Brighton, Andrew
    Towards a Command Culture: New Labour's Cultural Policy and Soviet Socialist Realism 36-41
British Broadcasting Corporation (BBC) 14, 24, 26, 60,

142-3, 160-1
    Promenade Concerts 10, 15, 58-9
British Council 19, 142, 144
British Film Institute 147, 162, 163
Britten, Benjamin 14
broadcasting 14, 15, 24, 58-9, 142-3, 156-7, 159-61, 165
Brough, Colin 155
Buffy House 54

C

Cage, John 136-8
Capa, Robert 49
Carter, Kevin 49
Centre for the Arts in Development Communications 69
Centre for Visual Arts, Cardiff 48-53
Channel 4 14, 45, 160
Chernyshevsky, NG 37
Chodzko, Adam
    Cleaner (A Story) 94-5
    Meeting 64
Chrisi Bailey Award 118-19
Cicero 132
cinema see film
City of Birmingham Symphony Orchestra 14, 34
Clancarty, Earl of 54-5
class
    arts audience 18, 21, 40, 149, 159-61, 166-71
    British State and ruling class 157
    politics of 112-13, 125
collectors, private 29
commercial success, legitimation by 104
Commission on Architecture and the Built Environment 15
communications 112
community arts and development 68-9, 156, 160-1
    Community Arts Working Party Report (1974) 148
community halls 15
complaint, culture of 34
Conceptualism 26, 126, 127, 128
conservatism 17
Conservative Party 166-8
    An Arts Policy? (Amis, 1979) 150-5
    Politics and the Quality of Life (Eccles, 1970) 147
    Thatcherism 24, 39, 114, 120, 132
consumerism 24
Cook, Roger
    Pierre Bourdieu, William Blake and the Battle for the Autonomy of the Arts 104-5
Coomaraswamy, Ananda 114
copyright 160
    Public Lending Right 155
    resale royalties 111
Council for the Encouragement of Music and the Arts (CEMA) 142
Cox, Oliver C
    Caste, Class & Race 125
Craddock, Sacha

Art Between Politics and Glamour 130-1
Crafts Council 162
creative economy 10, 15, 16, 18, 20-1, 24, 114, 120-1, 162, 170
Creative Industries Mapping Document 15
Creative Nation 120
creativity 16, 76, 150
Creed, Martin
    Funding Application for an Outdoor Work 84-5
    Work no. 203 86-7
critics 101, 130
Cubism 128, 138
Cultural Concern 120
cultural diversity 14, 16, 17, 76-7, 88, 121
cultural provision 162
cultural rights and development 68-9
Cunningham, Jack 120
curator, role of 11, 92, 101, 132-4
Curtis, Penelope
    Letter to Peer 101

D

dance 14
Davies, Terence 44
Debord, Guy
    The Society of the Spectacle 115
Degas, Edgar 29
    'degenerate' art 32
Deller, Jeremy
    Unconvention 48, 49
Department for Culture, Media and Sport 10
    Agreement between Arts Council of England and 20-1, 61, 92
creation 24
design 15
Dicks, Terry 166-8, 170
disabled, access by 21
Drummond, John 10, 58
Duchamp, Marcel 29, 128, 133, 136-8
Dumas, Marlene 130

E

Eccles, Rt Hon Viscount
    Politics and the Quality of Life 147
economics
    The British Art Market (Heathcoat-Amory) 122
    creative economy 15, 16, 18, 20-1, 24, 114, 120-1, 162, 170
    legitimation by commercial success 104
education 11, 14-15, 60-1
    art schools 28, 106-9
    arts, role of 32, 114, 156
    museums, role of 92, 116
    as predictor of art audiences 40
    truancy, reducing 57
    visual arts 144
egalitarianism 28

Eliot, TS 61
elitism 10, 15, 17, 28, 37, 59, 61-2, 159-61, 162-3, 166-71
employment in cultural industries 18
English language 15, 61
English National Opera 58
environmental issues 163
Equal Opportunities 77
ethnic minorities 21, 40, 46, 160, 161
    cultural studies 112-13
European Union, funding by 21
everyday life, aestheticisation 112
excellence, encouragement of 20, 32, 114, 151, 163-4

F

fashion 15
Fernie, Jes
    I Ate Prunella Clough 98-9
    Soup 100
Festival of Britain 144
film 14, 15, 42-7, 59, 147, 156, 160
Film Council 14, 43-7
Film Four 45
fine arts 14, 15
Fisher, Jean
    The 'Proletarianisation' of Art 112-13
Fisher, Mark 101
Forum for Cultural Rights and Development 68-9
free market 55
Freeze exhibition 130, 132
Freud, Lucian 14, 29
Freyberg, Lord 55-6, 106-7
Fuller, Roy 151, 154
Furlong, William
    Conversation Piece 136-8

G

Galleries of Justice, Nottingham 57
Gateshead Music centre 34
gay and lesbian culture 160
General Will, concept of 25
Gibson, Ben
    The Art of the State, or Laisser-Faire Eats the Soul: British Film Policy 42-7
Gibson, Lord 35
Gilbert and George 26
Gill, Eric 150
Gill, Peter 61
Gimple, René
    Statement 110-11
global economy 32
Gogh, Vincent Van 127, 145
Gormley, Antony
    Total Strangers 80-1
Gould, Helen
    Creative Exchange: The Forum for Cultural Rights and Development 68-9
government policy 14-15

Grayson, Richard
    Greek 65
Greenberg, Clement 28
Greenfield, Susan 127
Guiliani, Rudolph 32

H

Haggerston School, Hackney 14
Haines, Bruce 48
Hamlyn, Lord 57
Hampshire, Stuart
    Innocence and Experience 61
Hare, David
    Amy's View 59-60
Harle, John 58
Hartcliffe Boys' Dance Company 57
Hazlitt, William 14, 15
Heaney, Seamus 14
Heathcoat-Amory, David
    The British Art Market 122
Hegel, Georg Wilhelm Friedrich 37
Heidegger, Martin 128
Hepworth, Barbara 14
Hewitt, Peter 14, 34
hierarchy of artforms 156-7, 159-61, 162-3, 166-71
Higgin, Graham
    Lotting the Lottery 115
Higgs, Matthew
    Unconvention 49
Hilton, Tim 28
Hirst, Damien 26, 114
Hitchcock, Alfred 44
Hoggart, Richard 35, 60, 157
Home, Stewart
    Why Public Subsidy and Private Sponsorship Can't Save Art from Complete and Utter Irrelevance 125
Hounslow Borough Council Community Recreation Outreach 57
Howard, Jo 60
Hughes, Robert 28, 29
Hughes, Ted 14

I

identity, community 25
Impressionism 137
Independent Television Network Centre 60
Index on Censorship 67
innovation, encouragement of 14, 20, 32, 114
installations 126
institutionalisation 32
Internet 61, 121

J

James, C Vaughan
    Soviet Socialist Realism: Origins and Theory 36, 40
Jarman, Derek 43, 44
Jefferson, Thomas 158

Jenkinson, Peter 55
Judd, Donald 72

K

Kaiser, Michael 15
Kant, Immanuel 36-7
Katha 69
Keating, Paul 120
Keswick Theatre by the Lake 34
Key, Joan
  Statement 88
Keynes, Lord 15, 24, 36
  The Arts Council: Its Policy and Hopes 142-3, 158
Kippenberger, Martin 49
klássovost 36, 37, 39
Koons, Jeff 114
Kundera, Milan 37

L

Labour Party 36-41, 159-61
  The Arts and the People (1977) 149, 150
  Election Manifesto (1997) 37
Larkin, Philip
  The Whitsun Weddings 60
Leavis, FR
  Mass Civilisation, Minority Culture 61-2
Lee, Jennie 56
  A Policy for the Arts: The First Steps 146
Leighton, Lord 26
Lewis, CS 61
Lewis, Wyndham
  Bread and Ballyhoo 144
liberty and responsibility 158
library service 101, 155, 165
Lipton, Stuart 15
literature 60-1, 62, 156, 157, 163, 165
Livingstone, Ken 111
Lloyd, Lord 144
local authorities
  arts policies 25
  funding by 21, 170-1
Locke, John 158
London 143, 145, 149, 158
London Symphony Orchestra 34
Look Ahead hostel, Aldgate 15
lottery funding 14, 15, 25, 56, 66, 70, 75, 120, 121, 130,
  167-8, 171
Luce, Richard 10, 162
Lyotard, François 128

M

McCullin, Don 49
McIntosh, Lord 56-7
McKellan, Ian 18
Macmurray, John 36-7
Madden, Michael
  A Warning from a Trade Unionist 114

Manic Street Preachers 49, 50
Mansell, Christopher
  8+3 = 11, 6+5 = 11 88-9
Marxist-Leninism 39-40
Matarasso, François 60
  Freedom's Shadow 70, 72
Matisse, Henri 130
Maybury, John
  Love is the Devil 42
media
  influence 112
  policy towards 160, 162-5
memory banks, museums as 92-3
Mendes, Valerie 92
Michael Powell Prize 42
Millenium Dome 92, 101, 103, 110, 121
Millenium Photographic Exhibition 50
Miller, Dr Roland
  Extract from a Letter to Peer 75
Milne, Paula 60
Mulgan, Geoff 164
  Saturday Night or Sunday Morning? (with Worpole)
  159-61, 162
multimedia 15
Munch, Edvard 49
Murdoch, Iris 14
Murdoch, Rupert 120, 121, 160, 164
Murray, Nicholas
  Culture and Accessibility 58-63
museums 55-6
  access to, government review 40
  attendance figures 90-1, 130, 162
  curators 92, 101, 132-4
  display policies 130-1
  educational role 92, 116
  free access 116, 160
  leisure attractions, as 92
  Museum as Memory Bank (Smith) 92-3
  regional, funding 14
  visitors to, classification 40
Museums and Galleries Access Fund 56
Museums and Galleries Commission 101
Museums and Galleries Social Inclusion Group 57
Museums, Libraries and Archives Council 101
music 14-15, 58-9, 88-9, 160
Music for Change 69

N

naródnost 36-7
Nash, Paul 144
National Advisory Council on Creative and Cultural
  Education 15
National Arts and Media Strategy Monitoring Group 39
National Endowment for Science, Technology and the
  Arts (NESTA) 14, 107
National Foundation for Youth Music 14
National Insurance Contributions 14

National Portrait Gallery 93
National Theatre 34, 57
  Hamlyn week 14
Natural History Museum 92, 114
New Audiences fund 14, 21
New Deal 14, 18
New Generation Audiences Scheme 15
Nietzsche, Friedrich 128
Noble, Richard
  Accessibility for All. Freedom for the Few 76-7

O

Oldman, Gary
  Nil By Mouth 42
opera 14, 15, 58, 159, 166-7
Oppenheim, James 15
orchestras 14-15, 34

P

Parker, Alan 43
Parliamentary debates
  Art Colleges (House of Lords, 12 October 1999) 106-9
  The Arts (House of Commons, 5 May 1994) 166-71
  The Arts (House of Lords, 10 February 1999) 34-5
  Arts and Sport (House of Lords, 10 November 1999)
  54-7
Parris, Janette
  Plank Drawing 96
partîinost 36, 39
patronage 11, 144, 156
Pawlikowski, Paul 42
Pendyrus Male Choir 49
performance art 126, 156
performance indicators 10, 20
photography 113, 156, 163
Picasso, Pablo 24, 49, 127
Pick, John
  The Two Faces of Chris Smith 120-1
Pilgrim Trust 142, 144
Pitt Rivers Museum, Oxford 93
poetry 60-1, 62, 155
Policy Action Team 15, 54, 57
politics and the arts 10, 149, 150
  An Arts Policy? (Amis) 150-5
  Lecture at the RSA (Smith) 14-15
  political responsibilities of artists 70, 72, 132, 160-1
  Politics and the Quality of Life (Eccles) 147
Pollock, Jackson 49
popular culture 18, 26, 112-13, 125, 126, 127, 133,
  159-61, 162-3
popularity 29
postmodernism 58, 112
Poussin, Nicolas 29
Powell, Michael 44
Pressburger, Emeric 44
Priestley Report 158
public art 15

Public Lending Right 155
public policy and cultural activity 10, 24-5, 26, 70
 arm's-length principle 10, 24, 35, 156-7
 art schools 106-9
 funding 66, 70, 84-5, 96, 98-9, 116-17, 125, 151, 154-5
 Lecture at the RSA (Smith) 14-15
publishing 15, 59, 60, 155, 157, 160, 161, 165
Puttnam, David 16

Q

quality, assessment 10, 39, 162-5
Quality, Efficiency and Standards Team (QUEST) 14, 40
Quine, Willar Van Orman 127, 128

R

rave scene 133
Rees, Helen 163
Rees-Mogg, Lord
 The Glory of the Garden 158
Regional Arts Boards 14, 162
regions 25, 34, 46, 55, 130, 143, 145, 149, 158
Reith, Lord 11, 60
relativism 24
relevance 16
Rentoul, John 36
Reynolds, Joshua 104
Robinson, Gerry 14, 16, 34, 39, 40
 An Arts Council for the Future 18-19
 The Creativity Imperative: Investing in the arts in the
 21st century 129
Rogers, Lord 15, 61
 Towards an Urban Renaissance 67
Rousseau, Jean-Jacques 25
Royal Festival Hall
 Open Foyer Policy 66
Royal Fine Arts Commission 15
Royal Opera House 15, 34
Royal Shakespeare Company 14
Russell, Bertrand 128
Russell, John 28
Ryan, Mark
 Manipulation Without End 16-17

S

Saatchi, Charles 29, 127-8, 132, 133
Said, Edward 61
Sainsbury, Alex
 The Total Quality Culture 116-17
Saint-Exupéry, Antoine de 49
St John-Stevas, Norman 150
St Martin-in-the-Fields 54
Santacatterina, Stella
 Clarification of a Few Political Points 32
Saumarez Smith, Charles
 Museum as Memory Bank 92-3
Saville, Jenny 49
Scargill, Arthur 49

Unconvention 50
Scruton, Roger 24
Sedgemore, Brian
 Politics and Culture: The State and the Artist 24-5
Sensation exhibition 32
Shakespeare, William 67, 159
Shaw, Sir Roy 154
Shcherbina, Vladimir, Gei, Nikolai and Piskunov, Vladimir
 Socialist Realism and the Artistic Development of
 Mankind 37
Sir John Soane's Museum 93
site-specific artworks 49
Situationists 49
Smith, Bob and Roberta
 Postcard 12-13
Smith, Chris 10, 32, 34, 40, 61, 109
 Creative Britain 24, 37, 39, 114
 Lecture at the RSA 14-15
 The Two Faces of Chris Smith (Pick) 120-1
Smith, WH 60
social exclusion and inclusion 16, 17, 54-7, 68-9, 70, 75
Social Exclusion Unit 15, 54, 57
Socialist Realism 26, 29, 36-41, 76
social policy, arts as instrument of 36
South Bank Centre 14
Southgate, Colin 15
South London Art Gallery 90-1
Soviet Socialist Realism see Socialist Realism
Spitalfields Project 56
sponsorship 14, 20-1, 125, 130
Stalinism 17
Steiner, Professor George 18, 60-1
Strachey, Lytton 61
Street Symphony 69

T

Tate Gallery 144
Tate Modern 130-1
Tattoo 132
Tavernier, Bertrand
 Amis Americains 59
technology, digital 112
television 59-60, 113, 156-7, 159, 160-1, 164
Thatcherism 10, 24, 39, 114, 120, 132
theatre 14-15
Theatre for Development 69
Titian 29
totalitarian regimes 32, 36-41, 76, 104, 150
tourism 18, 158, 159
Truffaut, François 42
Turner Prize 102, 112, 130

U

Unconvention exhibition 48, 49, 50
urban environment 15

V

Victoria & Albert Museum 92
Virgil 10

W

Walden, George
 Contemporary Art, Democracy and the State 26-9
Wallinger, Mark 11
 Fool Britannia: not new, not clever, not funny 132-4
Walsall Museum and Art Gallery 55-6, 93
Warhol, Andy 49, 127, 136-8
Warnock, Mary 10
Weiner, Lawrence 49
Whistler, James McNeill 26
'white cube' gallery 101
Wider Picture, The 121
Williams, Raymond
 The Arts Council 156-7
women's culture 160, 161
women's studies 112-13
Worpole, Ken
 Saturday Night or Sunday Morning? (with Mulgan)
 159-61, 162
 When Worlds Collide 66-7

Y

youth culture 133, 160
Youth Music Trust 34

Acknowledgements

We are enormously grateful to all of the contributors to this publication, who responded so generously to our call for submissions. They have made this an exciting, provocative and relevant book, for now and for the future. Huge thanks are also due to the designer Stuart Smith who, in response to our brief, has taken this project beyond the realms of an academic or theoretical publication; we must also thank Wyndham Lewis, whose 1914 journal BLAST provided the initial inspiration. Much of the work in setting this project up in its early stages and in researching the historical material was carried out by Janice Kerbel, Jaal Lopes and Laura Moffatt. Special thanks are also due to Melissa Larner, who not only edited the texts, but provided invaluable advice and assistance throughout.

Many others have helped shape the book with their advice, material or feedback; they include Anne Beech, Juliet Steyn, Eileen O'Brien and Andrew Wilson. Thanks are also due to Michaela Crimmin and Sarah Isles at the RSA and to Abigail Appleton and Timothy Prosser at the BBC for hosting and organising the debate Art for All?, which brought many of the issues to the fore. This debate was held at the RSA, London on 21 November, 2000, and broadcast on Radio 3 Nightwaves on 14 December, 2000.

In addition to reproduced material in the public domain, we would like to thank the following for permissions given. Parliamentary copyright material from Commons Hansard and Lords Hansard is reproduced with the permission of the Controller of Her Majesty's Stationery Office on behalf of Parliament. An Arts Policy? is © 1979 Kingsley Amis, reprinted by kind permission of Jonathan Clowes Ltd, London, on behalf of the Literary Estate of Sir Kingsley Amis. Extracts from The Creativity Imperative by Gerry Robinson are reproduced with the kind permission of the New Statesman. The extract from A Market under Threat by David Heathcoat-Amory is reproduced with the kind permission of the Centre for Policy Studies, London. The extract from Bread and Ballyhoo is © Wyndham Lewis and The Estate of the late Mrs GA Wyndham Lewis Memorial Trust (a registered charity). The extract from The Arts Council is © The Estate of Raymond Williams. Considerable effort has been made to trace and contact copyright holders and to secure replies prior to publication. However, this has not been possible in all instances, particularly with old material. The editors and publisher apologise for any inadvertent errors or omissions. If notified the publisher will endeavour to correct these at the earliest opportunity.

Unless otherwise stated, all texts are dated 2000. Footnotes include only the information provided in the original source.

PEER
Shoreditch Town Hall
380 Old Street
London
EC1V 9LT

ISBN 0-9539772-0-X

First published in 2000
© PEER 2000
All rights reserved

All texts and works of art © the authors and the artists

Designed by SMITH
Copy-edited by Melissa Larner
Printed and bound in Great Britain by Dexters

Printed in 170 gsm Munken Pure and 300 gsm Munken Pure

Peer is a registered charity under the name The Pier Trust No. 1035789